S0-AIM-167

Arabs and Jews in Israel

Arabs and Jews in Israel

Volume 1
Conflicting and Shared Attitudes in a Divided Society

Sammy Smooha

Westview Press

BOULDER, SAN FRANCISCO, & LONDON

LIBRARY
COLBY-SAWYER COLLEGE
NEW LONDON, NH 03257

DS
119.7
.S622
1989
vol 1

#17874122

9/91

Westview Special Studies on the Middle East

This Westview softcover edition is printed on acid-free paper and bound in softcovers that carry the highest rating of the National Association of State Textbook Administrators, in consultation with the Association of American Publishers and the Book Manufacturers' Institute.

All rights reserved. No part of this publication may be reproduced or transmitted in any form or by any means, electronic or mechanical, including photocopy, recording, or any information storage and retrieval system, without permission in writing from the publishers.

Copyright © 1989 by Westview Press, Inc.

Published in 1989 in the United States of America by Westview Press, Inc., 5500 Central Avenue, Boulder, Colorado 80301, and in the United Kingdom by Westview Press, Inc., 13 Brunswick Centre, London WC1N 1AF, England

Library of Congress Cataloging-in-Publication Data
Smooha, Sammy.
  Arabs and Jews in Israel / by Sammy Smooha.
    p. cm.—(Westview special studies on the Middle East)
  Bibliography: p.
  Includes index.
  Contents: v. 1. Conflicting and shared attitudes in a divided
society—v. 2. Change and continuity in mutual intolerance.
  ISBN 0-8133-0755-4 (v. 1). ISBN 0-8133-0756-2 (v. 2).
  1. Jewish-Arab relations—1973-   —Public opinion. 2. Israel—
Ethnic relations—Public opinion. 3. Public opinion—Israel.
4. Palestinian Arabs—Israel—Attitudes. 5. Jews—Israel—
Attitudes. I. Title. II. Series.
DS119.7.S622 1989
956.94'004924—dc19   88-14266
                                                                          CIP

Printed and bound in the United States of America

(∞) The paper used in this publication meets the requirements of the American National Standard for Permanence of Paper for Printed Library Materials Z39.48-1984.

10   9   8   7   6   5   4   3

107009

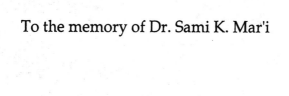

To the memory of Dr. Sami K. Mar'i

Contents

Part Two
TYPOLOGIES

Part Three
CONCLUSIONS

Part Four
APPENDIXES

Tables

Preface

On December 9, 1987, the Palestinians on the West Bank and Gaza Strip launched the most serious challenge in this century to non-Arab rule in the area West of the Jordan river. A genuine grassroots movement against protracted occupation and for self-determination, the Intifadeh has already inflicted many losses and scored many gains. By the first anniversary of the uprising, the toll for the revolting Palestinians was at least 280 dead, 4,000 wounded, 5,500 detainees, and some deportations and house demolitions. The substantial suffering and privations also entailed numerous beatings, curfews, arrests, searches, cuts in basic services, closings of schools, and losses of income. The Israelis have had 10 killed, 1,150 wounded, a minimum of a 1.5% drop in the Gross National Product, the stress of a people's army fighting civilians of an occupied nation, increased international isolation and censure, and the straining of relations with the Diaspora.

The gains of the Intifadeh were also impressive. The national pride, morale, and efficacy of the Palestinians were boosted. Sympathy for the Palestinian cause all over the world increased and the Palestinian question was pushed higher on the agenda of the parties to the conflict and of their allies. The uprising has also prompted the PLO to declare the State of Palestine in the West Bank and Gaza Strip on November 15, 1988, to accept UN resolutions 242 and 338 as bases for negotiations, and to renounce the use of terrorism. It drove Jordan to sever its ties with the West Bank and then to recognize the State of Palestine. It finally brought the United States on December 14, 1988, to recognize the PLO and open official talks with it, leaving Israel the only state in the world to reject the PLO. This war of children, stones, and occasional petrol bombs has thus exposed the hidden costs of occupation for the Israelis and made them impatient with the status quo and more open to other options.

How has the Intifadeh affected the Arab minority of Israel? Have these Palestinian citizens of the Jewish state, which they believe has denied their people the right to self-determination and engaged in a large-scale repression of a legitimate liberation movement by their brethren in the occupied territories, joined the Intifadeh?

Jews were quite alarmed by the Israeli Arab response. In fact, Jews started to grasp the full scale and severity of the Intifadeh to some extent as a result of the Israeli Arab general strike on December 21, 1987, when it was held to demonstrate solidarity with the revolting Palestinians. Many Jews felt that the Arab citizens stabbed the Jewish state in the back by identifying publicly with its avowed enemies.

Nationalist and ultra-nationalist Jewish public figures interpreted Israeli Arab behavior as clear evidence confirming their fears and warnings. To quote just a few of them, Knesset Member A. Lin, a specialist of Israeli Arab affairs, branded the December 1987 strike as "The Violence Day strike," as opposed to its official name, "Peace Day strike" (*Kol Hatsafon*, January 1, 1988). Concurring with him, Papu, the ultranationalist, denounced it as a further step in the exacerbation of Arab irredentism (*Beeretz Yisrael*, February 1988). Gilboa, the Prime Minister's Advisor on Arab Affairs, considered the Intifadeh as only a catalyst of the ongoing processes of Palestinization, pressure for autonomy, and dissociation from Israel, but concluded that "it is a new dangerous situation" (*Meorav Yerushalmi*, March 17, 1988). Cabinet Minister Sharon wrote on the 12th anniversary of the Land Day strike, held on March 30, 1988, that Israeli Arabs have to show complete loyalty to and identification with the state. "Instead, resurgence of Palestinian nationalism is taking place among part of Israeli Arabs....Today instead of fighting together with us, as loyal Israeli citizens, against those who seek to destroy us, they join and abet them" (*Yediot Aharonot*, March 30, 1988). Zeevi, the founder of the Moledet Party, which stands for the transfer of the Arab population from Eretz Israel, cautioned against the "public, comprehensive nationalist mobilization of all Israeli Arabs who aspire to emphasize secession from the state" (*Yediot Aharonot*, July 26, 1988), and called for their voluntary departure from the country (*Harretz*, July 25, 1988, editorial).

It is no wonder that the reaction of the common Jew and Jewish hardliners was hostile. But what about sympathetic Jewish observers? Let me mention some statements made by Israeli doves who saw the Intifadeh as eroding and likely to shatter Arab-Jewish coexistence. Soffer, a political geographer, declared that Israeli Arabs have been building separate, autonomous institutions, and that the Intifadeh is permeating the Green Line (*Kol Haifa*, November 18, 1988). Padhatzur, a senior journalist, regarded the Arab general strike ("The House Day strike") on November 15, 1988, not a protest against demolition of illegal houses in the town of Tayba but rather a thinly disguised solidarity strike with the declaration of the State of Palestine by the PLO on that day. He saw this as another step of Arab radicalization and dissociation from Israel (*Haaretz*, November 24, 1988). The noted Harkabi issued the following warning on this matter:

> The Arabs of Israel have become accustomed to the state and its ways, and even to Hebrew culture, with which many of them are more familiar than their own culture. That was a tremendous achievement. But as the dispute grows more severe, the process of Palestinization will increase, and with it, the gap between them and the state, to the point of secession. Those who strive for the untenable are liable to lose what is within reach. Thus, the increased investment of money and manpower in the West Bank may weaken our grasp on Galilee (*The Jerusalem Post International Edition*, February 13, 1988).

Peri, a political scientist, projected a "Belfastization of Israel" as the most probable scenario if the Intifadeh continues: "Many Israeli Arabs will join the rebelling residents of the territories. Jewish society will unite against them and a civil war between Jews and Arabs will develop in every part of the Land of Israel....This situation could last a very long time, as in Ireland" (*New Outlook* 31, 6, June 1988:13). For Benvenisti, a reputed "prophet of doom," Belfastization has already taken place. "Israel's Apocalypse Now" and the unity between Palestinians on both sides of the defunct Green Line are a solid fact (*Newsweek*, January 25, 1988).

Are these fears, expressed by Israeli Jewish hawks and doves, borne out by the experience of the first year of the uprising? Not really. Israeli Arabs waged two general strikes in proclaimed solidarity with the Intifadeh, staged rallies and demonstrations, issued protest statements, and sent relief to the territories. There were also a number of cases of stone throwing, blockades of roads, clashes with the police, dissemination of recorded cassettes instigating revolt, and several forest arsons. From October 1, 1987, to November 30, 1988, 93 sabotage rings were detected by the Shin Bet, only 4 of which were within the Green Line (quoted by Mansur, *Haaretz*, December 11, 1988).

This limited impact of the Intifadeh was further evident in Arab voting patterns. Participation in the Knesset elections has been high and even increased in November 1988. The rate was 70% in 1981, 74% in 1984, and 76% in 1988. In 1988, the PLO called on Israeli Arabs to vote for any party that supports negotiations with the PLO under UN auspices. This was the first time that the PLO endorsed parties which may be Zionist. The high participation in the national elections demonstrates that the Arabs are eager to integrate fully into Israeli politics and that they have not heeded recurrent calls by extremists to boycott the elections.

Neither was there any leap in Arab voting for non-Zionist parties in 1988. Knesset Member Abdul Wahab Darawshe presented Rabin's policy of "force, might and beatings" as a last straw in his tenuous position within the Labor Party. He broke away to found the Democratic Arab Party, which received 11% of the Arab vote (mostly at the expense of the Labor Party, whose share dropped from 31% in 1984 to 17% in 1988) and won a seat in the 12th Knesset. The Rakah-led Democratic Front for Peace and Equality (DFPE) maintained its portion of one-third of the Arab vote (33% in 1984 and 34% in 1988) and its 4 seats, while the Progressive List for Peace declined from 18% of the Arab vote in 1984 to 14% in 1988 and lost one of its two seats.

I conducted in March-April 1988 a representative survey of the Arab population, a fourth in a series of comparable surveys aiming to gauge Arab opinion and monitor trends over time (over one-fifth of all respondents in these surveys are Druzes and Bedouin who are more moderate than the average). A majority of 76% of all respondents felt that the Intifadeh adversely affected their attitude toward Israel (similarly, 78% in the 1985 survey felt the same about Israel's War in Lebanon, which they viewed as directed also against the Palestinians, not just the PLO). A rise in various indicators of politicization and activism is evident. To cite just a few examples, the proportion of Arabs who identify themselves in Palestinian terms was 57.5% in 1976 and 54.5% in 1980, rising to 68% in 1985 and 67% in 1988. The endorsement of general strikes as a means for Israeli Arab struggle was 63% in 1976 (the year of the first Arab general strike), 55% in 1980, 61% in 1985, peaking at 74% in 1988. Support for the Committee of Heads of Arab Local Councils, which emerged over the years to be a representative, independent, national leadership of Israeli Arabs, soared from 48% in 1976, to 55% in 1980, to 63% in 1985, and to 71% in 1988. Throughout the period, a clear majority, ranging from 64% in 1980 to 76.5% in 1988, favored the formation of a Palestinian state in the West Bank and Gaza. The trend is well captured in the proportion of Arabs classified as "oppositionists" (that is, while accepting Israel, they support a militant struggle for peace and equality) which was 44% in 1976, 40% in 1980 and 1985, rising to 52% in 1988.

Along with this rise in political activism and solidarity with the Palestinians, there is no evidence for growing extremism and rejectionism among Israeli Arabs. To indicate just a few highlights from the above surveys, Arabs denying Israel's right to exist amounted to 20.5% in 1976, 11% in 1980, 18% in 1985, and 13.5% in 1988. Endorsement of violence as a means of struggle was 18%, 7.5%, 8%, and 8%, respectively. The respective figures for Arabs who define themselves as Palestinians without any reference to Israel were 33%, 26%, 29%, and 27%. More explicit forms of dissociation from the state even show a certain decline: Arabs unwilling to have Jewish friends dropped from 42.5% in 1976, to 31% in 1980, to 37% in 1985, and to 34% in 1988; and Arabs who would move to a Palestinian state if it were established in the West Bank and Gaza declined from 14% in 1976, to 8% in 1980, and to 7.5% in 1988. Finally, Arabs classified as "rejectionist" (i.e., they reject Israel and their minority status in it) constituted 13.5% of the sample in 1976, 6% in 1980, 11% in 1985, and 10% in 1988.

The rationale underlying these various reactions to the Intifadeh is telling indeed. Israeli Arabs are a Palestinian national minority, destined to live permanently in the Jewish state. They avail themselves of Israeli democracy to wage a struggle for greater equality and integration. They are bilingual and bicultural, Israeli Palestinian in identity, and are in solidarity with the submerged Palestinian nation, but loyal to Israel. They support the PLO and a two-state solution to get their people settled and their own national aspirations fulfilled, but their fate and future are firmly linked to Israel.

The key concepts for understanding Israeli Arab patterns of behavior are militancy, not radicalism; opposition, not resistance; acceptance, not rejectionism; integration, not separation; and institutional autonomy, not irredentism. By the same token, the change in their behavior is conveyed by politicization, not radicalization; and an increase in political activism, not a rise in rejectionism.

The Intifadeh is the hardest test of loyalty Israeli Arabs have ever had, and by its first anniversary they have successfully passed the test. This is well expressed by Suleiman Shakur of the village of Sakhnin in the Galilee who is the brother of Imad, who left Israel to serve as Arafat's advisor on Israeli affairs. Suleiman dismissed statements by Israeli politicians who accused Israeli Arabs of aiding and abetting the uprising: "They will not manage to draw the Intifadeh into the Green Line. There is a difference between players and fans. We are the fans. Our goal is to live in Israel with equal rights, while the aim of the residents in the West Bank is to form a separate state" (*Yediot Aharonot*, December 2, 1988). No less revealing is the fact that the leader of the Islamic Resistance Movement in Gaza condemned the Palestinian declaration of independence, whereas a leader of the Israeli Islamic fundamentalists praised it (*Haaretz*, November 22, 1988).

For those who either hoped or feared that the Green Line has already faded out, obliterating the distinctions between Palestinians living on its two sides, the Intifadeh is a timely reminder that the Green Line is as firm as ever. Over 40 years, Israeli Arabs have emerged as a new entity, a distinct segment of the Palestinian people, tied to Israel. They have not joined the Intifadeh because, unlike their brethren across the Green Line, they do not endure occupation, do not seek liberation, and can wage a democratic struggle. In contrast to other Palestinians, they want more equality and integration as Israelis, rather than complete separation and sovereignty.

In a historical perspective, Israel has failed after 1967 to annex the West Bank and Gaza Strip and their Palestinian population, but it has succeeded after 1948 in fully and irreversibly annexing the Galilee and Triangle and their Palestinian population. This is why the two questions of Israeli Arabs and other Palestinians must be settled differently. The problem of the Palestinians in the territories and the Diaspora can be resolved by Israeli withdrawal and allowing a separate entity or state to arise there. On the other hand, the Israeli Arab issue is an internal one and can considerably be reduced by equalizing rights and opportunities for Arabs and Jews. Paradoxically and contrary to common conceptions, Israel would consolidate rather than compromise its Jewish-Zionist character by recognizing the Arabs as a Palestinian national minority with full rights, including institutional autonomy.

In a nutshell, this is the bottom line of this book, which summarizes part of a larger, ongoing research project that began in 1975. A major component of the project are four surveys of Arab and Jewish populations and leaderships conducted in 1976, 1980, 1985, and 1988. A monograph devoted to the 1976 survey was published in 1984. The present volume sums up the 1980 survey and the next volume will cover the 1985 and 1988 surveys.

These survey data provide basic information about Arab and Jewish attitudes toward each other over time. They can serve a number of purposes. First, they can dispel misconceptions and promote understanding between Arabs and Jews. Second, they can be a base for a policy shift from control over Arabs to compromise and to a certain degree of power-sharing. And third, the survey findings are a reliable source about Israeli Arabs' views and desires. This is crucial if their status is to be considered in future negotiations between Israel and the Palestinians, in conjunction with the unsettled status of the Arabs in East Jerusalem and Jewish settlers in the West Bank and Gaza Strip.

SAMMY SMOOHA
Brown University
Providence, Rhode Island

Acknowledgments

There are certain books which need extensive cooperation, substantial funding, and a long period of time to produce. As a result, their authors accumulate overdue debts. Conceived a decade ago, this book fits this special category.

The book is mostly based on a survey of the Arab and Jewish populations and public leaderships conducted in the summer of 1980. Majid Al-Haj helped in the translation of the Arabic questionnaire. In addition to helping with the Arabic translation, Nimr Smer with Michel Gantus served as fieldwork supervisors. The Dahaf Research Institute, directed by Dr. Mina Zemah, was responsible for interviewing the Jewish sample. Without the effort of scores of interviewers and the cooperation of thousands of respondents, including 178 public figures, this study could never have been completed. To all of them, I am grateful.

Administrative services were provided by Sara Tamir, Executive Director of the Jewish-Arab Center, under whose auspices the study was carried out, and by David Bukay, Executive Director of the Research Authority, University of Haifa.

A preliminary draft of the manuscript was written during my 1980-81 sabbatical year at the Sociology Department, State University of New York at Binghamton. The final version (including some revised portions from several of my published articles) was prepared during my 1987-88 sabbatical year in the Program in Judaic Studies at Brown University. I am thankful for the facilities extended to me by both universities, especially to three of my colleagues there whose encouragement and support proved to be most rewarding to me: Professor Don Peretz from SUNY-Binghamton and Professors Calvin Goldscheider and Ernest Frerichs from Brown University.

Richard Platkin, Asher Goldstein, Gershon Greenbaum, David Newman, and Susan Lundgren copyedited various sections of the typescript. Joshua Bell, of Verbatim Word Processing Services, was responsible for turning a messy manuscript into a neat, camera-ready copy; and Barbara Ellington and Rebecca Ritke, of Westview Press, oversaw publication.

Many of the ideas in the book have been tried on numerous students in seminars and on people at countless public and academic lectures that I have delivered on Arab-Jewish relations in contemporary Israel. Their thoughtful reactions have forced me to rethink and reformulate my position.

This project would not have been possible without a special grant for the year 1980-81 from the Ford Foundation, International Division, Middle East and Africa. The trust and help of Dr. Anne M. Lesch and Richard Robarts, both program officers at the time, and William Carmichael, Vice President, are greatly appreciated. Steven Riskin, also program officer at the Ford Foundation, arranged for subsequent funding. A grant from the Jaffe Foundation was necessary to bring the project to completion. It reflected Edward Jaffe's firm commitment to Arab-Jewish coexistence. The financial support of all these foundations is gratefully acknowledged. I am confident that the real reward for all those associated with the project will be the contribution this book might make in promoting understanding between Arabs and Jews.

Of course, these acknowledgments in no way absolve me of the responsibility for the faults remaining in the book.

This book is dedicated to the memory of Dr. Sami K. Mar'i, a caring colleague, a fine scholar, and a true believer in Arab-Jewish coexistence. Serving in 1976 as a director of the Institute for the Research and Development of Arab Education at the University of Haifa, he provided me with the support to conduct the first in a series of surveys of Arab-Jewish attitudes. I certainly miss our challenging exchanges.

S. S.

1

Introduction

The population of 5.1 million under Israel's control in 1980 was deeply divided into Palestinian aliens vs. Israeli citizens (a demographic ratio of 27:73), Arab vs. Jewish Israelis (15:85), Oriental vs. Ashkenazic Jews (55:45), and Orthodox vs. non-Orthodox Jews (20:80).[1] If the Palestinian-Israeli division is considered part of the external conflict, then the Arab-Jewish split is Israel's gravest internal problem.

Many have been alarmed by the Israeli Arabs' support of the PLO and a number of court convictions for the murder of Jews on nationalistic grounds and by the racism and political intolerance of some Israeli Jews. Both developments are feared as threats to democracy and to the strained, yet governable, relations between the Arab minority and the Jewish majority.

This study aims to explore the orientation of Arabs and Jews toward each other and the change it has undergone over time. By examining in detail the opinions of both sides after over thirty years of coexistence, the study will attempt to critically evaluate the widespread conviction that the major trend is a process of growing, mutual estrangement.

Before proceeding to the research findings, it is essential to scrutinize the prime factors shaping the orientation of Arabs and Jews. Since the views they express in the public opinion surveys are anchored in their distinct features and general orientations as a minority and a majority sharing the same state institutions, these features and orientations are discussed in this chapter.

[1]Since the survey on which the study is based was conducted in 1980, the quoted population figures are for this year. The total population under Israeli administration was 5.8 million in 1987. The demographic ratios between population groups have remained essentially the same.

Distinct Features of the Arab Minority

The Arab citizens of Israel within the pre-1967 borders numbered around 513,500 persons in 1980: one seventh of the Israeli population (of 3.8 million, excluding the 115,000 Arabs of East Jerusalem); less than one third of all Arabs under Israeli control (1.8 million); and about one eighth of all Palestinian Arabs (around four million).[2] These demographic ratios serve to underline the fact that Israeli Arabs live in two conflicting worlds: Israel and the Palestinian people.

The Arabs are a significant and restive minority within the Jewish state for the following reasons:

1. They are a territorially concentrated, indigenous group that feels firm ties with, and rights to, the land; that is growing steadily (from present indications there will be 1 million Arab citizens, one fifth of all Israelis, by the end of the century); and that is becoming increasingly important electorally (they account for nearly ten percent of the eligible voters in a highly competitive multi-party system).

2. The Arabs are a permanent, nonassimilating minority clearly distinguished from the Jews, and they possess all the institutions necessary to preserve a separate existence, the most essential being all-Arab local communities, schools, mass media and, of course, highly cohesive families (Tessler, 1980).

3. As a working-class minority in a predominantly middle-class society, a politically peripheral minority in a highly centralized state, and an Arabic-speaking minority amid a Hebrew-speaking majority, the Arabs lack the resources to compete with the Jews on an equal footing. As a result, they experience absolute and relative deprivation.

4. The Arabs are a dissident minority. They reject two crucial aspects of the fundamental ideology of the Israeli regime: the mission of the state vis-à-vis the Jewish world and its stance in the dispute with the Arab world. The Arabs object to Israel's *raison d'être* – the implementation of the goals of Zionism – which involves bringing to Israel as many Jews as possible, maintaining its nature as a Jewish and Zionist state, and defending the Jewish cause all over the world. They are understandably opposed to the idea that Israel is the homeland of all Jews in the world, not just of its Jewish and Arab residents, and that within it only the Jews enjoy the right to national self-determination. Arabs also resist the concept that Israel exists for the sake of the Jewish people and that its official institutions, symbols, emblems, and

[2]In 1987 Israeli Arabs numbered 650,000, one seventh of the Israeli population (4.3 million, excluding 135,000 Arabs of East Jerusalem) less than one third of all Arabs under Israeli administration (2.2 million).

holidays are Jewish. They want Arabic to be as widely accepted as Hebrew, and they would have Israel do away with the Law of Return, unrestricted Jewish immigration, Jewish settlement in Arab areas, and the precedence given to the Jewish sector in development programs. In Jewish eyes, Arab rejection of Israel as a Jewish-Zionist state implies total negation of the state's very existence.

The Arabs likewise oppose the Jewish consensus on the Israeli-Arab conflict and support a solution based on a PLO-headed Palestinian state in the West Bank and Gaza Strip. This is usually understood to mean Israeli withdrawal to the pre-1967 boundaries, the redivision of Jerusalem, recognition of the PLO, and the right of repatriation for the Arab refugees. Such a solution is anathema to the vast majority of Jews who regard it as evidence of Arab dissidence and even disloyalty.

5. As far as the state and the Jews are concerned, the Arabs tend to be seen as a hostile minority, sympathetic to the enemy and a potential fifth column if not effectively contained. The authorities base their treatment of the Arabs on the assumption of their potential disloyalty and, thus, exempt them from compulsory military service (except for the Druzes, who are subject to the draft, and the Bedouin, who may volunteer for the regular army) and so place them under close surveillance. Arab dissidence provides Jews with *prima facie* evidence of Arab disloyalty and legitimizes Jewish control.

This profile of the Arab minority serves as a convenient point of departure for the Arab radicalization perspective.

The Arab Radicalization Perspective

Various theoretical and ideological approaches lead to the conceptualization of the Israeli Arab response in terms of radicalization (*haktsanah,* in Hebrew); i.e., Arabs are regarded as having become increasingly radical, rejectionist, hostile, disloyal, and anti-Israel over the years. The Jewish public, specialists of Arab affairs, and other observers point to a rapid process of radicalization among Israeli Arabs since 1967 (Tehon, 1979). Deep-seated Arab extremism is found in a steadily mounting range of expressions and actions against the state. These bear witness to a change in most Arabs from passive loyalty to reluctant compliance and, in some aspects, to active and violent dissidence.

Despite their fundamental disagreements as general schools of thought, modernization, internal colonialism, and control theories concur that various conditions and developments eventually cause the radicalization of Israeli Arabs.[3] Peres is the first Israeli sociologist to single out modernization as a major source of Arab radicalization. Israeli Arabs who adopt modern values and behavior also embrace nationalism which supplies a new common denominator for Arabs from different backgrounds and constitutes a barrier against assimilation into the Jewish majority. In consequence, "modernization draws Arabs and Jews together on the personal level, and simultaneously repels them on the political and ideological level" (Peres, 1970:482). Contrary to the naive Zionist belief that Arabs would be less hostile to Jews once they were liberated from repressive traditionalism, Peres (1971) shows in his surveys that the more educated, urbanized, and younger the Arabs were, the more radical they became. He concludes:

> It has been demonstrated not only that modernization does not eliminate hostility towards Jews, but that nationalism seems to fill some of the psychological needs arising in the wake of modernization. If our findings are valid, one can hardly avoid the pessimistic implication that further modernization will aggravate the conflict in and around Israel (Peres, 1970:492).

Other social scientists also capitalize on modernization as a chief agent of Arab radicalism. Best representative of this tendency is the political scientist Landau (1969, 1981, 1984) who maintains that political alienation among Arabs has been growing since 1967 as a result of advancing modernization and nationalism.

Radicalization is also the outcome of certain developments to which Israeli social geographers point in their studies. The political geographer Soffer (1986, 1987, 1988), for instance, asserts that Israeli Arabs are gaining a sense of overwhelming power as part of the Arab and modern world and, especially, as a component of the Palestinian population in Greater Israel whose impending demographic parity with Jews is threatening the Jewish and democratic integrity of the state. In view of the Jewish failure to de-territorialize them, to develop their communities, and to win them over, many Israeli Arabs squat on state lands and move to Jewish towns, multiplying the points of friction with Jews. Furthermore, they still constitute 75% of the heart of the Galilee which serves as their geopolitical base. "Within Israel," Soffer warns, "a majority of Arabs will increasingly demand cultural and political autonomy and a minority will also demand separation from Israel" (1988:23).

---

[3]For a review of theories of modernization as an agent of ethnic mobilization, see See and Wilson, 1988:236-38.

The traditional Arab local, *hamula* (clan), and sectarian identities are negatively correlated with Palestinian national identity and positively correlated with Israeli civil identity. This is the main finding of a 1977 survey, conducted by the sociologist Mi'ari, from a sample of 292 Arab university graduates. He concludes:

> Assuming that traditional loyalties will continue to be weakened as a result of the process of modernization and social change, I expect that in the future Israeli identity will also continue to weaken, while Palestinian identity will continue to be strengthened. If this hypothesis is confirmed, one must raise a serious question about the future of Arab-Jewish "coexistence" in Israel (Mi'ari, 1987:42).

The Orientalist Rekhess has further articulated, updated and popularized the radicalization perspective drawing on modernization, the Israeli-Arab conflict, and other main forces. He holds that since 1967 Arabs have steadily become Palestinian in both their national identity and in their approach to Israel. In consequence, they now reject their minority status, have extended their struggle for equal civil rights to a demand for national rights, and have taken increasingly anti-Israeli stands (1976, 1977). The Arab intelligentsia has also become greatly involved in the new militancy (1979). Although Rekhess avoids the term "radicalization" in his most recent writings, he continues to focus on the factors leading to Arab extremism. The major internal factors at work here, in his view, are rapid population growth, which makes the Arabs feel both more powerful and more in need, the widening socioeconomic gap between Arabs and Jews, and the continuing policy of neglect toward the Arab minority. Together with the dramatic rise of the Palestinians, these changes have lent the Arab villages in Israel the status of national political centers (1986a), with Rakah (the Arab-dominated Communist party) and the PLO their champions (1986b).

Scholars and other critics, such as Jiryis (1976, 1979), Zureik (1979), and Nakhleh (1977b, 1980, 1982), who portray Israel as a colonial settler state in which the Arabs are a suppressed national minority in the process of forming a national liberation movement, regard Arab radicalization as an inevitable development. For them, the Arabs are a structurally unadjustable minority heading toward confrontation with the Jews in the coming years.

For the sociologist Zureik, the emergence of an anti-colonial, liberation consciousness and the formation of a resistance movement are gradual, but inevitable, processes in a settler society like Israel. It is only a matter of time, in this view, before increasing politicization of the Arabs directly challenges and confronts the repressive Israeli regime. Meanwhile, radicalization is evident in "identification with the Communist party, an attempt to establish a nationalist movement, and an increase in the Arab intelligentsia's involvement in the political affairs of the Arab community" (Zureik, 1979:186-87). For his part, the anthropologist Nakhleh (1980) criticizes the Israeli Arab intelligentsia, finding that it is still compromising, petit bourgeois, and tacitly accepting of the "occupier's paradigm" of the Arabs as a minority in a Jewish state. He feels that the Arabs have already reached a stage that enables them to shift to a revolutionary, rejectionist, "liberation-prone mentality."

Arab radicalization also looms large in Lustick's (1980) control model. The point of departure for his analysis is the all-embracing institutional discrimination. The resulting reservoir of discontent is put in abeyance by a water-tight "system of control" based on segmentation (the isolation and fragmentation of the Arabs), dependence (economic subordination), and cooptation (the capture of the elites and leadership). He nevertheless spells out three challenges (which he then underplays as "aberrations") to control. These are the steady erosion of traditional beliefs and behavior, the Palestinization of the group identity, and the crystallization of politically militant organizations such as the Communist party and the Sons of the Village Movement (1980:237-38). Radicalization is unavoidable in the long run because the authorities are unlikely to change their policy of control and because even a solution of the Palestinian problem – either by annexation of the West Bank and Gaza Strip or by the creation of a separate state – will, paradoxically, further radicalize the Arabs in Israel. This result would be caused, in this view, by the increase in their relative deprivation (in comparison to the ample opportunities open to their brethren in the new Palestinian state) and by the further consolidation of Israel's Jewish-Zionist character (in order to prevent its assimilation into the region) (ibid.:266).[4]

Radicalization is also seen by many as a direct offshoot of the post-1967 occupation. The reunion with the Palestinians in the West Bank and Gaza Strip, the intensification of contacts with them, and the gradual blurring of the Green Line have, it is argued, steadily diminished the differences between Israeli Arabs and other Palestinians. According to Horowitz, occupation has forced Israeli Arabs into an unenviable position for being simultaneously occupiers (as

[4]In his recent writings, Lustick has apparently abandoned this earlier position and advanced a new formulation to be discussed shortly. He maintains that rather than changing his own mind, he has updated his position in order to account for the change of Israeli Arabs and Israel in the early 1980's.

Israelis) and occupied (as Palestinians). "This paradoxical situation entailed an increased alienation of the Arab minority in Israel from the social and political framework of the state to which they are affiliated as citizens" (Horowitz, 1987:23). Benvenisti goes a step further. He claims that de facto annexation has reached a point of no return, replacing the State of Israel by the State of Eretz Israel. In this Second Republic, the critical division separates Jews from Palestinians, regardless of whether the latter are citizens or aliens. All Palestinians under Israel's jurisdiction share a common destiny and Palestinian nationalism, defy Jewish control, are engaged in communal strife with Jews, and are becoming increasingly hostile to the repressive and exploitive Jewish state (Benevenisti, 1987:66-80).

Jewish nationalists paradoxically subscribe to this unflattering image of Israel. For example, the main thrust of Rabbi Meir Kahane's books, *They Must Go* (1981) and *Uncomfortable Questions for Comfortable Jews* (1987), is that in a Jewish state, which is intentionally geared to serve Jews, Arabs are bound to be discriminated against and alienated and, hence, antagonistic. Although most Israeli Jews stop short of Kahane's conclusion that emigration is the only solution to the Arab minority, they share his assumptions and expectations. In fact, press commentators and policymakers tend to interpret Arab attitudes and protest actions as signs of intensifying radicalism.

Jointly considered, these various approaches point to five major unrelenting sources of Arab radicalization:

1. *The Israeli-Arab conflict.* It is argued that the conflict has reinforced the solidarity of Israeli Arabs with the Arab world and that the gradual Palestinization of the conflict since 1967 has de-Israelized them. According to the radicalization perspective, continued occupation of the West Bank and Gaza Strip has blurred the distinctions between Palestinians on both sides of the Green Line, the PLO has moved to claim the support of Israeli Palestinians as well, and Israel's War in Lebanon against the PLO and Palestinian institutions has further alienated Israeli Arabs.

2. *Arab modernization.* A rise in the level of education, standard of living, and urbanization (without migration to towns) transforms Arab identity. It substitutes a radical, unifying, nationalist identity – "Arab identity" before 1967 and "Palestinian identity" thereafter – for accommodating, divisive, parochial identities. In the first generation, modernization also boosts Arab natural increase dramatically (fertility remains high while mortality drops substantially) creating high demands on the meager family resources and underdeveloped community services. Greater needs and higher expectations intensify

the sense of relative deprivation and, in turn, augment radicalism among Israeli Arabs.

3. *Zionism.* The more modern and Palestinian Arabs become, the more hostile they feel toward Zionism. The problem of identification with the exclusionary Jewish state, namely, a state exclusively designed for Israeli and Diaspora Jews, increasingly strains the lives of the politicized Israeli Arabs.

4. *Policies.* Long-standing policies and practices of unfair distribution of public funds, surveillance over activists and leaders, mass expropriation of Arab lands and lingering land disputes, denial of control over certain Arab institutions, exclusion from the higher echelons of the economic and political power structure, and discrimination in white-collar jobs continue to make Israeli Arabs disgruntled and disillusioned with Israel. Instead of launching a crash program to close the pre-existing large Arab-Jewish gap, continued governmental neglect has allowed it to grow and, hence, to intensify absolute and relative deprivation.

5. *Jewish ethnocentrism.* It entails Jews' strong suspicion, negative stereotyping, avoidance of personal or close contacts with Arabs, and expectations for preferential treatment by the state. Higher levels of ethnocentrism among Jews generate feelings of rejection among Israeli Arabs.

The Arab radicalization perspective does not only count on these unfailing causes of radicalism and extremism but also draws on a plethora of direct evidence. First, the Arabs are becoming more Palestinian and less Israeli in identity, concerns, contacts, and support for the PLO (Israeli, 1980; Schölch, 1983). Second, their vote for Jewish-Zionist parties and affiliated Arab lists (over 75% prior to 1967) has declined steadily, manifesting growing disenchantment with the Jewish state (Cohen, 1985). Third, the traditional Arab leadership was replaced by an independent and semi-independent leadership operating through many organizations that emerged in the seventies and that have constantly challenged the authorities. And fourth, Arab protests have become widespread, recurrent, and even hostile, as reflected in several general strikes since 1976, a good many court convictions for sabotage after 1967, and the flourishing of nationalist literature.

Despite my awareness of its merits, especially its keen grasp of the gravity of the problem, its plausibility and its attractiveness, I reject the Arab radicalization perspective. In a series of studies and publications since 1976, I have attempted to develop and empirically confirm an alternative view – the Arab politicization perspective.[5]

The Arab Politicization Perspective

The Arab politicization perspective begins with the following critique of the Arab radicalization perspective:

1. The radicalization perspective is overly deterministic. Arab radicalization is assumed to be inescapable and persistent: Arab-Jewish relations, in this view, are bound to create strains and eventually collapse as a result of the continued conflict with the Arab world, institutional discrimination in the Jewish-Zionist state, and internal developments, e.g., Arab modernization and demographic growth, a Jewish drift to the nationalist right and toward hardened intransigence. In contrast, the politicization perspective leaves the course of development open and stresses overall historical processes that have positively influenced Arab-Jewish coexistence.

2. The radicalization perspective applies a blanket maximalist definition in its analysis of radicalism. The recent discrediting of moderate leaders, the general strikes, the rejection of the Jewish-Zionist character of the state, the emphasis on Palestinian national identity, the endorsement of a Palestinian state alongside Israel, and the support for the PLO are unjustifiably defined as indicators of radicalism. Rather, they should be seen as the legitimate protest or dissent of a national minority in a democratic state. In contrast, the politicization perspective adopts a narrower and minimalist approach defining Arab radicalism in such terms as the rejection of Israel's right to exist, advocacy of violence and terror, and support for a Palestinian or binational state in place of Israel.

3. The radicalization perspective mistakenly singles out only one trend among the Arabs, as if other counterbalancing developments had not occurred. The politicization perspective corrects this by examining radicalization in relation to other trends in the Arab response that run counter to it.

According to the latter perspective, politicization rather than radicalization is the key to understanding the Arab situation and the processes of change. As Arabs become increasingly politicized, they avail themselves of the political means to participate on an equal basis in Israeli society. Politicization is thus the major response to the structural contradictions present in the Arabs' situation in Israel: they

[5]These two perspectives were introduced for the first time in my monograph *The Orientation and Politicization of the Arab Minority in Israel* (1984a; first edition appeared in 1980) which was based on a survey conducted in 1976.

are simultaneously both inside and outside Israeli society and politics. They constitute a dissident yet loyal minority, a vulnerable yet rising group, whose capacity for adjustment is still undetermined.

The Arabs face multiple handicaps: lower status in a rapidly crystallizing class structure, insufficient Westernization in a transplanted European society, being non-Jewish and non-Zionist in a society designed for Jews and Zionists, as well as being regarded as a security risk in a state under siege. All these impediments make the Arabs as a group the single largest threat to the status quo in Israel and the proponents of the most radical change.

To maintain law and order, the authorities have subjected Arabs to effective control ever since the establishment of the state. Control is a machinery of ever-diminishing efficiency based on economic dependence and the political regulation of Arab behavior (Smooha, 1980, 1982). It is inherently subject to erosion because Israel is basically democratic. By the 1980's, control had lost so much of its effectiveness that many of the mechanisms expounded by Lustick no longer apply (for instance, most Arab leaders today are not coopted).

How one defines the problem of Arab-Jewish coexistence varies in accordance with one's starting point. For the Jews, it is how to contain the restive and dissident Arabs; for the Arabs, it is how to effect change without being branded disloyal; for the system as a whole, it is how to reconcile the Jewish-Zionist character of the state with political democracy while not jeopardizing national security. The main question for analysis is whether it is realistic to expect a peaceful transition from a situation of control over the Arabs to one in which the Arabs are accepted as a new group in legitimate (coalition) politics and can benefit from the arrangements of compromise and partnership (consociationalism).

To advocate the politicization perspective does not mean to ignore the existence of countervailing forces and divergent trends in Arab-Jewish relations. Arab politicization involves, at one and the same time, Israelization, factionalization and increasing militancy. "Israelization" is reflected in the Arabs' growing bilingualism and biculturalism, their acceptance of Israeli standards and styles, and their view of themselves as an integral part of Israel.

Factionalization means the internal division of the Arabs into four political streams: accommodationists, reservationists, oppositionists, and rejectionists. The accommodationists accept the status quo, seek concessions through the system, and draw on the dominant Zionist establishment for ideological and organizational support. As non-partisans, the reservationists are the least crystallized ideologically and organizationally; they are critical but ready to cooperate with the authorities through such bodies as the Committee of Heads of Arab Local Councils.[6] The oppositionists approve of Arab-Jewish coexistence but insist on radical change; they are most attracted to the articulate ideologies and leaderships of the Israeli Communist party (Rakah) and the Progressive List for Peace (PLP). The rejectionists repudiate Israel and their minority status in it and follow the Sons of the Village Movement, which supports the Rejection Front within the Arab world.

In view of their growing Israelization and factionalization, heightened militancy for the overwhelming majority of Arabs is not rejection of Israeliness, but rather a challenge to the status quo and an attempt to negotiate new terms of coexistence with the Jews.

The Arab politicization perspective is also accepted and applied by Al-Haj in his work on how Israeli Arabs are changing and how they relate and compare to the Palestinians in the West Bank and Gaza Strip. While the latter use a "survival strategy" to withstand occupation and to extract themselves from Israel, the former adopt an "accommodation strategy" for gaining greater incorporation into Israel (Al-Haj, 1988b). Al-Haj assumes the simultaneous reinforcement of two orientations among Israeli Arabs: one is an internal civil orientation which prompts them to select Jews as a reference group and insist on equality and integration with them; the other, an external, national orientation pushes Arabs to adopt outside Palestinians as a reference group and fight for an independent Palestinian state alongside Israel for these outside Palestinians. He concludes:

> We may hypothesize that considerable change in the status of Arabs in Israel is inevitable. Given the conspicuous processes of modernization and politicization that are taking place, it will be increasingly difficult to control the Arab minority. On the other hand, that minority is becoming ever more attached to Israel for the simple purpose of safeguarding its achievements. Any remoteness from Israeli society would entail a high price (Al-Haj, 1988a:116).

Lustick's revised perspective on the Arab minority is closer to politicization than to the radicalization perspective. He observes considerable change in both Israeli Arabs and Israel:

[6]It is likely that the newly established Democratic Arab Party, that won a seat in the Knesset in the 1988 elections, will provide the kind of ideology and leadership that reservationist Arabs need. The fledgling party is led by Knesset Member Abdul Wahab Darawshe, a self-styled, Moslem Arab moderate who broke away from the Labor Party in January, 1988 in protest of Rabin's clampdown on the Intifadeh and Labor's failure to effect a significant change in the Arab sector.

In the 1970's Israeli Arabs were calling for non-discrimination and civil rights, as did the American Negroes in the 1950's and early 1960's. In the 1980's Israeli Arabs are demanding their share of political power, as did American Blacks in the late 1960's....The gradual entry of Israeli Arabs into Israeli politics as an independent force presages even more dramatic, if unrecognized, changes in the face of Israel. For political relations between Jews and Arabs are being determined less and less by control, and more and more by bargaining....What this means, in a phrase, is creeping binationalism (Lustick, 1988b:14).

In this restatement of his position, Lustick concedes that the "system of control," presented as robust in his 1980 book, has been dismantled by and large in the 1980's (1988a). Furthermore, he emphasizes the transformation of Israel from a Jewish-Zionist to a binational state, especially as a result of the demographic growth and political rise of non-Zionist ultra-Orthodox Jews, Israeli Arabs, and Palestinians in the territories (1988c). He also cites two additional key factors. "One is the bold, adroit leadership of the Arabs who have reached political maturity within Israel." The other factor is the continuation of occupation which has polarized the Jews into two evenly and sharply divided political camps. Jewish political polarization has increased the dependence of the Labor Party and the small Zionist leftist parties on the Arab vote. For this reason these parties have substantially liberalized their policies toward Israeli Arabs in order to win their support. In response, Israeli Arabs switched in 1981 from protest or patronage to strategic voting, i.e., voting intended to put Labor in power. This new political role of Israeli Arabs is of course feared and resented by the Likud camp.

Lustick's updated formulation is, however, as imbalanced as his prior account. According to his earlier analysis, "intransigent" Zionism has turned Israel into a sort of Herrenvolk democracy for Israeli Arabs, whereas in the later version, "flexible" Zionism is supposedly losing ground to triumphant democracy. Both portrayals of Israel are equally untenable. Zionism and democracy have been two pillars of Israeli society constantly engendering tensions and contradictions in the treatment of Israeli Arabs. Rather than slighting either one of them, as Lustick does, the Arab politicization perspective takes both seriously and analyzes their dynamics over time and their implications for the Arab minority.

To shed further light on the politicization perspective, let me distinguish it from the radicalization perspective with regard to Arab orientation. The politicization perspective defines radicalism narrowly to mean extremism and rejectionism, arguing that Israeli Arabs are neither radical nor radicalizing in this sense. Rather, they are becoming "politicized," i.e., active and militant. It intends to make a specific contribution by introducing this conceptual distinction. On the other hand, proponents of the radicalization perspective would probably reject this distinction because they prefer a broader definition of radicalism which includes politicization.

The list of indicators of radicalization and politicization, as seen by the politicization perspective and summarized in Table 1.1 captures the main differences between the two perspectives.

Table 1.1 Selected Indicators of Radicalization vs. Politicization

Arab Radicalization Perspective	Arab Politicization Perspective
1. Rejection of Israel's right to exist	Acceptance of Israel's right to exist
2. Desire to restrict contacts to Arabs, or to operate only in independent, national Arab organizations	Willingness to have unrestricted contacts with Jews or to integrate into Jewish or mixed organizations (short of assimilation)
3. Support for all means of struggle, including illegal and violent means, if necessary	Support for democratic, parliamentary or extra-parliamentary, but legal means of struggle only
4. The struggle for civil equality is considered as part of the struggle for national liberation	The struggle for civil equality is considered as a struggle for equal rights and opportunities between Arabs and Jews
5. Israeli Arabs have a right to self-determination; their fate and future are tied to the Palestinian people; and their status as a minority in Israel is rejected	Israeli Arabs do not have a right to self-determination; their fate and future are tied to Israel; and their status as a minority in Israel is accepted
6. Rejection of the territorial integrity of Israel in its pre-1967 borders, including the separation of the Galilee and Triangle from Israel	Acceptance of the territorial integrity of Israel in its pre-1967 borders, including the retention of the Galilee and Triangle as parts of Israel
7. Support for a non-Israeli Palestinian identity for Israeli Arabs	Support for an Israeli Palestinian identity for Israeli Arabs
8. Repudiation of the existence of a Jewish nation in Israel	Recognition of the existence of a Jewish nation in Israel
9. Support for a secular-democratic or a Palestinian state in all of Mandatory Palestine in place of Israel	Support for a Palestinian state in the West Bank and Gaza Strip alongside Israel
10. Support for the Rejection Front	Support for the PLO mainstream
11. The PLO is the sole, representative body of all Palestinians, including Israeli Arabs	The PLO is the sole, representative body of the Palestinian people, excluding Israeli Arabs

The Arab politicization perspective builds on three socio-historical forces that have channeled Israeli Arab orientation into politicization (political mobilization and the struggle for integration) rather than radicalization (extremism and dissociation from the state). These forces are as follows:

1. *The Palestinian shift away from rejectionism.* The Six Day War ushered in a long process of Palestinization of the Israeli-Arab conflict (Kelman, 1988). With the official exit of Egypt from the conflict in 1979 and the de facto non-belligerency of Jordan after 1967, the dispute was reduced to its Palestinian-Jewish core and was quasi-internalized by Israel through the occupation of the territories. The defeat of the Arab military option and Pan-Arabism paved the way for the rise of a genuine Palestinian national movement under the PLO. The new Palestinian movement has gradually shifted away from a long-standing, uncompromising rejection of any Jewish national right to any part of Eretz Israel/Palestine to a pragmatic two-state solution (Abraham, 1983; Harkabi, 1988). The further Palestinization of the conflict by Israel's direct onslaught in 1982 on the the Palestinian entity in Lebanon, the Intifadeh of 1987/88, and King Hussein's policy of July 1988 to sever ties with the West Bank prompted the Palestinian National Council on November 15, 1988 to declare the independence of the State of Palestine, to accept UN resolutions 242 and 338, and to renounce terrorism while keeping the right to the armed liberation of the West Bank and Gaza Strip. A month later, Arafat, Chairman of the PLO, moved to explicitly acknowledge Israel's right to exist and relinquish the use of terrorism in all its forms. The United States responded immediately on December 14, 1988, by agreeing to open official talks with the PLO. This historical breakthrough left Israel as the only state still adamant not to recognize the PLO. In sum, the Palestinians have moved away considerably from historical rejectionism.

Contrary to the Arab radicalization perspective which takes a dim view of this post-1967 transformation of the external conflict, the Arab politicization perspective considers the balance sheet to be positive for Israeli Arab accommodation to the state. Rakah, which has emerged as a dominant political power during this period, has played a central role in this regard. Rakah is explicit about acknowledging Israel's right to exist and insisting on a strategy of legal parliamentary and mass politics for Israeli Arabs. It also endorses a political strategy, rather than armed struggle, and a two-state solution for the Palestinians across the Green Line. More importantly, Rakah legitimizes these principles by the claim that the PLO itself stands for them. Furthermore, Israeli Arabs believe that this is indeed the case despite the PLO's lingering ambivalence and ambiguity on these issues till recently. To generalize, the objective, partial Palestinian shift away from rejectionism and its perception by Israeli Arabs as reconciliation with Israel have pushed Israeli Arabs during the 1970's and 1980's to accept the Jewish state and to seek suitable means to integrate into it.

2. *Democratization of Israeli society.* From its inception, Israel was established as a liberal democracy extending automatic citizenship to all its residents, including the Arabs,[7] and to all the new Jewish immigrants. Democracy under the resolute, charismatic leadership of Ben-Gurion was nevertheless quite limited. Among its main weaknesses were a single, dominant party system with a delegitimization of the permanent opposition parties, firm party machines which dominated the electorate and controlled nominations, the heavy censorship of the press and the state-run radio broadcasts, ineffective extra-parliamentary politics, a military government over the Arab minority, and a Labor oligarchy of Ashkenazic veterans ruling over all institutions and equating its sectional interests with the public good.

These shortcomings have diminished considerably in the post-Ben-Gurion era, especially since the mid seventies. Political parties lost their machines and nominations became contested; the ascendency of the Likud to power in 1977 inaugurated a new era of government changeovers; the freedom and influence of the press, radio, and television grew substantially; the military government over Israeli Arabs was abolished in December 1966; pressure and protest groups have flourished since 1967 (Schnall, 1979); the Oriental majority appreciably increased its political representation; and the ruling elite was forced to open up and to diversify.[8]

The deoligarchization and opening up of Israeli society in the two decades following the Six Day War were facilitated by a sharp rise in the standard of living and education, the ascent of a new class of professionals, technocrats, managers and businessmen, and the strengthening of ties with and orientation toward the West. Democratization took place, however, alongside a shift of the Jewish population to the right, to nationalistic and pro-annexationist politics, alongside deep, internal political polarization, and alongside other lingering flaws of Israeli democracy.

---

[7]Some of the Arabs – those dislocated during the 1948 war or those who returned illegally to Israel after the war – were initially denied citizenship. In the course of time, however, they were naturalized.

[8]For a review of political change in Israel, see Arian, 1985; Shimshoni, 1982; Galnoor, 1982; Shapira, 1977; and Elazar, 1986.

Nonetheless, the overall positive effect of the democratization process for Israeli Arabs cannot be overemphasized. It enabled them to join the general movement for change already under way in Israel and to wage a peaceful, militant struggle without risking governmental repression and Jewish backlash.

3. *Ultimate Jewish control.* Israel was established as a Jewish state and the Jewish consensus on keeping it Jewish has remained intact over the years. Since Israeli Arabs are the single, gravest, internal danger to Israel's Jewish-Zionist character and national security, they have been put under a machinery of control. This consisted of fragmentation, selective isolation and integration, economic dependence, the cooptation of their leaders, the repression of active dissidents, ongoing surveillance, and other means to prevent mobilization and to insure overt compliance.

This strategy was changed because of serious obstacles encountered in the seventies. It was weakened by the lifting of the military administration over Israeli Arabs who then seized upon the democratization of Israeli society to stage massive protests and to defy restrictions. At the same time the ability of the authorities to counteract the challenge by expanding and perfecting control over Israeli Arabs was attenuated by the urgent need to build a new, larger system of control in the occupied territories. This required a shift of resources and personnel from inside to outside the Green Line. Facing these exigencies, the authorities had to appreciably scale down control over the Arab minority, discard routine surveillance, and concentrate their efforts on curbing extremist activities or barring political actions that in their judgment would likely lead to subversion. While the authorities continued to treat Israeli Arabs as potentially disloyal, control shifted from a micro to macro level, was applied more selectively, and aimed primarily to contain apparent defiance. To illustrate, contrary to common expectations for the tightening of controls over Israeli Arabs, the first 1977-81 term of the Likud government pursued a policy of benign neglect. But it moved swiftly by barring the convening of both a representative Arab congress in Nazareth in December 1980 and a statewide, coordinating committee of local organizations affiliated to the rejectionist Sons of the Village Movement in early 1981.

The change in the control pattern has encouraged Israeli Arab accommodation. As daily surveillance and interference in Arab life eased, fewer Israeli Arabs were harassed and hurt. Moreover, they have learned from experience that Israel is here to stay; that Jewish control is firm, even when restrained and remote; that more liberal treatment by the authorities is not a compromise of Israel's Jewish-

Zionist character; that any Arab defiance will be detected and severely punished; that they have real, pervasive stakes in Israel; that they are bound to lose by destabilizing Israel; and that they do not have a better, viable alternative to life as a minority in a democratic, Jewish Israel. Convinced of effective, ultimate Jewish control, Israeli Arabs have nilly willy become more expedient, pragmatic, and moderate in their orientation toward Israel.

Distinct Features of the Jewish Majority

Like the features of the Arab minority, the traits of the Jewish majority tend to impede friendly Arab-Jewish relations as evident from the following account:

1. Jews are "a mino-majority"; i.e., a minority that turned recently into a majority (Seliktar, 1984b). As such, their psychology has remained fraught with feelings of inadequacy, insecurity, suspicion, anxiety, and hostility that are often associated with their previous minority position. The shift to majority status is also problematic for Israeli Jews because they are a part of a people who are largely scattered as minorities outside Israel (73%) and because they are a tiny minority in the region (3.6 million Jews versus 180 million Arabs).

2. Jews are a threatened majority. They live in a hostile environment that presents a fatal threat to their very survival. The traumas of the Holocaust and the 1973 War reinforce their apprehension over the grave external danger. Since they regard Israeli Arabs as part of the wider menacing Arab world, they experience a real difficulty in developing trust and tolerance toward them. At the same time, past persecutions restrain Jews from contemplating extreme actions against the Arab minority.

3. Jews are a Zionist majority. Except for fringe ultra-Orthodox and marginal leftist groups, they adhere to the Zionist ideology and entrust the state with the task of implementing it. The status of a non-Jewish and non-Zionist minority in such a state is inevitably problematic because Jews expect, and indeed obtain, preferential treatment and promotion of their institutions and interests at the expense of others.

4. Jews are a non-secular majority in a non-secular state. Most Jews are either Orthodox or traditional (observing religion selectively). In view of the lack of separation between state and religion, religious symbols and traditions are widely propagated in the society and they deeply penetrate the mind and behavior of Jews (Leibman and Don-Yehiya, 1984). Since Judaism is a monoethnic religion (Jews have only one religion and the Jewish faith claims only one people), which also happens to be non-proselytizing and nonassimilationist, religious

observance unavoidably breeds intolerance of Arabs. These ethnocentric effects of Judaism are only partially mitigated by its high morality.

5. Jews are ethnically divided. The division into an Ashkenazic dominant minority and an Oriental nondominant majority generates considerable tension among Jews (Smooha, 1987b). The placement of the Arab minority at the bottom of the ethnic hierarchy fulfills a vital tension-release function for the Jews. It validates the membership and increases the acceptability of the deprived Orientals in the Jewish mainstream, confers on them a higher standing, makes it easier to give them preferential treatment in employment and resource-allocation, exempts them from staffing certain undesirable jobs, and creates certain posts (surveillance over Arabs) that they are more likely to fill. The Orientals are also more disposed to intolerance because they are more religious and less educated than Ashkenazim. (For these and other explanations, see Smooha, 1978:102-03; Seliktar, 1984b; Peri and Goldberg, 1985). Furthermore, their less favorable orientation is enhanced by the hardline Likud, to which they are firmly allied. Under these circumstances and short of a radical reduction of the Ashkenazic class and cultural dominance, a significant improvement in the position of the Arab minority will not be attempted lest it hurt the rising Oriental majority.

6. Jews are democratic and Western in their basic orientation. They believe that all citizens are entitled to equal rights and freedoms and they also support the state democratic institutions, political parties, and the press. This attachment is reinforced by their view of Israel as belonging to the free world, by their being part of the Jewish people who predominantly live in the West, and by their realization that Israel's heavy dependence on the Western bloc requires the maintenance of acceptable democratic standards.

The commitment of Israeli Jews to democracy is, however, weakened by counter-forces. First, in the absence of a constitution, there exists insufficient protection of individual and minority rights. Second, the 1945 Emergency (Defense) Regulations – introduced by the British Mandatory authorities – which are still in force, can easily be and frequently are used to infringe civil rights. Third, equal rights can also be denied on the grounds that by not serving in the army, the Arabs do not fulfill equal duties. Fourth, the immediate and present danger from the outside offers a ready-made formula for imposing various restrictions. And fifth, hailing mostly from Eastern Europe and the Middle East, Jews lack a Western democratic tradition (Shapira, 1977).

These characteristics of the Jewish majority provide a basis for the Jewish intransigence perspective.

The Jewish Intransigence Perspective

The Jewish part in the study of Arab-Jewish relations is usually neglected. When the attitudes of the Jewish public are considered, they tend to be confined to the narrow question of stereotyping and social distance. The tendency to single out the Arab minority, as does the Arab radicalization perspective, is reminiscent of the notorious tradition of blaming the victim. Needless to say, the devotion of equal attention to both sides is a prerequisite for arriving at a realistic and balanced account of the complex issues involved.

Although nowhere explicitly formulated, it is commonly believed that the Jewish standing on coexistence is characterized by intransigence and a growing rejection of Israeli Arabs. Jewish intransigence feeds on the above sources within the Jewish majority: its past experience as a persecuted minority, the threat from the rejectionist Arab world, the Zionist ideology that sanctifies Israel as a Jewish state, the excessive influence of religion, internal ethnic tensions, and political intolerance which focuses on Arabs.

According to this Jewish intransigence perspective, not only do most Jews have an anti-Arab orientation, but they are also becoming increasingly alienated from Israeli Arabs since 1967. Several primary factors lie underneath the hardening of the Jewish position. These are: (1) Jews' perception of the Arabs as becoming increasingly radical and anti-Jewish; (2) the historical shift of Israeli society after 1967 to the right, to hawkishness, and to an erosion of democracy; and (3) alteration of ethnic relations within the Jewish population resulting in the enhancement of the status, power, and daily impact of the more anti-Arab Oriental majority.

The fact that the Arabs are a dissident minority is not lost on the Jews. They know that most Israeli Arabs reject Zionism and advocate a two-state solution to the Palestinian question. In other words, most Jews perceive Israeli Arabs as opposed to the Law of Return and Jewish immigration, as equating Zionism with racism, calling on Israel to retreat to the pre-1967 borders to allow the formation of an independent Palestinian state there, and as claiming a Palestinian national identity. All these Israeli Arab views are considered subversive by most Jews.

As to the macro-change of Israeli society after 1967, there is an agreement among Israeli social scientists that a gross shift to the right took place. Eisenstadt (1985), who dates the process earlier and sees it as inevitable, conceptualizes the transformation in terms of "the disintegration of the Labor-Zionist institutional mold." This mold entailed revolutionary spirit, innovation, creativity, pioneering, secularism, tolerance, civil equality, rule of law, human and labor orientations, and modern values. The fall of the stagnant Labor ethos opened the way to countervailing pressures.

Some speak of the strengthening of particularistic dimensions in the Israeli collective identity. Kimmerling observes a competition, in the eighties, between a civil (or "State of Israel") and primordial (or "Eretz Israel") identity. The civil outlook enshrines Israel proper, equality among all Israeli citizens, individual achievement, rule of law, and realpolitik. In contrast, the primordial approach to the Israeli collective identity sanctifies Greater Israel, Jews, and Judaism, blurs the differences between individuals and society, and treats non-Jews unequally and suspiciously.

Liebman elaborates on Kimmerling's thesis. He suggests that the Jews relate to Israel more and more as "a community" ("built on status, on past performance and future expectations, on degrees of kinship ties, on loyalty and commitment," and hence on inequality) and less and less as "a state" (impersonal, egalitarian). He then draws the implication of this shift for the treatment of Arabs:

> Since membership in the community of Israelis is defined by Jewish identity, the non-Jewish minorities, almost by definition become second-class citizens.
>
> There is no question, in our opinion, that the primary threat to the rights and status of the Israeli Arabs stems from the Jews' fear for their security and the threats their Arab neighbors pose. But, we suggest, this threat by itself, is not the immediate cause for the reluctance of so many Israelis to view the Arabs as equal members of the society. This reluctance, we believe, stems from the political culture that encourages conceptions of community at the expense of conceptions of state (Liebman, 1988:102).

Similarly, Cohen (1983) notes a dangerous erosion of universalism as the main source of legitimation in Israeli society as a result of the concomitant rise of Revisionist Zionism and Oriental Jews. This intensification of ideological and ethnic particularism will reduce Israel's chances to reach a peace settlement with the Arab world and come to terms with the Arab minority.

Shafir (1984) detects a dynamics leading to deep change in Zionist values because of the open frontier on the West Bank. Israeli nationalism is becoming "integral," i.e., territorialist, authoritarian, chauvinistic, xenophobic, and intransigent. Shafir poses an alarming question: "Can the Israeli personality, institutions and forms of domination created in the West Bank be prevented from filtering through into the mainstream of Israeli society and subverting the spirit, even if not necessarily the formal expressions, of its democracy?" (ibid.:824).

Political scientists and political sociologists stress the political realignment of forces as one major outcome of the pervasive transformation of Israel. Israeli politics changed from a system ruled by a dominant party whose power rested on a broad mass base to a system in which two opposing, socially distinct, political camps compete strongly.

Shamir (1986) offers a detailed analysis of this realignment by comparing the development before and after 1967 (the following figures are quoted from her article). There was a growth of the right. The right-wing parties nearly doubled their Knesset seats – from 26 in 1965 to 47 in 1984. Self-identification with the right rose from 8% in 1962, 16% in 1969, 35% in 1981, to 38% in 1984, while that with the left declined from 31% in 1962 to 23% in 1984. Most of the public became hawkish: throughout the period, 80% to 90% have opposed withdrawal from most of the territories.

Political polarization also took place. The emergence of two nearly equal political camps looms large in election results. The Labor camp of today, which included the religious parties before 1967 but not since 1977, won 73% of the vote in 1965 and only 43% in 1984. The Likud bloc won 21% of the vote in 1965, but with the affiliated religious parties it grew to 47% in 1984. This polarization was most evident in the public images of Labor and Likud. Whereas 32% of the Jewish public in 1973 viewed Labor as left-wing and 37% as right-wing, in 1984, Labor was more uniformly labeled as left-wing (61% and 10%, respectively). On the other hand, the Likud was perceived as left-wing by 10% and as right-wing by 76% in 1973, and 7% and 77%, respectively, in 1984. The popular meaning of left and right is favoring or opposing compromise on the occupied territories.

Furthermore, there was an increase in the convergence of political and other cleavages in Israeli society. The social base of both political camps has become more homogeneous. By the 1984 national elections, the Likud drew heavily on Orientals, on working and lower classes, and on observant and traditional Jews, while the reverse has been true for Labor. "The close relationships among ethnic origin, religiosity, position on issues relating to the Israeli-Arab conflict and voting patterns, make it hard to disentangle causal processes" (ibid.:279). Shamir's analysis, however, shows that the realignment in Israeli politics was caused by both the ideological shift of the Jewish public to the right after 1967 and the rise of the Oriental majority.

According to the Jewish intransigence perspective, this hardening of Israeli ideology and politics has spilled over on to public policies and to Jewish public opinion with regard to the Arab minority. Despite the Arab struggle for equality, the long-standing "policies by default" have virtually been left unchanged; namely, a failure to design and to implement a crash program to bring the Arab sector to a par with the Jewish population and a reluctance to do away with various discriminatory practices.

Furthermore, certain hardline steps were adopted since 1975, including the plan to expropriate Arab lands that triggered the Land Day strike in 1976, the establishment of 30 watchpost settlements as part of the Judaization project of the Galilee, and the legislation of a number of laws to consolidate the Jewish-Zionist character of the state. The latter includes legal amendments to make the traditional Hebrew law a mandatory source in case of lacunas in the law, to criminalize the public display of signs of identification with the PLO, to ban contacts with PLO officials, and to deny participation to any election list unless it accepts Israel as a state of the Jewish people.

As to the impact of the rise of Oriental Jews, various studies (e.g., Peled and Bar-Gal, 1983) have shown that their stands are more anti-Arab than those of Ashkenazic Jews. The growth in the Oriental influence has inescapably unleashed personal manifestations of prejudice and discrimination. For instance, lower and working class Orientals constituted the bulk of the voters for Kahane in 1984 and of the hooligans around him.

Although these indications in support of the Jewish intransigence perspective are factual, they are at best only circumstantial. Rather than directly demonstrating that most Jews are intransigent vis-à-vis Israeli Arabs and that they are becoming more so over time, they point to certain conditions and developments that pressure Jews in this direction. A closer examination, however, reveals counterbalancing conditions and developments. Direct observation and some evidence on Jewish orientation toward Israeli Arabs suggest that an alternative perspective may be as plausible and valid. This is the Jewish accessibility perspective to which I subscribe.

The Jewish Accessibility Perspective

The Jewish accessibility perspective complements the Arab politicization perspective. It proposes that rather than responding by intransigence and backlash, the Jews and Jewish institutions have increasingly yet reluctantly become more accessible and even more responsive to Israeli Arabs, whose major orientation is to join and participate in the system.

The complementary Jewish accessibility and Arab politicization perspectives are grounded on the general assumption that in genuine political democracies full citizenship is an effective weapon at the disposal of subordinated minorities and is bound to erode the machineries of control. It is, therefore, assumed that the formal extension of citizenship to the Arabs in 1948 is the prime mover of later developments. Despite its varied shortcomings, Israeli democracy greatly influences Arab-Jewish relations by laying down useful procedures of political, rather than violent, conflict management. Since the early 1970's, the Arabs have been skillfully employing these means to further their cause. It is due to the ground rules of democracy and the democratization of Israeli society since the mid sixties that the Jewish reaction has been piecemeal concessions and partial openness rather than tightening control and outright repression.

The overall process of growing Jewish accessibility, like the process of Arab politicization, has three components: inclusiveness, factionalization, and ambivalence. Inclusiveness implies that more and more Jews are finding themselves coming together with Arabs in public facilities, organizations, institutions, and localities and consequently losing the sense of Jewish exclusivity. They are increasingly aware of the presence of Arabs in many areas and rungs of the society. They can communicate more readily with the Arabs, who are becoming more bilingual and bicultural. As a result, a larger number of Jews realize that they have to reconcile themselves to the existence of a permanent Arab minority in the Jewish state, and a mounting proportion do so.

Like the increasing factionalization of the Arabs by their attitudes toward the Jews, the Jews are also becoming more divided among themselves with regard to the Arab minority. Four Jewish types, echoing four political streams, can be identified: the conciliationists, pragmatists, hardliners, and exclusionists. The conciliationists, whose position is best represented by the small Zionist leftist parties, insist on extending full equality to the Arabs but without compromising the Zionist character of the state. While leaning in this direction, the pragmatists, who are attracted mostly to the Labor ideology, favor the granting of more concessions to Arabs and the liberalization of control over them. The hardliners are close to the Likud approach, which advocates a stiffening of surveillance over the Arabs while appeasing the "loyal" Druzes and others. Infused with Kahane's spirit, the exclusionists reject Arabs as part of Israel and wish to bar and subordinate them as much as possible.

The overall Jewish orientation is, nevertheless, switching from negation to ambivalence. Jews have been forced to indulge in less stereotyping, to be more discerning in their perception of the different types of Arabs, more careful in their statements about Arabs, and more defensive with regard to Arab affairs. They are more ready to consider

Arab grievances, less self-confident about their deep-seated stands, and more receptive to concessions made to the Arabs by the authorities. Jewish self-righteousness has been diluted by some guilt feelings and the admission of some wrong-doing. A growing number of Jews are realizing that Israel must ameliorate the conditions and actual rights of its Arab citizens.

The moderate improvements in the Israeli Jews' orientation vis-à-vis the Arab minority will be more properly appreciated in face of their general reluctance to allow Arabs to freely enter Israeli society, lest they have to recast Israel's Jewish-Zionist character and considerably relinquish their power and privileges. But it is against the foil of the two other constraints – racism and political intolerance – that the modest move of Jews toward Israeli Arabs stands out.

Some anti-Arab racism, i.e., a predisposition among some Jews to categorically deprive all Israeli Arabs of equal treatment, to label them as incorrigibly inferior, and to hate them as group, is unavoidable in a society that shapes its institutions in Jewish molds and strives, as part of its survival strategy, to maintain "qualitative superiority" over its belligerent Arab environment. Although embarrassing, Jewish racism is not a serious problem because of its limited incidence and unanimous censure by the elite.

Of much greater consequence for Arab-Jewish coexistence is political intolerance, which enjoys wide currency and legitimacy among Jews and thrives on the weak points of Israeli democracy (Shamir and Sullivan, 1983; Sullivan, Shamir, Roberts, and Walsh, 1984; Seligson and Caspi, 1983). The Jewish public hardly distinguishes between legitimate dissent and illegitimate subversion. As a result, the Arabs serve as the main target of Jewish political intolerance. The Arabs are regarded by most Jews, who apparently think in terms of the Arab radicalization perspective, not only as dissident but also subversive because of their affiliation with the enemy, endorsement of a Palestinian state on the West Bank and Gaza, recognition of the PLO as the true representative of the Palestinians, and rejection of Israel's Jewish-Zionist mission. Jews either disregard or fail to realize that the Israeli Arabs, whom they regard as enemy-affiliated Arabs, are seldom engaged in hostilities against Israel; that they desire a Palestinian state alongside, and not in place of, Israel; that they support the PLO but not its National Charter and its resort to terror against civilians; and that they deny Israel's Zionist zeal but accept its right to exist.[9]

[9]Shipler (1987) provides an incisive report on both Arab and Jewish sides in Israel and Hareven (1983) reproduces personal Arab testimonies.

The Research Project

In the mid seventies, I launched a long-term research project that aimed at gaining a deeper understanding of the way the Arab minority and the Jewish majority in Israel view each other and of the conditions each group regards as necessary for peaceful coexistence. While the accomplishment of this aim will not be sufficient either to confirm or reject the Arab radicalization and Jewish intransigence perspectives in contrast to the Arab politicization and Jewish accessibility perspectives, it will elucidate points of contention between the two sets of perspectives and throw some light on their relative validity.

Various studies have been carried out within the framework of the project, but the four surveys undertaken in 1976, 1980, 1985, and 1988 loom largest among them.

The Four Surveys

The four surveys of attitudes of Arab-Jewish relations consist of the following groups:

1. *The 1976 survey*. The first of its kind in Israel, the 1976 survey was based on a national representative sample of 656 adult Arabs and a sample of 148 adult Jews from two towns. Despite its limitations, the Jewish sample was roughly representative of the adult Jewish population with regard to age, education, and ethnic origin.

2. *The 1980 survey*. Interviews for the 1980 survey were completed with 1,140 adult Arabs and 1,267 adult Jews, representing the entire adult population of Israel within the pre-1967 borders.[10] The survey also included 88 Arab and 90 Jewish public figures, representing three political streams in each population.

3. *The 1985 survey*. It drew on interviews with 1,203 Arabs and 1,205 Jews, as well as 137 Arab and 144 Jewish public figures, representing four political streams in each population.

4. *The 1988 survey*. Consisting of 1,200 Arabs and 1,209 Jews, this survey was conducted in March/April 1988, i.e., 4-5 months since the uprising in the occupied territories on December 9, 1987.[11]

[10]Originally, the first two Arab samples also included 16-17 year old youths (66 in 1976 and 45 in 1980), but they are excluded from the present analysis for the sake of comparability with the later surveys which consist of adults only.

[11]Funding for the surveys was received from the following sources: the 1976 survey was funded by the Institute for the Research and Development of Arab Education (University of Haifa) and a grant from the Ford Foundation received through Israel Foundations Trustees; the 1980 survey was underwritten by the Ford Foundation (the headquarters in New York City); the 1985 survey was supported by a grant from the Ford Foundation received through Israel Foundations Trustees, a direct grant from the Ford foundation (the

These surveys were conducted according to common procedures. The Arab surveys drew on national samples taken from complete official voter rolls in a cross section of localities. Face-to-face interviews were administered by Arab interviewers at the respondents' homes, applying a standard questionnaire in Arabic. The 1980-88 Jewish surveys followed the usual practice, i.e., in this case, the interviewing of 1,200 adult Jews by Jewish interviewers through a standard questionnaire in Hebrew. The samples in these Jewish surveys were weighted according to age, education, and ethnic origin in order to correct the demographic biases (the population parameters were derived from the labor force surveys conducted by the Central Bureau of Statistics). The cooperation of the population was satisfactory.

Contrary to initial and lingering doubts, it was shown that the Arab surveys met all the criteria of survey research and yielded results whose reliability, validity, and significance matched those of the Jewish surveys.

The 1976 Arab survey and the 1980 Jewish survey served as a baseline for the later surveys. Comparability was obtained by using similar procedures of data-collection, including questionnaires containing a common core of questions. The 1976 survey was summarized in a monograph (Smooha, 1984a). The present volume is devoted to the 1980 survey and the next volume to the 1985 and 1988 surveys.

The 1980 Survey

Appendix A discusses in detail the methodology of the 1980 survey, and Appendix B reproduces a full text of the questionnaire translated into English.

The target population for the 1980 survey was adult Arab and Jewish citizens residing within the Green Line. The Arab sample consisted of 1,140 adults who were randomly selected from the official list of eligible voters in each of 42 localities. These localities were systematically chosen to represent all Arab communities according to religion, region, municipal status, population size, level of services, and votes for the Democratic Front for Peace and Equality in 1977.

Like all samples of 1,200 persons, the Arab sample has an average error of 3%. Because of its superior technique – drawing a systematic

Headquarters in New York City), and a supplemental grant from the National Council for Research and Development; and the 1988 survey was funded by the DFG (Deutsche Forschungsgemeinschaft) received through the Arnold Bergstraesser Institut, Freiburg, Federal Republic of Germany. The financial assistance of all these foundations is greatly acknowledged.

random sample from a full list of names – it is demonstrably representative. The following percentages reflect more or less the correct proportions of a cross section of the entire Israeli Arab population:

Gender: 51% were men and 49% were women.

Age: 35% were 18-25 years old, 27% 26-35, 18% 36-45, and 19% 46 years or older.

Education: 20% had no formal schooling, 48% primary education only, 24% post-primary education, and 8% post-secondary or higher education.

Religion: 10% were Druze, 72% Moslem (subdivided into 11% Bedouin and 61% non-Bedouin), and 18% Christian.

Region: 66% lived in the Galilee, 19% in the Triangle, 7% in the Negev, and 8% in the Coastal Strip and central region.[12]

Municipal Status: 10% lived in mixed Arab-Jewish towns, 12% in Arab towns, 27% in large Arab local councils, 24% in small Arab local councils, and 27% in unincorporated, agricultural, or temporary Arab localities.

The Jewish sample contained 1,267 adults from 34 urban and rural localities, representing the Jewish communities according to region, population size, municipal status, and voting patterns. In each town or village chosen, streets were sampled; in each of the chosen streets, households, and within each household, persons were selected at random for interviewing.

While achieving representativeness, this ecological sampling technique resulted in certain biases. Although the incorrect proportions in age, education, and ethnic origin were corrected by weighting, the final sample still underrepresents new immigrants, those with poor knowledge of Hebrew, and religious Jews. As a result, there is a slight liberal bias in the sample.

The 1980 Jewish sample is composed of the following population categories:

Gender: 51% were men and 49% were women.

Age: 20% were 18-25 years old, 27% 26-35, 15% 36-45, 12% 46-55, and 25.5% 56 or older.

Education: 3.5% had no formal schooling, 30% primary education only, 44% post-primary education, and 23% post-secondary or higher education.

---

[12]Haifa, Shefaram, Daliat-Al-Karmel, Acco, and Maker were classified in 1980 as part of the Galilee, whereas in 1976 as part of the Coastal Strip and the central region.

Ethnic origin: 47% defined themselves as Oriental or Sephardic, 47% as Ashkenazic, and 6% as mixed; the father's country of birth of 5% was Israel, 11% Morocco, 6% Iraq, 9% Yemen, 18% Poland, 9% Soviet Union, 9.5% Roumania, and the rest other countries.

Religious observance: Some 5.5% defined themselves as very religious, 12% as religious, 41% as traditional, and 41% as secular.

District: 9% lived in the Northern district, 15% in the Haifa district, 24.5% in the Central district, 35% in the Tel Aviv district, 8% in the Jerusalem district, and 8% in the Southern district.

Municipal status: 81% lived in municipalities (cities and big towns), 11% in local councils (small towns), and 8% in regional councils (villages).

In addition to the 2,407 interviews with rank and file Arabs and Jews, the 1980 survey included 178 interviews with some 30 public figures who represent each of the following six different political streams:

1. Establishment-affiliated Arab leaders: Arab functionaries in the separate Arab departments in government offices and the Histadrut, Arabs active in Zionist political parties, and heads of Arab local governments identified with the authorities. This is obviously an accommodating leadership group.

2. Rakah-affiliated Arab leaders: Arabs who hold ranking positions in or offices on behalf of the Democratic Front for Peace and Equality (DFPE), which is dominated by the Israeli Communist Party (Rakah). These leaders are anti-Zionist, militant in the struggle for Arab civil rights, and supporters of a Palestinian state alongside Israel.

3. Rejectionist Arab leaders: Arabs who are active in the Progressive National Movement and the Sons of the Village Movement which are involved in student and local Arab politics. They reject the State of Israel and wish to see it replaced by a democratic-secular, or a Palestinian state in the entire area of Palestine.

4. Dovish Jewish leaders: influential Zionist Jews in Shelli, Mapam, Labor, Shinui, Citizens Rights Movement, and Peace Now who have "a dovish reputation."

5. Hawkish Jewish leaders: influential Zionist Jews in the Tehiya party (an ultra-nationalist party which includes secularists and Gush Emunim who are committed to Greater Israel and opposed to the Peace Treaty with Egypt), and top figures in the National Religious Party and Likud who have "a hawkish reputation."

6. Jewish Arabists: Jewish high officials who run the separate Arab departments and other Jewish politicians or functionaries who are directly associated with Arab minority affairs. In their political outlooks they fall in between the Jewish doves and hawks.

This volume sums up the findings of the 1980 survey. More specifically, it will present an analysis of the key issues dividing Arabs and Jews, construct typologies of Arabs and Jews according to their orientation toward each other, and tentatively monitor and establish trends in Arab and Jewish orientations over time by comparison with earlier evidence.

While reading through the book, the reader is advised to bear in mind that the reported findings refer to the 1980 survey, if not otherwise indicated. Hence, tables without a cited source, as are most tables in this book, contain figures from the 1980 survey. All the reported percentages ignore non-responses (don't know) and are adjusted accordingly (with a few exceptions, missing data do not exceed 3%).

The findings from the 1980 survey, which constitute the core of this volume, will be supplemented by some data from the 1976 survey and from the Van Leer survey. The latter is a survey of Jewish attitudes toward Israeli Arabs, based on a sample of 1,223 adult Jews and conducted in January 1980 (six months before our survey) for the Van Leer Jerusalem Foundation. The figures quoted here from the Var Leer survey differ slightly from those in the original summary report (Zemah, 1980) because they have been adujsted for non-response and sampling biases.[13]

Importance of the Survey

What difference does it make what Israeli Arabs say or feel about their minority status, the Jewish state, and the Jewish majority? Does it really matter what the Jews say or feel about Arabs? If not, it casts grave doubt on the importance of the obtained survey information, even if it is accurate.

Good surveys generate data which are "nationwide, quantifiable, replicative, cumulative, comparative, fairly reliable and genuinely social scientific," yet "...no effort can do away with the problems and limitations which inhere in survey research" (Hanson, 1979:659). Aware of this criticism, I wish to comment briefly on the usefulness of these survey data, and by doing so, respond to some major objections to surveys in general.

1. *Triviality.* A common criticism, that surveys produce trivial information, usually attitudes toward minor questions, simply does not

---

[13]I wish to thank Alouph Hareven for making the Van Leer survey data available to me.

apply to the current survey. I have made a strenuous effort to cover the most fundamental issues in Arab-Jewish relations.

2. *Neglecting behavior and hard facts.* The criticism that surveys focus on inherently less salient attitudes, rather than on concrete behaviors and life-situations, is partially applicable to the present study but for good reason. First, personal Arab-Jewish interactions are not extensive, so there are little variable data to record. Second, Arab radicalism is more likely to be expressed in attitudes than behavior because of the restrictions on Arabs. Since the study focuses on radicalism, views are a more suitable measure than actions. Nonetheless, reported behavioral indicators were covered when possible, including interethnic contacts, media exposure, protest activities, and actual privation.

3. *Overlooking elite ideologies.* The criticism that surveys over-emphasize mass attitudes at the expense of the more crucial elite ideologies does not apply to this inquiry. Having been aware of the danger that the absence of a parallel study of elite views makes the attitudes of the general public appear as unduly important, the 1980 survey of the Arab and Jewish populations also included a sample of leaders from the two sides, so that both mass and elite views can be considered and compared.

4. *Empiricism.* The criticism that survey data and analysis yield subjective descriptions divorced from broad structural contexts and theoretical considerations probably does not hold for the survey under discussion. For me, survey data are an aid to, not a substitute for, macro-sociological analysis. As against pollsters who monitor transient public opinion or shifting salient issues, my approach is that of a political sociologist exploring underlying trends in social structure. What is of interest is not any single survey question; the answers to which may alter with rewording or fluctuating public mood. The aim is, rather, to reconstruct a pattern from a series of responses, as well as to identify the structure underpinning the pattern. This is why these survey findings from the beginning of the eighties have not become dated by the end of the decade.

5. *Poor guide to policymakers.* The criticism that survey research is a poor guide to policymaking does not apply to this study. The study is replete with valuable information about how Arabs view their conditions and which changes they desire and how Jews also see these areas. This material can serve any interested person or body, ranging from the Israeli authorities to their opponents on the right or left, Arab or Jewish. More specifically, the survey findings are relevant to a change of policy toward the Arab minority and to the settlement of the broader Palestinian question of which Israeli Arabs are one component.

Part One

KEY ISSUES

2

Selecting the Key Issues

Intergroup relations are usually strained by open or tacit disagreements that may be referred to as "issues." Issues concern those problem areas that are potentially disruptive to minority-majority relations and can be either dormant or operative.

In societies where there is a strong dominant group, this group defines the public issues. It exercises power to suppress certain matters that are critical for the subordinate group. Because of minority unwillingness or powerlessness, many disputed questions appear to be nonexistent. For this reason, it is essential for the researcher to study both the "issues" and the "non-issues." In this way, key problems are not left out and justice is done to both dominant and nondominant viewpoints (Bachrach and Baratz, 1962).

This is the rationale underlying the selection of Arab-Jewish issues included in the survey. It must be emphasized that some of them are not even perceived as such by the dominant Jewish majority and others are not pressed as public concerns by the nondominant Arab minority. In any event, the selected matters are judged here to be significant enough to divide Jews and Arabs.

Thirteen key issues are identified and the opinions of the public of both sides on each issue are ascertained. They will be discussed in the following order:

1. *Ethnic stratification.* To what extent are Israeli Arabs resigned to their lower position in the class structure of Israeli society and to what extent are Jews prepared to place on the national agenda the achievement of Arab-Jewish equality?

2. *Cultural diversity.* To what extent do Arabs accept Israel's Western and Jewish culture or feel the strains of cultural dominance? Are Jews willing to promote institutional bilingualism and biculturalism as a means of accommodating Israeli Arabs?

LIBRARY
COLBY-SAWYER COLLEGE
NEW LONDON, NH 03257
107009

3. *Legitimacy of coexistence.* Does each community recognize the legitimate presence of the other? Do Israeli Arabs acknowledge Israel's right to exist and do they reconcile themselves to its Jewish-Zionist character? Are Jews receptive to having an Arab minority with full civil rights in their midst?

4. *Israeli-Arab conflict.* Is there an operative consensus among Jews on how to resolve the regional Israeli-Arab conflict and especially how to settle the Palestinian question, and do Israeli Arabs share this?

5. *Collective identity.* How widespread are various Palestinian versus Israeli concepts of identification among Israeli Arabs? Do Israeli Arabs and Jews agree on the definition of the Arab national identity?

6. *Institutional separation.* Do Israeli Arabs and Jews approve of the status quo of institutional separation, or does either side want greater integration?

7. *National autonomy.* Do Israeli Arabs claim the right to some sort of self-determination and, if so, what are its desired expressions, particularly control over Arab institutions, regional self-rule, and irredentism? What degree or form of national autonomy is the Jewish public ready to grant Arabs?

8. *Group goals.* What goals are sought by Israeli Arabs and Jews vis-à-vis each other: exclusion, domination, equal opportunity, consociationalism (compromise and partnership), secession, or non-sectarianism?

9. *Leadership credibility.* How much credibility do various local Arab leadership groups and the PLO enjoy among Israeli Arabs and Jews?

10. *Educational goals.* Do Israeli Arabs wish Arab cultural heritage, biculturalism, and Palestinian nationalism to become goals for Arab education? Do Jews consent to the educational goals desired by Israeli Arabs? What goals do both sides consider as suitable for Jewish education?

11. *Strategies for change.* Do Arabs and Jews concur on the legitimacy of the different means adopted to improve Israeli Arab conditions – parliamentary politics, extra-parliamentary politics, and extra-legal politics?

12. *Ethnocentrism.* To what degree do Israeli Arabs and Jews show intolerance toward each other?

13. *Deprivation and alienation.* How rampant are Israeli Arab feelings of being individually and collectively discriminated against and of being treated as outsiders? Do Jews see any basis for the sense of deprivation and alienation felt by Israeli Arabs?

The ensuing detailed examination of the Arab-Jewish differences of opinion on these key issues aims to clarify the dominant Jewish views and the degree and nature of Arab dissent from them.

3

Ethnic Stratification

In deeply divided societies where a system of ethnic stratification is present, the critical question arises as to how the nondominant group reacts to its disadvantaged position. Its responses may range from resigned accommodation to flagrant resistance.

In Israel there is a system of ethnic stratification in which Ashkenazic Jews occupy the top strata and Israeli Arabs the bottom with Oriental Jews falling in between. Essentially, Arabs encounter the same lower-class handicaps which Oriental Jews face, although to an even greater extent (Smooha, 1976).

As a Third World minority in an advanced industrial society, Arabs are understandably at a disadvantage in commanding the necessary competitive resources. To cite some of the quantitative evidence, in 1979 (around the time the survey was conducted) only 22% of the Arabs as compared to 77% of the Jews lived in towns which usually provided better services and opportunities than villages. The dependency rate, i.e., persons under 15 and over 64, was 51% among Arabs and 40% among Jews (C.B.S., *Statistical Abstract of Israel 1980*, No. 31, 1980:41, 55). Discrepancies in living standards were also considerable. At that time per capita income of Jews was double that of the Arabs; 37% of the Arabs, in contrast to 2% of the Jews, lived in overcrowded dwellings (housing density of three or more persons per room) and a sizable minority of Arabs, compared to a negligible proportion of Jews, lacked basic household facilities such as baths or showers and washing machines (Table 3.1).

The poorer housing conditions of the Arabs are also reflected in the large percentage living in extended households. Although it is no longer their preference (Table 4.3 in the next chapter), 44% of the Arabs in 1976, compared to only 13% of the Jews, lived in some type of extended

household (Table 3.2). Of the married couples, 21% of the Arabs and only
1% of the Jews, had lived or were still living with their parents.

Table 3.1 Living Conditions

	Arabs	Jews
Index of average gross money income (base: Israeli Jews born in Europe-America 100.0)		
Per urban employee's household (1979)	73.2	93.2
Per capita of urban employee's household (1979)	12.2	24.6
Housing density – number of persons per room (1979)		
1 person or less	14.4	57.0
1.01-2.00	31.1	37.1
2.01-2.99	17.1	4.0
3 persons or more	37.4	1.9
Households in dwelling units that lack		
Flush toilet (1978)	13.4	0.9
Bath or shower (1978)	27.2	1.5
Electrical refrigerator (1977)	25.5	1.0
Washing machine (1977)	66.5	25.9
Television set (1977)	29.1	10.6
Telephone (1977)	92.6	53.6[a]
Private car (1977)	90.2	72.6

[a]For all (Jewish and Arab) households.

Source: Central Bureau of Statistics, *Statistical Abstract of Israel,1980*, no. 31, 1980:268, 275, 283, 293; CBS, *Society in Israel*, 1980:206-07.

Table 3.2 Extended Households

	Arab Public	Jewish Public
Composition of the household		
Living in non-extended household	55.6	86.8
Married couple accommodating a relative	16.6	8.8
Married couple without children living with parents	4.1	1.5
Married couple with children living with parents	11.8	1.5
Other extended households	11.9	1.5

Source: The 1976 survey.

Socioeconomic measures for the 1960's and 1970's show a dramatic
rise in standards for both Arabs and Jews, but the gaps have remained
substantial (Table 3.3). To indicate only the highlights: 60% of the Arabs
in 1961 lived in households with 3 or more persons per room, dropping
to 18% by 1979, compared to 37% and 2% of the Jews, respectively. The
proportion of Arabs employed in professional, managerial, clerical, and
commercial occupations increased from 15% in 1961 to 23% in 1979,
while the rise among the Jews was from 35% to 55%; the Jews in 1979

were still better off, at a ratio of 2.4 to 1. Despite the appreciable Arab educational accomplishments since 1949, by the late seventies Jews had a lead of 2:1 in the rate of high school attendance and 5:1 in the rate of university attendance. Jews also scored much higher on achievement and intelligence tests (Lieblich, 1983).

Table 3.3 Socioeconomic Measures, 1960's and 1970's

| | 1960's | | 1970's | |
	Arabs	Jews	Arabs	Jews
Education				
Years of schooling (1970, 1979)				
0	49.5	12.6	19.8	6.7
1-8	41.4	42.9	45.3	26.2
9-12	7.6	34.6	28.1	47.0
13+	1.5	9.9	6.8	20.1
Post-primary education rates per 100 persons aged 14-17 in age-specific population (1966/67, 1976/77)	22.4	62.0	44.9	74.8
Graduates of matriculation examinations – rates per 100 persons aged 18-24 in age-specific population (1959/60, 1977/78)	0.2	1.4	1.6	3..2
Higher education – rates per 100 persons aged 20-29 in total population (1970/71, 1977/78)	0.9[a]	7.9[a]	1.7[a]	8.9[a]
Employment (1961, 1979)				
White-collar occupations (professional, managerial, clerical, commercial)	15.1	35.4	23.2	55.0
Services	6.5	12.9	9.9	11.1
Blue-collar occupations	35.9	37.3	54.6	29.0
Agriculture	42.4	14.4	12.3	4.9
Living conditions				
Index of average gross money income (base: Israeli Jews born in Europe-America 100.0) Per urban employee's household (1970, 1979)	61.1	90.0	73.2	93.4
Per capita of urban employee's household (1970, 1977)	9.5	23.1	12.2	24.6
Households with 3 or more persons per room (1961, 1979)	60.1	17.8	37.4	1.9
Households in dwellings without flush toilets (1961, 1979)	51.1	5.0[b]	13.4	0.9
Households in dwellings without bath or shower (1961, 1978)	88.5	14.8[b]	27.2	1.5

[a]Estimates, not exact age-specific rates.

[b]For all (Jewish and Arab) households.

Source: Central Bureau of Statistics, *Statistical Abstract of Israel 1962*, No., 13, 1962:178, 391; No. 23, 1972:43, 599; No. 31, 1980:275, 283, 578; CBS, *Society in Israel*, 1980:164, 170; CBS, *Population and Housing Census 1961, Housing in Settlements*, No. 23, 1965; 11, 13.

Israeli Arabs are also denied participation in the top and middle-rank decision-making echelons of the country. As Table 3.4 clearly shows, they are absent from the governing elite of the state, the Histadrut, the Jewish political parties, and various national public organizations. They are present, yet powerless, in the Knesset and Histadrut bodies. Arabs enjoy power only in local governments, although it is constitutionally quite limited.

These privations are augmented by lack of industrialization and insufficient funding which leave the Arab local communities underdeveloped, suffering from ongoing surveillance, job discrimination, denial of institutional autonomy, and frequent intervention in their internal affairs.

The situation has not improved significantly by the late eighties. The overall rise in the standards of the Israeli population has not necessarily diminished the large Arab-Jewish socioeconomic gap. For instance, the post-1967 entry of over 100,000 Palestinian cheap laborers from the West Bank and Gaza Strip into the Israeli labor market pushed Israeli Arabs, Oriental Jews, and Ashkenazic Jews upward, but left the inequality among them almost intact (Lewin-Epstein and Semyonov, 1986).

Given the low class position of Israeli Arabs, the issue is whether they accept the status determinants and aspirations dominant in Israeli society. If they do, they are bound to feel very discontent with their status and to look for the opportunity to challenge it. The question for the Jews is the strength of their commitment to substantially reduce Arab-Jewish inequality.

The data show that Arabs do perceive their status to be determined by almost the same criteria that apply to status attainment by Jews in Israel (Table 3.5).Education is perceived as the single most crucial factor by 52.5% of the Arabs and 50% of the Jews. The achievement criteria of education, occupation, and money are regarded as the most important status determinants by 81% of the Arabs and 90% of the Jews. Arabs seem to depart from the traditional status determinants of family distinction and property (land), as indicated by their minor support (10%). This finding is essentially the same as that of an earlier study (Mar'i, 1978:156-57).

It is remarkable that although Israeli Arabs in 1949 were 80% illiterate and of peasant origin with limited access to formal education, they presently have an exceptionally high regard for education. A majority of 92.5% of the Arabs, as compared to 89% of the Jews, desire higher education for their children, and 85% and 83%, respectively, are willing to finance it (1976 survey figures). The 7% of the Arabs in the sample who have some higher education should be contrasted with the 92.5% who want complete university schooling for their children. This

Table 3.4 Power Positions

	Arabs	Jews
State (1979)		
President	0	1
Cabinet ministers	0	17
Deputy ministers	0	3
Knesset members	7	113
Supreme Court justices	0	11
Directors-General	0	18
Histadrut		
Central Committee (1980)	3	32
Executive Committee (1977)	8	177
Secretaries-General of trade unions (1978)	0	37
Hevrat Haovdim Executive (1978)	1	28
Hevrat Haovdim Secretariat (1978)	3	67
Parties		
Labor Party (1979)		
Bureau	0	65
Central Committee	20	840
Mapam (1979)		
Steering Committee	2	25
Secretariat	9	111
Central Committee	27	415
National Religious Party (1978)		
Secretariat	0	14
Executive Commitee	0	76
Narrow Central Committee	0	65
Broad Central Committee	0	277
Herut		
Executive Committee (1979)	1	49
Central Committee (1978)	7	693
Liberal Party		
Executive Committee (1978)	0	42
Central Committee (1977)	0	196
National Public Bodies		
Industrialists Union (1978)		
Steering Committee	0	17
Executive Committee	0	70
Broadcasting Authority (1979)		
Steering Committee	0	7
Plenum	2	29
Council on Higher Education (1979)		
Plenum	0	24
Public Council on Culture and Arts (1979)		
Plenum	4	82
National Bar Association (1979)		
Central Committee	0	15
Council	0	43
Localities		
Heads of local governments (1978)	54	100
Heads of regional councils (1973)	1	47
Secretaries-General of Workers' Councils (1978)	3	67

demonstrates that long-distance, inter-generational social mobility is sought by the great majority of Arabs in Israel, as well as by the Jews (19% and 89%, respectively). This corresponds to the situation in other class, achievement-oriented, industrial societies.

Table 3.5 Status Determinants

	Arab Public	Jewish Public
Hold that the most important factor determining the social status of Arabs in Israel today is[a]		
Education	52.5	50.0
Occupation	19.6	21.8
Connections	8.8	4.9
Money	8.6	18.3
Family distinction	7.2	2.8
Property (land)	3.2	2.1

[a]In the question for Jews, the words "of Arabs" were deleted.

Source: The 1976 survey.

The same picture holds true for the occupational sphere (Table 3.6). A great majority of both Arabs (85%) and Jews (94.5%) would encourage their children to enter high-status occupations (i.e., scientific, professional, technical, and managerial). They would also prefer to be self-employed (74% of the Arabs compared to 55% of the Jews). Since only a small minority are engaged in such top-ranking positions (9% of the Arabs and 25% of the Jews) or are self-employed (28% and 24%), long-distance occupational aspirations are far-reaching indeed.

The Arab adoption of Western status criteria and aspirations is further demonstrated by their occupational preferences. All in all, a profession requiring university training is preferable to a job that merely pays well (69% favor the former as opposed to 14% preferring the latter among the Arabs in the 1976 survey, and 71% and 15%, respectively, among the Jews). A decided majority (80% of Arabs and 91% of Jews) also opt for the scientific and technological tracks in high school rather than for humanistic studies. For most, education should train women for skilled employment outside the home.

Because Arabs occupy the lowest rank in the system of ethnic stratification, yet have high aspirations for social mobility, the nature of Arab reference groups becomes critical. Like minorities in other societies, Israeli Arabs face the dilemma of either accepting or rejecting the dominant Jewish majority as a positive reference group.

Two types of reference groups are relevant here: (1) the comparative group, which creates a context for evaluating one's own achievements and those of others – hence a potential source of relative deprivation; and

(2) the normative group, which sets values and thereby becomes a moral model to emulate (Merton, 1957:283-84). In choosing a reference group, most individuals both compare their own status attainment to that group and identify with its values, consequently striving to join that group.

Table 3.6 Occupational Distribution vs. Occupational Aspirations

	Arabs Actual[a]	Arabs Aspired[b]	Jews Actual[a]	Jews Aspired[b]
Occupation				
Scientific and academic	1.2	58.8	7.5	62.5
Other professional, technical	7.4	18.6	13.4	28.5
Managerial	0.4	7.2	4.3	3.5
Clerical	4.3	7.6	18.6	2.8
Sales	7.1	2.6	8.2	0.0
Service	9.7	0.3	11.6	0.0
Skilled in industry, building, transport	41.9	2.8	25.6	1.4
Unskilled in industry, building, transport	11.8	0.6	5.4	0.0
Agricultural	16.2	1.4	5.4	1.4
Employment status				
Employee	71.6	8.8	76.3	33.1
Self-employed	28.4[c]	73.7	23.7[c]	54.9
No preference	—	17.5	—	12.0

[a]Actual distribution of occupations and employment status in 1976, CBS, *Statistical Abstract of Israel 1977*, No. 28, 1977:301, 326.

[b]Aspired "occupation" refers to the occupation desired for one's children; aspired "employment status" refers to oneself.

[c]Including other non-employee status (employer, cooperative member, Kibbutz member and unpaid family member).

Source: The 1976 survey.

Since Arabs in Israel are simultaneously a part of different worlds, they have a wide choice of potential reference groups. Being Israeli citizens, their immediate milieu is that of the Jews. At the same time, they may relate to the Arab world in general and the Palestinian people in particular. Moreover, they have to come to terms with Western cultural penetration.

The actual selection of a particular reference group not only poses an immediate dilemma for Israeli Arabs but also affects their relations with Jews. More specifically, the adoption or rejection of Jews as a positive reference group bears heavy repercussions for Arab-Jewish coexistence. It is evident that the majority of Arabs accept Jews as a comparative group (Table 3.7). A majority of 58% of the Arab public compare their socioeconomic standards to those of Jews in Israel who, for the Arabs, represent the Western world. An additional 9% compare themselves directly with Westerners; thus a total of two thirds of the sample looks toward high socioeconomic standards. The remaining one third have lower levels of aspiration.

Table 3.7 Arabs' Comparative Groups

	Arab Public	Establishment Affiliated Arab Leaders	Rakah Affiliated Arab Leaders	Rejectionist Arab Leaders
In assessing one's socioeconomic achievements today, comparison is made to				
Palestinian Arabs in Mandatory Palestine	13.2	8.3	0.0	8.3
Arabs in the West Bank and Gaza Strip	5.6	0.0	6.5	29.2
Arabs in Arab countries	13.8	0.0	6.5	8.3
Jews in Israel	58.3	91.7	80.6	45.8
Inhabitants of the Western world	9.1	0.0	6.5	8.3

The strong socioeconomic orientation toward Israeli Jews and the West is even more pronounced at the leadership level. As many as 92% of the Arab leaders affiliated with the Zionist establishment, 87% of the Arab leaders affiliated to Rakah, and 54% of the rejectionist Arab leaders (i.e., activists in the Sons of the Village Movement or the Progressive National Movement) select Israeli Jews and Westerners as their framework of comparison. The fact that this holds a majority even among the rejectionist Arab leaders testifies to the firm Israeli Arab commitment to Western socioeconomic standards, which are Jewish in this context.

Table 3.8 Size and Urgency of Closing the Arab-Jewish Socioeconomic Gap

	Arab Public	Estab. Affil. Arab Lead.	Rakah Affil. Arab Lead.	Rejec- tion. Arab Lead.	Jewish Public	Dovish Jewish Lead.	Jewish Arab- ists	Hawkish Jewish Lead.
Regard the present socioeconomic gap between Arabs and Jews as								
Large	51.8	40.0	93.8	96.8	38.7	43.8	17.2	13.6
Medium	40.6	52.0	6.3	3.2	44.0	37.5	58.6	68.2
Small	7.6	8.0	0.0	0.0	17.3	18.8	24.6	18.2
Consider the closure of the present socioeconomic gap between Arabs and Jews as an urgent state goal	86.5	96.0	100.0	83.9	15.5	55.9	24.1	25.0

The Arabs are keenly aware of the discrepancy in status attainment between themselves and the Jews: 52% of them view the gap as big, 41% as medium, and only 8% as small (Table 3.8). The more radical Arab leaders are unanimously convinced that the inequality is enormous. All Arabs, both rank and file and leaders, agree that Israel should adopt the closure of the Arab-Jewish socioeconomic gap as an urgent national goal.

This too reconfirms their objections to the existing institutionalized ethnic hierarchy in Israel.

In contrast to the Arabs, only a minority of the Jewish public (39%) and of the Jewish leadership (ranging from 14% to 44%) regard the Arab-Jewish socioeconomic gap as wide. Most importantly, having a stake in the status quo most Jews fail to see the bridging of the gap as an urgent state objective, although a majority of the dovish Jewish leaders wish to see the gap closed by state policies. In fact, 56% of them, as opposed to only 15.5% of the general Jewish population, wish the state to act promptly upon this matter (Table 3.8).

An acute sense of relative deprivation among Arabs is logically bound to result from the clear contrast between their low achievements and the high aspirations which are derived from their choice of Jews as a comparative group. The Arabs' frustration is conceivably intensified by their gloomy expectations for social mobility as reflected, for instance, in their apprehension about the occupational future of Arab youths and their suspicion that governmental policies do not serve their needs (this deep sense of deprivation will be discussed in Chapter 15). Hence, it appears that far from being resigned to their lot as the lowest ethnic stratum, Israeli Arabs manifest a vast vested interest in revamping Israel's system of ethnic stratification. This Arab drive for equality is countered by putative Jewish stakes in the status quo of inequality as evidenced by the reluctance to reorder national priorities or to commit the necessary resources.

4

Cultural Diversity

Plural societies are usually multi-cultural societies in which the dominant group retains cultural dominance. The degree of this dominance depends on whether the minorities are subject to cultural repression and involuntary assimilation, whether they acquire the "core culture" necessary for coping in the society-at-large, and whether the dominant group is willing to recognize and partially integrate the subordinate culture into the national culture.

These questions are applicable to the plural society of Israel which is modern and Jewish in culture, thereby placing the Arab minority in a subordinate cultural position. Yet Israel accepts the Arabs as a linguistic, cultural, and religious minority and allows them to have the required means for full culture retention: separate Arab schools, media, places of worship, and all-Arab communities. Since the undesirability and improbability of cultural assimilation between Arabs and Jews are agreed upon, the issues are whether the two sides are developing any common core culture and how divided are they about Israel's national culture and the status of the Arab culture within it.

By the early eighties the cultural results of the ongoing, historical process of Israelization of the Arabs are clearly noticeable. While preserving their language and culture, Israeli Arabs have adopted certain patterns of the dominant Israeli culture which are vital for getting along in Israeli society, economy, and politics. Most Arabs have become bicultural in using Hebrew as a second language, in mixing their traditions with modern values, and in obtaining Jewish practices in addition to their own. This cultural change has no doubt facilitated not only Arab adjustment to Israel but also Arab-Jewish communication, understanding, and cooperation.

The survey data show that Arabic-Hebrew bilingualism and Arab-Jewish biculturalism are quite advanced, but are mostly limited to

Israeli Arabs. The figures are impressive indeed: 70% of all Israeli Arabs can speak both Arabic and Hebrew, and 63% can read and write in both languages (Table 4.1). Bilingualism is universal among Arab men aged 18-25 (98% can speak, and 93% can read and write both Arabic and Hebrew), and among Arab public leaders (with the exception of the vanishing traditional notables), indicating a rapid acceptance of bilingualism as an established standard among the Arabs in the foreseeable future. In contrast, bilingualism is partial and somewhat on the decline among the Jews. In 1980, only 37% of the Jews (59% of the Orientals vs. 14% of the Ashkenazim) knew how to speak Israel's two official languages and just 10% could use them for reading and writing. The diminishing trend is evident in the reduced retention of Arabic by Oriental sabras. For example, 70% of foreign-born Moroccan Jews could speak Arabic as compared to only 57% of their Israeli-born offspring.

Table 4.1 Knowledge of Hebrew and Arabic

	Arab Public	Jewish Public
Know how to speak Arabic	100.0	37.2
Know how to read and write Arabic	77.6	10.3
Know how to speak Hebrew	69.9	100.0[a]
Know how to read and write Hebrew	62.9	92.9
Know how to speak Arabic and Hebrew	69.9	37.2
Know how to read and write Arabic and Hebrew	62.7	10.3
Know how to speak, read and write in Arabic and Hebrew	60.6	8.1

[a] Since interviews with Jews for the survey were conducted in Hebrew only, all respondents obviously speak Hebrew. It is estimated that about 85% of the Jews in Israel are Hebrew speakers.

Table 4.2 Media Exposure

	All Arabs	Arab Potential Users	All Jews	Jewish Potential Users
Recipients of Arabic foreign news broadcasts on a regular basis[a]	58.5	58.5	11.5	31.5
Recipients of Arabic Israeli news broadcasts on a regular basis[a]	53.1	53.1	20.9	55.4
Recipients of Hebrew Israeli news broadcasts on a regular basis[a]	27.7	46.2	95.7	95.7
Readers of Arabic newspapers	43.2	56.0	0.7	8.2
Readers of Al-Anba	30.6	39.7	0.4	4.5
Readers of Al-Ittihad	20.2	26.2	0.1	1.1
Readers of East Jerusalem newspapers	13.4	17.4	0.3	3.4
Readers of Hebrew newspapers	42.0	68.1	86.3	93.7

[a] The 1976 survey.

The Israelization of the Arabs is also manifested in their media exposure. Although a majority of them follow foreign radio and television broadcasts (from Jordan, Monte Carlo, PLO, etc.), they also use the Israeli Arabic and Hebrew media extensively (Table 4.2). To quote the main figures, 58.5% follow foreign Arabic news broadcasts, 53% listen or watch Israeli Arabic news broadcasts, and 42% read Hebrew newspapers. Jews do not read Arabic newspapers but a sizable minority of them watch Arabic broadcasts, mostly because the Hebrew television offerings are insufficient.

Arabs are also becoming closer to Jews culturally in their adoption of modern values and the move away from traditionalism, but the gap between the two communities has remained significant. Family norms are a good measure of both the cultural change Arabs have undergone and the gap still separating them from Jews. To illustrate, whereas 62% of the Jews support family planning, 39% of the Arabs do so (Table 4.3). The status of women is the most sensitive area. Although Arab

Table 4.3 Family Norms

	Arab Public	Jewish Public
Preferred residence after marriage		
Apart from parents	58.2	93.0
No preference	16.3	3.5
With parents	25.5	3.5
Degree of family planning preferred		
Full	38.7	62.2
Partial	26.0	23.8
None	35.2	14.0
Desired number of children		
1-3 children	20.5	42.8
4-5 children	44.3	45.8
6+ or as many as possible	35.3	11.5

Source: The 1976 survey.

women in Israel are permitted much more freedom of movement, rights and mixing with men than in traditional Arab society, only half of the Arabs would allow a young single Arab girl to participate in coed cultural activities or to wear trendy fashions (Table 4.4). The main bastion of tradition is female chastity. Only 14% of the Arabs, as compared to 92% of the Jews, would let a young girl have a boyfriend. These figures echo the cultural revolution Oriental immigrants have undergone; in the fifties most of them held attitudes similar to those held in the eighties by Israeli Arabs. Unlike Oriental Jews who were transplanted overnight from traditional Arab countries into a modern

Jewish society, cut off from Arab cultures and forced to assimilate, Israeli Arabs have continued to live in their original communities, to maintain cultural contacts with the Arab world particularly after 1967, and to enjoy the facilities to keep their distinct traditions.

Table 4.4 Behavior Permitted Young Single Arab Girls[a]

	Arab Public	Jewish Public
Participation in mixed (men and women) cultural activities		
Permit	52.8	89.5
Permit to some extent	27.2	6.3
Do not permit	20.0	4.2
Going out with girlfriends away from place of residence		
Permit	49.3	79.4
Permit to some extent	32.0	7.1
Do not permit	18.7	13.5
Wearing trendy fashions – mini, maxi, etc. – as styles change		
Permit	41.7	83.0
Permit to some extent	35.2	10.6
Do not permit	23.1	6.4
Having a boyfriend		
Permit	13.7	91.6
Permit to some extent	15.0	3.5
Do not permit	71.4	4.9

[a] For Arab respondents: "Young single Arab girls"; for Jewish respondents: "Young single girls."
Source: The 1976 survey.

A high endogamy points to considerable continuity with past practices. As many as 25% of the Arabs are married to paternal first cousins, 48% to relatives (hamula members), and 76% to residents of the same locality (Table 4.5). These rates reach 36%, 62% and 89.5%,

Table 4.5 Cousin, Hamula, and Locality Endogamy among Arabs

		Cousin	Hamula	Locality
Total	24.6	47.9	75.6	
Number of hamula members living in one's locality				
Fewer than 100 persons		16.0	30.4	64.8
100-499		25.3	50.8	76.7
500-999		28.8	62.2	81.1
One thousand or more		35.9	62.4	89.5
Community				
Christians		17.1	30.2	69.8
Non-Bedouin Moslems		23.8	49.2	75.6
Druzes		22.7	38.5	89.8
Bedouin		39.8	72.0	72.9

respectively, among members of big hamulas and are particularly high among the more traditional Bedouin: 40%, 72% and 73%. The fact that they are also high among the more urbanized and educated Christian Arabs (17%, 30% and 70%, respectively) reveals the moderate pace of change in the Arab sector.

Arab attitudes are more modern than are the more complex traditional marriage practices. A majority of Israeli Arabs endorse Western values such as living apart from parents after marriage, money accumulation, and competitiveness (Table 4.6). They also favor modification or abolition of traditional Arab customs such as the right to cousin marriage, loyalty to the hamula, and blood vengeance (Table 4.7). They wish, nevertheless, to keep traditions which they consider noble, like lavish hospitality, neighborliness, and family honor. These fine distinctions among various values made by Israeli Arabs reflect the stage of cultural transition in which they find themselves during the eighties.

Table 4.6 Western Values

	Arab Public	Jewish Public
Western values acceptable for Arabs in Israel (for Jewish respondents: "for Israeli society")		
Woman's right to choose husband freely		
Accept as is	31.8	75.5
Accept with modification	43.2	17.5
Reject	25.0	7.0
To live apart from parents after marriage		
Accept as is	67.5	90.3
Accept with modification	23.2	5.6
Reject	9.3	4.2
To save, invest, and earn as much money as possible		
Accept as is	59.7	72.2
Accept with modification	34.9	20.8
Reject	5.5	6.9
To surpass one's co-workers or fellow-students		
Accept as is	64.3	72.5
Accept with modification	28.8	19.0
Reject	6.8	8.5

Source: The 1976 survey.

How do Israeli Arabs and Jews view the emerging bilingualism and biculturalism among individuals which have created a common cultural ground? They and their leaders fully concur on bilingualism for both Arabs and Jews. On the other hand, a consensus on biculturalism is still

Table 4.7 Arabs' Views of Traditional Arab Values

	Arab Public
The right to cousin marriage	
Retain as is	16.4
Modify	22.4
Abolish	61.2
Loyalty to the hamula	
Retain as is	28.6
Modify	28.0
Abolish	43.4
Blood Vengeance	
Retain as is	13.2
Modify	12.5
Abolish	74.3
Lavish and unstinting hospitality	
Retain as is	74.5
Modify	22.6
Abolish	2.9
Numerous neighborly commitments	
Retain as is	76.5
Modify	19.8
Abolish	3.7
Duty to protect honor of women in the family	
Retain as is	84.3
Modify	13.2
Abolish	2.4

Source: The 1976 survey.

lacking (Table 4.8). There is neither an Arab nor Jewish majority for the idea that Arabs should learn modern values and practices from the Jews, and that Arabs should espouse Jewish values and customs in addition to their own.[1] It seems that the Arabs are ambivalent toward biculturalism lest it dilute their original Arab culture, which it inescapably does to some extent. Although 61% of the Arabs desire Jews to embrace certain

[1]It is significant that a majority of Arabs do not take Jews as a normative group, yet a majority do take them as a comparative group. This finding is highlighted by the 68% of Arabs who do not think Arabs should learn modern values from the Jews (Table 4.8) in contrast to the 67% who compare their own socioeconomic achievements to the Jews' and Westerners' standards (Table 3.7). This peculiar pattern can be mainly explained by sheer vested interests. As a cultural minority, Arabs reject Jews as a source of values in order to preserve their separate existence and identity. On the other hand, by adopting the Jews as a comparative group the Arabs raise their socioeconomic standards, thereby becoming highly sensitive to relative deprivation and insistent in their demands for equality.

Arab cultural patterns, probably in reciprocity for the actual Arab move toward them, only 29% of the Jews agree.

Table 4.8 Values of Individual Bilingualism and Biculturalism

	Arab Public	Estab. Affil. Arab Lead.	Rakah Affil. Arab Lead.	Rejec-tion. Arab Lead.	Jewish Public	Dovish Jewish Lead.	Jewish Arab-ists	Hawkish Jewish Lead.
Hold that Israel should do its best to have most Jews and most Arabs master both Hebrew and Arabic	96.3	100.0	100.0	86.7	76.1	100.0	96.6	92.0
Hold that Arabs in Israel should learn modern values and practices from the Jews	31.7	68.0	43.8	48.4	49.2	60.0	84.6	33.3
Hold that Arabs in Israel should adopt Jewish values and practices in addition to their own	33.6	48.0	41.9	38.7	47.1	76.7	78.6	37.5
Hold that Jews should adopt Arab values and practices in addition to their own	61.4	56.0	62.5	48.4	29.4	71.4	82.1	36.0

The real divisive issue hinges, however, on the character of the national culture. Jews favor a modern Jewish culture and therefore oppose making Arabic as dominant as Hebrew and reject Arab culture as part of Israel's national culture. On the other hand, the Arabs want Israel to become a truly bilingual state and to make their culture part and parcel of the Israeli culture; hence they feel reserved about Israel's drive toward the West.

This disagreement is evident in responses to questions about institutional bilingualism and biculturalism. Arabs are found to be as strongly for them as the Jews are against them. Whereas 92% of the Arabs believe that Hebrew and Arabic should prevail equally in the public domain, only 24% of the Jews concur (Table 4.9). While 41% of the Arabs favor a modern culture for Israel, 63% of the Jews hold the same view. By the same token, 72% and 33.5%, respectively, agree that the Arab culture has to be treated as an important part of Israel's culture. Since the last statement suggests a public recognition of Arab culture alongside the dominant Jewish one, rather than turning Israel into an officially bicultural country, 70% of the dovish Jewish leaders and 54% of the Jewish Arabists endorse this kind of biculturalism as compared to only 33.5% of the Jewish public. In contrast, 79% of the rejectionist Arab leaders and 83% of the hawkish Jewish leaders are either against or reserved about such measures of institutional biculturalism because these nationalist leaders are unwilling to compromise the exclusive dominance of their own culture.

Table 4.9 Values of Institutional Bilingualism and Biculturalism

	Arab Public	Estab. Affil. Arab Lead.	Rakah Affil. Arab Lead.	Rejec- tion. Arab Lead.	Jewish Public	Dovish Jewish Lead.	Jewish Arab- ists	Hawkish Jewish Lead.
Hold that Hebrew and Arabic should prevail equally in public and state institutions	92.2	100.0	96.9	96.6	24.3	46.9	50.0	23.1
Hold that modern values and practices should prevail in Israel	41.4	52.0	56.3	87.1	63.0	86.7	91.7	36.8
Hold that Arab culture should be treated as an important part of Israel's national culture	71.9	92.0	96.9	21.4	33.5	69.7	53.6	17.4

To conclude, Arabs have the status of a linguistic and cultural minority in Israel. This absolves Israel from a cultural repression of the Arabs, yet it does not necessarily make the Jewish state a pluralistic society which treats all constituent cultures equally. Institutionalizing Jewish culture and orienting itself to the West, Israel despises the Arab culture and at best tolerates it as a culture for the Arabs only.[2] As we shall see later, to a certain degree Israel tries to contain the Palestinian expressions in the Israeli Arab culture because of the fear that Palestinian nationalism will spread among Israeli Arabs. Although Israeli Arabs have become increasingly bilingual and bicultural, they disagree with these cultural policies and wish to make Israel more Arab in culture and more responsive to their cultural needs.

[2]With regard to the contempt Israeli Jewish elites feel toward Arab culture, see Smooha, 1978: 88.

5

Legitimacy of Coexistence

The best sign of communal rift in plural societies is the disavowal of permanent coexistence between the constituent segments. The nondominant group may challenge the system totally by denying the state's very right to exist or partially by rejecting some of its laws and structures. Similarly the dominant group's opposition may be manifested by a desire to "dispose" of the minority altogether or a reluctance to grant it full rights. The plural structure of Cypress, Lebanon, and Northern Ireland, to name but a few, is noticeable in the virulent struggles over matters of legitimacy.

Both the Arab minority and Jewish majority present Israel with fundamental questions about legitimacy. Do the Arab citizens acknowledge Israel's right to exist? Do they approve of its constitutional character as a Jewish-Zionist state? These two related questions are sufficiently separate. Those, like the Rejection Front, who officially repudiate Israel do so not just because of its unique national identity. Conversely, there are those, like Rakah, who recognize Israel as a reality but at the same time disapprove of its Jewish-Zionist mold. The Jews encounter similar queries: do they consent to having an Arab minority or would they rather get rid of it? Are they willing to accord Arabs full civil and other rights? Willingness to incorporate Arabs into the state does not necessarily mean full civic or national equality.

The data clearly disclose doubts concerning the desirability or possibility of coexistence on both sides. First and foremost is the question of Israel's right to exist. Although Israel in 1980 was isolated in the international arena, its sovereignty was acknowledged by most states. The Arab world, with the paramount exception of Egypt, was the only bloc denying Israel's existence as a state. Most importantly, when the survey was conducted in 1980, the PLO officially rejected Israel although it was actually ambiguous and ambivalent. This formal repudiation of Israel by the organization that personifies the Palestinian national movement in the eyes of Israeli Arabs was of utmost significance. Only in late 1988 did the PLO move to accept Israel's right to exist.[1] The Arabs, being simultaneously Israeli citizens and part of the Arab world and particularly the Palestinian people, experience contradictory pressures on this issue. In reply to the simple, direct question: "Does Israel have a right to exist?," 59% answer in the affirmative, 30% have reservations, and only 11% reject this right (Table 5.1). It is difficult to assess how much of this unqualified acceptance of Israel as a state can be attributed to a genuine conviction of Israel's moral essence, to a sense of realism, or to pure expediency. It is indeed remarkable, however, that only a tiny minority of one tenth concur with the PLO's official rejection at that time of Israel's legitimacy as a state.

Table 5.1 Arab's Acceptance of Israel's Right to Exist by Arabs

	Arab Public	Establishment Affiliated Arab Leaders	Rakah Affiliated Arab Leaders	Rejectionist Arab Leaders
Acceptance of Israel's right to exist				
Yes	58.8	96.0	84.4	0.0
Have reservations	30.3	4.0	15.6	22.6
No	11.0	0.0	0.0	77.4

The degree of outright rejection of Israel's right to exist is very small and varies among population cross sections. The most accepting groups, with rejection below 10%, include Druzes and Northern Bedouin, Arabs not affected by land expropriations, Arabs who are on visiting terms with Jews, and those with political ties to the Zionist establishment (Table 5.2). Prominent among the latter are leaders tied to the Zionist establishment who unanimously accept Israel's existence (Table 5.1). Although none of the Rakah or DFPE leaders totally reject the existence of the state, their constituents do so to some extent: 9% of the Rakah members and 17% of the DFPE voters do not accept Israel's right to exist. The dissent of the activists in the Sons of the Village Movement and the Progressive National Movement is unmistakable: 77% totally reject Israel's existence, 23% have reservations, and none accept it.

[1]Within Israel only the tiny splinter groups of the ultra-orthodox *N'turei Karta* and some revolutionary socialists, certain factions within *Matzpen*-Israeli Socialist Organization, still withhold legitimacy from the State of Israel.

Table 5.2 Rejection of Israel's Right to Exist by Arab Population Groups

	% Rejecting
Less rejecting groups	
Aged 36-45 years	6.3
Druzes	1.8
Northern Bedouin	7.4
Not affected by land expropriations	7.9
Have visited Jewish friends	9.5
Residents of unincorporated villages	7.6
Live in localities in which over 79% of the vote won by Zionist parties or affiliated Arab lists	2.5
Members of Zionist parties	5.6
Voted for Zionist parties or affiliated Arab lists in 1977	5.7
Intend to vote for Zionist parties or affiliated Arab lists in 1981	6.6
More rejecting groups	
Aged 19-24 years	13.9
Moslems (excluding Northern Bedouin)	13.3
Much affected by land expropriations	15.4
Have no Jewish friends	15.0
Live in localities in which 20-39% of the vote won by DFPE (Rakah)	17.3
Members of Rakah	9.3
Voted for DFPE in 1977	11.2
Intend to vote for Rakah or DFPE in 1981	13.8

In a parallel vein, most Jews are prepared to endorse the Arab minority's right to live in Israel, just as the majority of Israeli Arabs accept Israel's right of existence.[2] When asked about a formula for the Arab minority situation, only 15% of the Jews in the survey insist on total Arab exclusion from the state (see Table 10.4 in Chapter 10). It is highly significant that only 4% of the hawkish Jewish leaders and none of the other Jewish leaders opt to bar Arabs. To be sure, most Jews' first choice is to have fewer Arabs around. For instance, in 1967-68, 91% to 93% of a sample from the Tel Aviv area agreed that "it would be better if there were fewer Arabs" (Peres, 1971: Table 12) and 83% in the 1976 survey felt the same. Similarly, in the 1980 survey 50% think that Israel should explore and seize every opportunity to encourage Arabs to leave the country, 31% have reservations, and only 19% object. Despite these preferences and occasional tacit threats by hardline public figures, a continued Arab presence is well safeguarded in Israel. The policy toward the Arabs is control rather than expulsion. In 1980 only Kach, Rabbi

[2]It can be argued that the equivalent question to the Arab recognition of Israel's right to exist is the Jewish recognition of the Palestinians' right to self-determination. This is no doubt true in the broader context of the Israeli-Arab conflict but not in the more focused area of minority-majority relations in Israel.

Kahane's splinter party, advocated the removal of all Arabs from the country. Kach was banned from participating in the 1988 elections and succeeded to some extent by Moledet ("Homeland"). Moledet, a more respectable party, won two seats in 1988 by calling for the mass transfer of the Arab population from the West Bank and Gaza Strip. Unlike Kach, Moledet does not preach the transfer of Israeli Arabs but calls on them to render a military or civil service in order to obtain full civil rights. The Tehiya and Zomet parties, which together won five seats in the Knesset in 1988, are sympathetic with this stance.

If coexistence is espoused in principle by both sides, then the real divisive issue of legitimacy concerns its terms. For the Arabs, the question is to reconcile themselves to Israel's Jewish-Zionist character and, by implication, to be resigned to a subordinate minority status. For the Jews, the problem is to compromise Israel's identity with equal status for the Arab minority.

Table 5.3 Arabs' Acceptance of Israel as a Jewish-Zionist State

	Arab Public	Establishment Affiliated Arab Leaders	Rakah Affiliated Arab Leaders	Rejectionist Arab Leaders
Acceptance of Israel's right to exist within the Green Line as a Jewish-Zionist state				
Yes	12.6	36.0	3.1	3.2
Have reservations	30.3	52.0	25.0	6.5
No	57.1	12.0	71.9	90.3
It is all right to use any means necessary to abolish Israel's Jewish-Zionist character				
Against	17.9	28.0	12.5	3.3
Have reservations	32.7	44.0	46.9	6.7
In favor	49.4	28.0	40.6	90.0

A majority of Arabs frown on Israel's Jewish-Zionist "constitution." While 59% of the Arabs accept Israel's right to exist, 57% flatly deny Israel's right to be a Jewish-Zionist state (Table 5.3). The contrast is even more striking among Rakah-affiliated Arab leaders of whom 84% condone the state but 72% spurn its Zionist mission. A substantial 77% of the rejectionist leaders repudiate the very existence of Israel and 90% reject its character. Equally dramatic is the discrepancy in levels of recognition by the establishment affiliated Arab leaders. Whereas 96% fully recognize Israel as a state, only 36% fully accept its right to be

Jewish-Zionist.[3] Furthermore, a majority of the Arab rank and file, and of Arab leaders, do not rule out the use of "any means necessary" to do away with Israel's Jewish-Zionist mold, thereby giving vent to their deep disaffection but not necessarily legitimizing violence (Table 5.3).

At first glance, Jews appear receptive to Arab minority rights. A majority of 55% of the Jewish public and virtually all the leaders grant the Arab minority the right to live in Israel with full civil rights (Table 5.4). Similarly, 47% favor the same rights to Jews and Arabs and 61% assent to equal duties (Table 14.9 in Chapter 14). Those who are more educated, older, politically aware, and of Ashkenazic background are expectantly more liberal than others (Table 5.5).

Table 5.4 Jews' Acceptance of Arab Minority's Right to Live in Israel with Full Civil Rights

	Jewish Public	Dovish Jewish Leaders	Jewish Arabists	Hawkish Jewish Leaders
Acceptance of the Arab minority's right to live in Israel with full civil rights				
Yes	54.7	97.1	93.3	88.5
Have reservations	28.6	2.9	6.7	7.7
No	16.6	0.0	0.0	3.8

Upon closer examination, however, Jews are actually less accepting of Arabs. Many Jews who agree to allow the Arab minority full civil rights have in mind a status quo in which Arabs are formally afforded such rights but denied them in practice. If this is true, then the 47% to 55% of the Jews who endorse equal rights for Arabs should be considered rather low in approval because it implies that the remaining half would not even put up with the existing restricted rights. This interpretation is amply borne out by the fact that an overwhelming majority of Jews favor preferential, rather than equal, treatment of Jews by the state (Tables 14.10-14.11).

Further probes unveil the profound division between Arabs and Jews on Israel's Jewish-Zionist nature. The Jewish commitment to Zionism is strong indeed (Table 5.6). Even when reminded of the presence of an Arab minority in their midst, 95.5% of the Jews reaffirm their conviction to retain or even strengthen Israel's Jewish-Zionist identity. Over two thirds approve of the use of "any means necessary" to defend it, and one third to a half would deny various civil rights to groups opposed to it.

[3]This finding is in line with the main conclusion that Geffner (1974) drew from her study of attitudes among Israeli Arab elites toward Israel. She found that those affiliated to the Zionist establishment overemphasize Israel's pluralistic, secular, and democratic nature and tend to ignore its Jewish-Zionist character.

Table 5.5 Arab Minority's Right to Live in Israel with Full Civil Rights by Jewish Population Groups

	% Rejecting
Less rejecting groups	
Aged 36-45 years	12.8
Have higher education	5.8
Have great interest in politics	12.5
Voted for small liberal parties in 1977[a]	2.6
Kibbutz members	5.2
Ashkenazim	9.3
More rejecting groups	
Aged 18-25 years	20.2
Have primary education or less	26.2
Have little interest in politics	24.6
Voted for Likud in 1977	18.0
Voted for the religious parties in 1977	25.7
Residents of development or immigrant towns	19.7
Orientals	25.0

[a] Democratic Movement for Change, Citizens Rights Movement, Independent Liberals, Shelli, Mapam members who voted for Labor.

Table 5.6 Importance of Israel's Jewish-Zionist Character to Jews

	Jewish Public	Dovish Jewish Leaders	Jewish Arabists	Hawkish Jewish Leaders
Hold that it is important to keep Israel a Jewish-Zionist state	95.3	100.0	100.0	100.0
Maintain that Israel should strengthen, or preserve as is, its Jewish-Zionist character despite having an Arab minority	95.5	100.0	90.0	100.0
Believe that it is all right to use any means necessary to retain Israel's Jewish-Zionist character	70.5	26.7	55.2	43.5
Endorse, without reservation, each of the following measures against groups that oppose Israel's Jewish-Zionist character				
Denial of a license to publish a newspaper	49.8	21.9	26.7	47.8
Denial of registration to be incorporated as a voluntary association	51.4	31.3	34.5	68.2
Use of administrative detention	33.0	9.1	37.9	50.0
Outlawing	42.6	25.0	39.3	52.4
Deportation from the country	38.2	6.3	29.6	45.5

Israel's plural structure is best manifested in the communal dissension over a variety of features that combine to make Israel Jewish and Zionist (Table 5.7). By large majorities, Jews agree and Arabs disagree that Israel is a homeland of Jews only rather than a common homeland of both Jews and Arabs. Jews and Arabs are also sharply divided on whether Israel should keep a Jewish majority, save the Law of Return as is, endeavor on behalf of Jewish immigration and world Jewry, retain Hebrew as the dominant language, preserve Jewish emblems and symbols of the state, and accord Jews a preferential treatment. There is further dissension about Zionism as a non-racist, national liberation movement. Although not questioned about the special status presently conferred on the Jewish Agency and National Jewish Fund, Jews are known to think well of it, whereas Arabs take a dim view of it.

Table 5.7 Israel's Features as a Jewish-Zionist State

	Arab Public	Estab. Affil. Arab Lead.	Rakah Affil. Arab Lead.	Rejec-tion. Arab Lead.	Jewish Public	Dovish Jewish Lead.	Jewish Arab-ists	Hawkish Jewish Lead.
Endorse each of the following features								
Israel as a homeland of Jews only	5.2	0.0	3.2	9.1	74.6	34.4	44.8	88.0
Jewish majority	18.2	45.5	3.2	0.0	97.7	100.0	100.0	100.0
Law of Return (retain as is)	6.0	4.2	0.0	0.0	73.3	87.1	93.3	96.2
Strenuous efforts for Jewish immigration and world Jewry	7.1	13.0	0.0	6.7	81.6	90.3	89.2	95.7
Jewish emblems and symbols of the state[a]	*	*	*	*	97.3	94.1	100.0	100.0
Hebrew as the dominant language	2.4	0.0	3.1	0.0	75.7	53.1	50.0	76.9
State's preferential treatment of Jews	3.4	4.2	0.0	0.0	83.9	28.5	50.0	54.6
Zionism as a non-racist movement	15.6	40.0	0.0	0.0	*	*	*	*

* Not asked

[a] Percent reserved or totally opposed to changing the state symbols, such as the flag and anthem, to facilitate Arab identification with Israel.

Both Arabs and Jews accept the principle of coexistence much more than the actual terms of it. Of the Arabs who fully acknowledge Israel's right to exist, only 21% unreservedly recognize its right to be a Jewish-Zionist state, 20% reject the charge that the Zionist movement is racist, and 7.5% assent to the retention of the Law of Return as is. The respective figures among the leaders who have thrown their lot in with the Zionist establishment are 37.5%, 42%, and 4%. The implication is that even Arabs who are prepared to live as a legal minority in Israel do not accept the present unequal circumstances.

By the same token, of those Jews who fully accept the Arab minority's right to live in Israel with complete civil rights 94% insist on maintaining or reinforcing Israel's Jewish-Zionist character despite the Arab presence, 64% regard Israel as an exclusively Jewish homeland, and 76% favor preferential treatment of Jews by the state. On the other hand, the dovish Jewish leaders, the Jewish group most predisposed to cooperative coexistence, take a more complex position. All of those favoring full rights for Arabs also reaffirm their commitment to Israel's Jewish-Zionist character notwithstanding the Arab minority. Yet, 66% of them regard Israel as the shared homeland of Jews and Arabs and 74% favor equal treatment of all Israeli citizens.

These liberal Jewish leaders express the long-standing official line that political democracy and Zionism are both compatible and present in the state of Israel. Although this is true in some cases, there are many situations where these two distinguishing features collide and Jews, as the dominant group, make choices for the entire society. Priorities are likely to be decided by Zionist values and by sheer Jewish self-interest as responses to the survey indicate. Indeed, the large majorities among Jews: 57.5% of the Jewish public, 70% of the dovish leaders, 71% of the Arabists, and 91.5% of the hawkish leaders, give precedence to Israel's Jewish-Zionist character when it contradicts with the democratic-egalitarian ethos (Table 5.8).

Table 5.8 Possibility of Equal Status for Arabs in Israel

	Arab Public	Estab. Affil. Arab Lead.	Rakah Affil. Arab Lead.	Rejec- tion. Arab Lead.	Jewish Public	Dovish Jewish Lead.	Jewish Arab- ists	Hawkish Jewish Lead.
If the egalitarian-democratic character of the state stands in contradiction to its Jewish-Zionist character and a choice need be made between them								
Would prefer the egalitarian-democratic character	*	*	*	*	42.5	30.0	28.6	9.5
Would prefer the Jewish-Zionist character	*	*	*	*	57.5	70.0	71.4	91.5
Arabs can be equal citizens of Israel as a Jewish-Zionist state and can identify themselves with the state								
Yes	25.0	40.0	6.3	0.0	27.3	42.4	56.7	64.0
Possible	23.4	32.0	9.4	3.2	26.1	30.3	16.7	8.0
Doubtful	23.7	28.0	46.9	0.0	22.7	21.2	20.0	16.0
No	27.9	0.0	37.5	96.8	24.0	6.1	6.7	12.0

* Not asked

In order to assess the overall impact of this finding on Arab status, all respondents were asked whether "Arabs can be equal citizens in Israel as a Jewish-Zionist state and can identify themselves with it" (Table 5.8). Both the Arab and Jewish publics are evenly split on the issue. On the other hand, a majority of all three types of Jewish leaders take a positive stand, once again conforming to the official belief in Arab-Jewish coexistence on Jewish terms. Although preferring a non-sectarian state, most establishment-affiliated Arab leaders also concur. In fact, for them the possibility of equal Arab status in a Jewish-Zionist state is a credo and basis for activity. In a sharp contrast, Rakah-affiliated and rejectionist Arab leaders are convinced that Israeli Arabs cannot be equal and cannot identify themselves with contemporary Israel.

To conclude, the issue of legitimacy of coexistence has by and large ceased to be a question of the right of Israel or its Arab minority to exist. It has become one of the proper conditions for mutual accommodation. However, even though Arabs and Jews increasingly accept coexistence, they remain sharply divided over Zionism, Israel's raison d'étre, and basic ideology. Arabs as a whole reject Israel's Jewish-Zionist character, while Jews are firmly committed to it. Israeli Arabs wish to transform Israel into a binational state, an old idea that leaders of both sides dismissed during the British Mandate and Jews continue to oppose vehemently. Since Jews have a higher regard for Israel's Jewish-Zionist identity than to its political democracy, they are reluctant to grant full equality to the non-Zionist Israeli Arabs.

6

The Israeli-Arab Conflict

The Israeli-Arab conflict is total and far-reaching. It is Israel's most critical problem cutting across all others: economic, social, and political. Naturally, it has become the focus for strong emotions and opinions and a yardstick for loyalty and patriotism. As such, it constitutes an inexhaustible source of Arab dissidence in Israeli society.

Issues

Of the plethora of issues pertaining to the Israeli-Arab conflict, three were selected for inquiry: the Israel-Egypt peace treaty, territorial matters, and the Palestinian question.

According to the 1978 peace treaty, Egypt is to cease belligerency, recognize Israel, and begin to normalize relations with it. In return, Israel is to withdraw from Sinai and negotiate the implementation of an autonomy plan to resolve the Palestinian question. Do these accords become a basis for understanding between Arabs and Jews or a new bone of contention? Respondents were asked to indicate their overall attitude toward the treaty.

The vast majority of Jews, 71%, fully endorse the treaty, while 21% have reservations and only 8% oppose it (Table 6.1). The treaty is endorsed by 88% of the dovish Jewish leaders and 72% of the Jewish Arabists, but only 48% of the hawkish Jewish leaders lend their complete support. These figures confirm what is already known about Jewish opinion. Most Jews approve of the treaty because they regard it as a historical breakthrough by Israel into a hostile Arab world. Jewish reservations and objections hinge, however, on two major points. One is the total withdrawal from Sinai that requires the dismantling of Jewish settlements and sets an "undesirable" precedent for future agreements on the West Bank and Golan Heights. The other point is the autonomy scheme that could eventually lead, as many Jews fear, to a separate Palestinian state.

Table 6.1 Israel-Egypt Peace Treaty

	Arab Public	Estab. Affil. Arab Lead.	Rakah Affil. Arab Lead.	Rejection. Arab Lead.	Jewish Public	Dovish Jewish Lead.	Jewish Arab-ists	Hawkish Jewish Lead.
Stand on the peace treaty								
In favor	49.1	88.0	3.1	0.0	71.4	88.2	72.4	48.0
Have reservations	27.7	12.0	34.4	9.7	20.6	11.8	24.1	32.0
Against	23.2	0.0	62.5	90.3	8.0	0.0	3.4	20.0

To date, there have been few data available on the views of Arabs in Israel regarding the peace treaty, and what is known tends to be negative. On the one hand, recognition of Israel by the strongest Arab state legitimizes accommodative efforts made by the Arab minority. It is also possible that permanent coexistence between Egyptians and Israelis will spill over to Arab-Jewish relations inside Israel. On the other hand, at the time of the 1980 survey, the treaty was rejected by the larger Arab world that censured and isolated Egypt and boosted its backing of the PLO. Most importantly, at that time, the Palestinians in the occupied territories and elsewhere were adamantly opposed to the treaty in which they found no remedy for their predicament. Within Israel, most Arab leaders were also harsh in their criticisms. Rakah severely denounced the treaty, which bypassed the Soviet Union, for being an imperialist plot and a betrayal of the Palestinian cause. The National Committee of Arab Students, the Progressive National Movement, and supporters of the Rakah-backed Democratic Front for Peace and Equality as well as independent Arab professionals also issued statements and demonstrated against the peace treaty (for some of the public statements, see Nakhleh and Zureik, 1980:216-20).

It is against the foil of these negative responses that the Arab sample answers should be regarded as quite favorable to the peace treaty. Half (49%) are fully supportive, 28% are reserved, and only 23% are opposed. The positive attitude of the majority of the establishment affiliated Arab leaders is as expected, as is the negative opinion of the majority of the other leaders. The contrast between the Rakah position and Arab public opinion on this question is striking indeed.

The peace treaty serves, therefore, as less of a barrier to Arab-Jewish coexistence than the public denunciations of many Arab leaders would suggest. The substantial support it receives, notwithstanding the reservations, testifies to the deep desire for peace in both communities.

The territorial question has many aspects, three of which are examined: settlements, borders, and East Jerusalem. When Israel consolidated its hold over the territories acquired in 1967, East Jerusalem and its immediate surroundings were annexed. Over 150 Jewish settlements have been established since then in the various territories, with the Labor government emphasizing the Jordan Valley, Golan Heights, and the Rafiah Salient in the Gaza Strip, and the Likud government adding scores of settlements in the densely populated areas of Judea and Samaria. In the 1970's Labor justified the settlements on defense grounds, whereas Likud added historical, ideological, and religious reasons. Israeli officials claim that the pre-1967 borders are indefensible and insecure and that they will not withdraw to them (Harris, 1980).

The controversies among Jews should not overshadow the fact that much of the public is behind the official policies and actions. Of the Jewish public as a whole, 72% lend at least some support for settlements in Judea and Samaria and 47% fully endorse the policy of the Likud government (Table 6.2). A clear majority favoring unrestricted settlement of the occupied territories is also reported in subsequent polls; for example, three quarters of the Jewish population favor continued settlement of the West Bank in surveys taken in April-May 1981 (*Jerusalem Post International Edition*, May 10-16, 1981:8). This support is strong in view of the soaring international censure of these settlements, especially those in sensitive, densely populated Arab areas. The public-at-large and even most dovish Jewish leaders (of whom 73% disapprove of the Likud settlement policy) would approve of selective, defense-based settlements.

The massive Jewish reluctance to cede all the occupied territories is clearly evident from related answers. As to which borders could be compromised for the sake of a peace settlement, only 10% of the Jewish population agree to pull back to the pre-1967 frontiers or beyond and 86% oppose the return of East Jerusalem even if this concession is deemed essential for peace. Jewish public opinion is closer to the views of the hawkish rather than dovish leaders on these matters (Table 6.2).

While most Jews are reluctant to stop settlement totally or to withdraw to the pre-1967 borders (including East Jerusalem), the overwhelming majority of Israeli Arabs favor these moves. Even accommodating Arab leaders dissent on this question from the Zionist establishment and agree with Arab public opinion. Furthermore, over one third of the Arabs want Israel to retreat to the UN Partition Resolution borders of 1947 (which do not include the predominantly Arab areas of the Triangle and the Western and central Galilee) or to be superseded by a new state in the entire territory of Mandatory Palestine.

Table 6.2 Settlements, Borders, and East Jerusalem

	Arab Public	Estab. Affil. Arab Lead.	Rakah Affil. Arab Lead.	Rejec-tion. Arab Lead.	Jewish Public	Dovish Jewish Lead.	Arab-ists	Hawkish Jewish Lead.
Settlements in Judea and Samaria								
In favor	2.3	0.0	0.0	0.0	46.9	0.0	26.9	80.0
Have reservations	13.1	16.0	0.0	0.0	25.6	27.3	38.5	20.0
Against	84.6	84.0	100.0	100.0	27.6	72.7	34.6	0.0
Borders with which one is prepared to compromise in order to reach a peace settlement								
All of Palestine in which a new state will be established	11.8	0.0	0.0	77.4	1.1	0.0	0.0	0.0
1947 UN partition borders	26.3	8.0	15.6	19.4	0.3	0.0	0.0	0.0
Pre-1967 borders, including East Jerusalem	41.5	48.0	71.9	3.2	1.1	3.1	3.7	0.0
Pre-1967 borders with certain modifications	8.8	40.0	12.5	0.0	7.8	43.8	14.8	0.0
Present borders with willingness to compromise also in Judea and Samaria	7.0	4.0	0.0.	0.0	31.2	53.1	66.7	17.6
Present borders with certain modifications	5.5	0.0	0.0	0.0	58.5	0.0	14.8	82.4
Giving up East Jerusalem if this is necessary to reach a peace settlement								
In favor	*	*	*	*	5.4	13.3	6.9	0.0
Have reservations	*	*	*	*	9.0	10.0	13.8	0.0
Against	*	*	*	*	85.6	76.7	79.3	100.0

* Not asked

Equally divisive is the Palestinian problem which constitutes the core of the Israeli-Arab dispute. The Jewish public concur with the official view of all post-1967 Israeli governments on the four questions presented on this issue (Table 6.3). Only one tenth unconditionally accept Israel's recognition of a Palestinian people, but one third would go along under certain circumstances. Some change is apparent among dovish Jewish leaders, including those affiliated with the Labor and Mapam parties; three fifths of them "acknowledge" the existence of the Palestinian people, but they stop short of acknowledging the Palestinians' right to self-determination. The other question concerns recognition of the PLO as the Palestinians' authoritative representative. On this question, 84% of the public at large, 53% of the dovish leaders, 73% of the Arabists, and 96% of the hawkish leaders are utterly opposed. There is similar opposition to the creation of a Palestinian state in the West Bank and

Gaza Strip alongside Israel and to granting the 1948 Palestinian refugees the right of repatriation to Israel within its pre-1967 borders.

Table 6.3 The Palestinian Problem

	Arab Public	Estab. Affil. Arab Lead.	Rakah Affil. Arab Lead.	Rejec-tion. Arab Lead.	Jewish Public	Dovish Jewish Lead.	Jewish Arab-ists	Hawkish Jewish Lead.
Israel should recognize the Palestinians as a nation								
Yes	80.2	72.0	93.8	100.0	11.1	58.8	31.0	4.2
Only under certain circumstances	16.1	24.0	6.3	0.0	34.5	26.5	37.9	25.0
No	3.7	4.0	0.0	0.0	54.4	14.7	31.0	70.8
Israel should recognize the PLO as the Palestinians' representative								
Yes	67.8	32.0	87.5	93.5	3.0	20.6	6.7	0.0
Only under certain circumstances	22.9	60.0	12.5	0.0	12.7	26.5	20.0	4.0
No	9.3	8.0	0.0	6.5	84.3	52.9	73.3	96.0
Favor the formation of a Palestinian state in the West Bank and Gaza Strip alongside Israel								
Yes	64.0	68.0	93.8	6.5	5.7	14.7	10.3	0.0
Only under certain circumstances	19.8	28.0	6.3	22.6	17.8	29.4	20.7	8.3
No	16.2	4.0	0.0	71.0	76.6	55.9	69.0	91.7
Israel should recognize the Palestinian refugees' right of repatriation to Israel within the pre-1967 borders								
Yes	78.0	36.0	90.3	100.0	5.8	0.0	3.6	0.0
Only under certain circumstances	17.6	56.0	9.7	0.0	20.3	35.3	21.4	12.0
No	4.4	8.0	0.0	0.0	73.8	64.7	75.0	88.0

By similarly large majorities, Israeli Arabs take the opposite stand. Of the Arabs surveyed, 80% favor without reservation Israel's recognition of the Palestinians as a nation, 68% want Israel to recognize the PLO, 64% support a separate Palestinian state, and 78% endorse the Palestinian refugees' right to return. These views correspond exactly with those of Rakah on the Palestinian problem. Other leaders show some deviation from this Arab mainstream. Rejectionist leaders oppose the idea of a mini-state in the West Bank and Gaza Strip. On the other hand, around two thirds of the establishment-affiliated Arab leaders are careful not to go so far as to advocate unconditional recognition of the PLO and the refugees' right of repatriation.

The autonomy plan advanced by the Likud government and incorporated in the Camp David accords was intended to resolve the Palestinian problem by granting the residents of the West Bank and Gaza Strip self-rule. This scheme fell into disrepute by 1980, as conflicting interpretations and expectations by Israel, Egypt, and the United States led the trilateral autonomy talks to a stalemate. Public opinion well reflects the general dissatisfaction. Some 61% of the Arab public, 56% of the establishment-affiliated leaders, and all Rakah-affiliated and rejectionist leaders are either reserved or opposed to the autonomy plan because they prefer Palestinian national sovereignty to an extended municipal authority. Fearing that home-rule might eventually lead to a separate Palestinian state (or to certain kinds of annexation in the case of some Jewish doves), 70% of the Jewish public, 82% of the dovish leaders, 67% of the Arabists, and 68% of the hawkish leaders have reservations or disapprove. The widespread dislike of the autonomy plan in both communities, though for different reasons, prevents it from turning into a divisive issue.

Ideological Positions

To gain a better sense of the range in disagreement between Israeli Arabs and Jews on the Israeli-Arab conflict, it is necessary to go beyond the examination of separate issues. To obtain a rough summary measure, an index has been constructed by scoring any "hawkish" answer 1 and any "nonhawkish" response 0.[1] Since 14 items are included (i.e., the 8 items discussed above and 6 related others), the index ranges from 0 to 14. It is found that Jews are skewed toward the upper (hawkish) end of the continuum, whereas Arabs are slanted toward the lower (nonhawkish) end. Specifically, 69% of the Arabs and 1% of the Jews score 0 to 3 points, and 72% of the Jews and 2% of the Arabs receive 11 to 14 points. This bimodal distribution leaves only 29% of the Arabs and 7% of the Jews in the broad middle, sharing compromising views. It shows that the Arab-Jewish disagreement on these vital matters reaches polarization, i.e., a majority in each side holds a position opposed to that of the other.

Identification of the main ideological positions on the Israeli-Arab conflict and classification of the respondents accordingly further clarifies the nature of dissension. Looking in 1980 at the Israeli political spectrum as a whole, it is possible to differentiate, with some simplification, the following six political streams, each of which takes a distinct stance:

(1) *Tehiya.* The Tehiya movement was formed in 1978 to oppose the Camp David accord. It includes dissenters who had belonged to the Likud and members of Gush Emunim, the Greater Eretz Israel Movement, and other splinter groups. This small, radical, right-wing

---

[1]"Hawkish" is defined as endorsement without reservation of non-conciliatory policies by Israel such as Jewish settlement of Judea and Samaria and total rejection of the Palestinians as a nation.

party opposes the Israel-Egypt peace pact and calls for the formal annexation and massive Jewish settlement of the territories. During the 1980's the Tehiya Party has become the main spokesman for the ultranationalist and annexationist circles in Israel.

(2) *Likud.* Under Begin's leadership, the Likud also adheres to the idea of Greater Eretz Israel. It therefore claims Jewish sovereignty over the West Bank and Gaza Strip and seeks their eventual incorporation into Israel. Except for East Jerusalem and the Golan Heights, it stops short of legal annexation. Although officially sponsoring the peace treaty and the autonomy plan, the Likud is in fact internally divided on these questions.

(3) *Labor.* The Labor party upholds settlements for defense only and objects to them in the populated areas of Judea and Samaria. In order to resolve the Palestinian problem, it is prepared in principle to make territorial concessions in the West Bank in order to permit a Jordanian-Palestinian confederation. Labor strongly opposes an independent Palestinian state west of the Jordan river.

(4) *Shelli.* This small, left-wing party is committed to Israel as a Jewish-Zionist state. But it supports a Palestinian state alongside Israel and it does not disqualify the PLO as a representative Palestinian body. It proposes to leave Jerusalem united but to have two sovereignties in the city. Furthermore, it calls for the resettlement of the Palestinian refugees in the proposed Palestinian state. Although Shelli disappeared as a party after 1981, its position has continued to represent the Zionist left on the Israeli-Arab conflict. Moving closest to the defunct Shelli's stance by 1988, the Citizens Rights Movement (CRM) has become the chief representative of the conciliatory Zionist left in Israel.[2]

(5) *Rakah.* Like the Soviet Union, the pro-Moscow Israeli Communist party recognizes the State of Israel, but opposes Zionism. It advocates total withdrawal from the occupied territories (including East Jerusalem), and proposes a Palestinian state on the West Bank and Gaza Strip. It also insists on the Palestinian refugees' right of return to pre-1967 Israel.

(6) *Sons of the Village Movement.* This small, radical ultranationalist Arab movement supports the Rejection Front within the Palestinian resistance movement. It neither recognizes the Jews as a nation nor Israel's right to exist. It also calls for the establishment of a secular-democratic or a Palestinian state in all of Palestine instead of Israel.

From an international perspective, these six ideological positions fall into four categories as summarized in Table 6.4. The Tehiya position is

---

[2]*Shelli* failed to win a seat in the Knesset in the 1981 national elections, and was split into two factions in 1984. One faction joined the CRM and another joined forces with Arab activists to found the Progressive List for Peace (PLP). Two of *Shelli's* leaders were elected to the Knesset in 1984 and one in 1988.

the Israeli-Jewish rejectionist stance and is on the fringe of Israel's operative consensus. The consensus is supported by the Likud, Labor, the religious parties, and others who agree on the most critical points in this survey. They generally: (1) accept the Israel-Egypt peace treaty, (2) oppose withdrawal to the pre-1967 borders, (3) refuse to alter Israel's annexation of Arab East Jerusalem, (4) oppose recognition of the Palestinians as a nation, (5) oppose recognition of the PLO, (6) oppose the establishment of a Palestinian state in the West Bank and Gaza Strip alongside Israel, and (7) oppose the extension of the right to repatriation to the 1948 Arab refugees. There is, however, no consensus between Likud and Labor on borders and settlements.

Table 6.4 Classification of Ideological Positions on the Israeli-Arab Conflict

	Tehiya	Likud	Labor	Shelli	Rakah	Sons of the Village Movement
Opposed to immediate annexation of the occupied territories	−	+	+	+	+	+
Opposed to settlements in Judea and Samaria	−	−	+	+	+	+
Favor territorial concessions in the West Bank	−	−	+	+	+	+
Favor withdrawal to the pre-1967 borders with certain modifications	−	−	−	+	+	+
Recognize the Palestinians as a nation	−	−	−	+	+	+
Recognize the PLO as the Palestinians' representative	−	−	−	+	+	+
Favor a Palestinian state alongside Israel	−	−	−	+	+	−
Favor withdrawal from East Jerusalem	−	−	−	−	+	+
Recognize the Palestinian refugees' right of repatriation	−	−	−	−	+	+
Do not recognize Jews in Israel as a nation	−	−	−	−	−	+
Deny Israel's right to exist	−	−	−	−	−	+
Favor a democratic-secular state in all of Palestine	−	−	−	−	−	+
Not opposed to the Palestinian National Charter and to the PLO's use of terrorism	−	−	−	−	−	+

Outside and to the left of Israel's operative consensus are the positions espoused by Shelli and Rakah. Although similar to the Tehiya stance in representing oppositionist and minority views, they have special significance because they coincide with what may be called the "world's operative consensus." Since 1967, opinions throughout the world regarding the Israeli-Arab conflict have converged sufficiently to reach a general consensus on several aspects of the dispute. Unlike the Israeli operative consensus, the vast majority of the world's states agree that Israel should (1) retreat to the pre-1967 borders, (2) repeal the annexation of Jerusalem, (3) recognize the Palestinians' right to national self-determination, (4) accept the PLO as a legitimate Palestinian representative, (5) permit the establishment of a Palestinian state in the West Bank and Gaza Strip, and (6) allow some Palestinian refugees to return. It is noteworthy that the United States, Israel's staunchest ally and the chief mediator in the conflict, as well as Egypt have assented to most of these points albeit with certain reservations and modifications. This fundamental disagreement with Israel has become abundantly and dramatically clear in December 1988 when the United States decided to open a substantive dialogue with the PLO.[3]

Despite its marginality in the Israeli context, the position of the Sons of the Village Movement is significant because its stands correspond with those of the Rejection Front consisting of certain intransigent rejectionist factions within the PLO and several Arab states. It rejects Israel's existence as a separate state, aims to replace Israel with a Palestinian state, adheres to the Palestinian National Charter, and advocates armed struggle.

From an Israeli perspective, these four ideological positions can be ordered on a scale of conformity-dissidence. Israel's operative consensus should naturally be considered as the mainstream and the stand of the nationalist Tehiya party must be regarded as pro-Israel dissidence. On the other hand, the world's operative consensus would be moderate dissidence because it accepts Israel but opposes its foreign policy, whereas the Rejection Front ideology is certainly strong anti-Israel dissidence.

As Table 6.4 shows, there is no single issue or even a combination of issues which could differentiate the four ideological positions, let alone the six political streams. Hence, in order to classify respondents by these positions on the independent basis of their views on the Israeli-Arab conflict instead of resorting to their self-classifications, it has been necessary to select different items to define each ideological position. For instance, the question on the Israel-Egypt peace treaty is essential for identifying subscribers to the Tehiya ideology but it is useless for specifying most of the other positions. Similarly, the question of Israel's

[3]There is however, no significant support in the United States for an independent Palestinian state in the West Bank and Gaza Strip and for return of any substantial number of refugees to Israel in its pre-1967 borders.

right to exist distinguishes adherents to the rejectionist ideology from the others but lacks any additional differentiating power.

A total of ten closed questions was required to categorize the respondents into mutually exclusive ideological positions on the Israeli-Arab conflict.[4] Each position is operationalized by a particular predetermined set of answers. This procedure assures clarity but inescapably leaves out respondents who either fail to answer some questions or whose responses diverge from the patterns of the categories used.

The following operational definitions (i.e., sets of answers) classify respondents according to one of the six ideological positions:

(1) Respondents are classified as "Tehiya dissidents" if they take all the following stands: (a) insist on retaining the post-June 1967 ceasefire borders, (b) favor unrestricted Jewish settlement in Judea and Samaria, (c) oppose the autonomy plan, and (d) object to or have reservations about the peace treaty.

(2) Respondents are assigned into the "Likud ideological position" if they consent only to the first two of the above four views.

(3) Respondents are considered as "Labor supporters" if they *either:* (a) do not favor settlements in Judea and Samaria yet (b) would not withdraw to the pre-1967 borders, *or* (a) endorse settlements but (b) would withdraw in order to reach peace. Thus, for the purpose of this study, Labor supporters are seen as conciliatory on either settlements or borders in contrast to Likud adherents who would compromise on neither and to Shelli followers who would concede both.

(4) Respondents who agree with the three following points are put into the "Shelli sympathizers" category: Israel should (a) allow a Palestinian state in the West Bank and Gaza Strip (or recognize the PLO), (b) withdraw to the pre-1967 borders, and (c) maintain its Jewish majority (or prevent Palestinian refugee repatriation).

(5) Respondents are considered "subscribers to Rakah ideology" if they accept only the first two of the above three points in the Shelli ideology.

(6) Respondents are defined as "rejectionists" (supporters of the Rejection Front within Israel) if they (a) deny Israel's right of existence (or view

[4]Listed in order of mention in the definitions below, these ten closed questions concern: (1) borders, (2) settlements in Judea and Samaria, (3) the autonomy plan, (4) the peace treaty, (5) a Palestinian state in the West Bank and Gaza Strip, (6) Israel's recognition of the PLO, (7) Israel's retention of a Jewish majority, (8) Israel's recognition of the Palestinian refugees' right of repatriation, (9) Israel's right to exist, and (10) Israeli Jews as a nation.

Israeli Jews as a religion, not a nation) and (b) endorse "a secular-democratic state" in all of Palestine in lieu of Israel.

A methodological testing of the resultant typology demonstrates several major points. First, the classification correlates very highly with numerous issues on the Israeli-Arab conflict, and as such, it can serve as a useful descriptive device. Second, the strict definitions of each type result in the exclusion of 18% of the respondents; some simply fail to respond, but most of this group give sets of answers that do not match any of the above six operational definitions. Third, it is clear that the bulk of the exclusion can be accounted for by inconsistency. To illustrate, of the excluded Arab respondents 93% favor Israel's withdrawal to the pre-1967 borders or further, but only 22% endorse the formation of a Palestinian state in the West Bank and Gaza Strip, compared with 87% and 72%, respectively, among the respondents who are included in the typology. Similarly, 79% of the unclassified Jews support Jewish settlement of Judea and Samaria but only 14% would like to retain the existing boundaries, compared with 41% and 65%, respectively, among the classified Jews. And fourth, most exclusions result from inconsistencies; it is unlikely that the overall categorization of the Arab and Jewish populations will be biased in either dovish or hawkish directions.[5]

The ideological distribution of Jews demonstrates a number of tendencies (Table 6.5). First, 88% of the Jewish public and 86% of the Jewish leaders fall into the Likud and Labor positions. They constitute Israel's operative consensus that rightly claims a huge and solid majority. Second, within the Israeli mainstream the less moderate (Likud) are outnumbered two to one by the more moderate (Labor). This is due to the fact that Jewish hawkishness varies significantly from one issue to another so that the percentage of Jews who are consistently hawkish cannot be high. For example, although 65% of all classified Jews are in favor of the present borders, no more than 41% may fall into the Tehiya and Likud positions because only 41% of all classified Jews support unrestricted settlement of the West Bank. The Labor ideology on the Israeli-Arab conflict, being more ambiguous and conciliatory than that of the Likud, conforms to the thinking of most Israeli Jews. In fact, the popularity of the Peace Now Movement stems from its basic espousal of

---

[5]A further examination shows that women, illiterates, persons aged 56 and over, Bedouin, those disinterested in politics, those unconcerned about the problem of Arab-Jewish relations, and the generally more accommodating are overrepresented among the Arabs who are excluded from the typology. On the other hand, among Jews no special differentiation can be made between the included and excluded.

the widespread Labor ideology which is attacked by the Likud, as well as from its avoidance of any explicit dovish stance.[6] And third, among the dissident minority of Jews, the "super hawks" (Tehiya supporters) outnumber the "super doves" (Shelli backers) by four to one. This reveals the staggering weakness of the Jewish super doves who can draw support only from the outside (Arabs in Israel or world public opinion).

Table 6.5 Distribution of Ideological Positions on the Israeli-Arab Conflict

	Arab Public	Estab. Affil. Arab Lead.	Rakah Affil. Arab Lead.	Rejec- tion. Arab Lead.	Jewish Public	Dovish Jewish Lead.	Jewish Arab- ists	Hawkish Jewish Lead.
Ideological position								
Tehiya	0.0	0.0	0.0	0.0	9.5	0.0	0.0	11.8
Likud	1.1	0.0	0.0	0.0	31.0	0.0	9.5	58.8
Labor	15.7	26.1	0.0	0.0	57.0	81.3	81.0	29.4
Shelli	6.1	21.7	3.3	0.0	1.8	18.8	9.5	0.0
Rakah	70.7	52.2	96.7	25.8	0.8	0.0	0.0	0.0
Sons of the Village Movement	6.4	0.0	0.0	74.2	0.0	0.0	0.0	0.0

Turning to the Arab distribution, several points are evident. First, 83% of the Arab population fall outside Israel's operative consensus, substantiating the image of Israeli Arabs as a dissident minority within the Israeli context. This is true even of the great majority of the accommodating leaders who are tied to the Zionist establishment. Furthermore, even conforming Arabs dissent on some sensitive issues: of the Arabs identified with Labor ideology, 49% recognize, nevertheless, the Palestinian refugees' right of return and 58% object to the notion of a permanent Jewish majority in Israel. Second, the Rakah ideology emerges as the core of the Arab approach to the Israeli-Arab dispute. It is even more popular among Arabs than the Labor ideology is among Jews. As such, it qualifies as the Arab mainstream. And third, while three quarters of the surveyed activists in the Sons of the Village Movement adhere to the Rejection Front ideology of eliminating Israel as a state, only 6% of the Arab population support this position. Israeli Arabs, as a whole, reject the ideology of the Rejection Front on the conflict, and accept, instead the world's operative consensus. Hence, their dissidence in Israeli society is moderate rather than strong.

[6]Peace Now Movement has radicalized considerably since the eruption of the *Intifadeh* on December 9, 1987. By late 1988 it called on Israel to withdraw from the occupied territories and hold talks with the PLO. It also ended its long-standing Jewish and Zionist exclusivity by incorporating Israeli Arabs and even Palestinians from the West Bank and Gaza Strip into its mass rallies and demonstrations.

The data show a good fit between the selection by Arabs of the political body that offers the best solution to the Israeli-Arab conflict and the objective classification of Arabs into ideological positions on the conflict. When they are directly asked to choose one of the six solutions to the conflict, the selection is clearly shaped by the ideological position of their preferred political body (correlation is 0.47; Table 6.6). For instance, 74% of Israeli Arabs with a Labor position compared to only 21% of those with a Rakah position choose mainstream (Likud or Labor) solutions.

Table 6.6 Ideological Positions on the Israeli-Arab Conflict by Political Body that Offers the Best Solution to the Conflict

	Total[b]	Tehiya	Likud	Labor	Shelli	Rakah	Sons of the Village Movement
The political body that offers the best solution to the Israeli-Arab Conflict[a]							
Arab Public							
Tehiya	0.9	*	*	2.4	0.0	0.4	3.6
Likud	3.7	*	*	10.6	2.3	1.5	3.6
Labor	28.4	*	*	63.4	63.6	19.5	3.6
Shelli	11.9	*	*	9.8	15.9	12.9	5.5
Rakah	21.4	*	*	4.9	6.8	28.2	7.3
PLO	33.8	*	*	8.9	11.4	37.5	76.4
Number of cases	(758)	(0)	(8)	(123)	(44)	(528)	(55)
Jewish Public							
Tehiya	15.7	50.2	27.8	3.3	8.9	*	*
Likud	29.5	20.4	46.5	22.6	4.2	*	*
Labor	52.2	28.3	25.1	71.5	59.9	*	*
Shelli	2.3	0.0	0.6	2.4	23.2	*	*
Rakah	0.1	1.0	0.0	0.0	0.0	*	*
PLO	0.3	0.0	0.0	0.1	3.8	*	*
Number of cases	(880)	(83)	(275)	(497)	(18)	(8)	(0)

* Insufficient number of cases.

[a] Response rate is 74% for the Arabs and 82% for the Jews. Nonrespondents do not differ from respondents on ideological positions.

[b] "Total" refers to respondents who answer the question and are classified on ideological positions.

A remarkable pattern stands out, however. Arabs who are ideologically identified with the Rakah's ideology concerning the conflict, as measured by the above criteria, are widely scattered in selecting their preferred solutions. Only 28% opt for the Rakah solution. Rakah's relative unattractiveness as a political symbol is striking when compared to the strong appeal of the PLO. The PLO attracts 9% of the adherents to the Labor ideology, 11% of Shelli, 37.5% of Rakah, and 76% of the Sons of the Village Movement. In fact, 34% of all Arabs prefer the PLO political solution compared to only 6% who actually take the ideological position of the Rejection Front.

The dissociation between the PLO as a political symbol and as a rejectionist ideology of sort is evident in other areas. While a growing proportion of Israeli Arabs identify themselves with the PLO, see it as the spearhead of Palestinian nationalism, and accept it as the representative Palestinian leadership, they as a whole repudiate any rejectionist ideas that the PLO may hold. On the one hand, 68% of all sampled Arabs call on Israel to recognize the PLO, 48.5% regard it as a representative of Israel's Arabs, and 57.5% justify Fedayeen actions in which Israeli Jews are killed. On the other hand, only 12% of Israeli Arabs favor the idea of a secular-democratic state in all of Palestine, 13% consider Israeli Jews to be only a religious (not a national) community, and 12% fail to urge the PLO to recognize Israel. Actually, few Israeli Arabs are willing to concede this apparent inconsistency, because they perceive the PLO as acting upon an ideology which is essentially non-rejectionist and indistinguishable from that of Rakah. This differentiated Arab view is reinforced by a dose of ambiguity that has been injected into the PLO position through certain pronouncements, actions, and inactions that diverge from the rejectionist Palestinian National Charter.

The simultaneous acceptance of the PLO leadership and the disapproval of harsh rejectionist ideas associated with the PLO have a far-reaching implication. This means that Arab identification with the PLO does not imply a rejectionist orientation toward Israel. Hence, the common Jewish perception that any Israeli Arab display of identification with the PLO is a declaration to damage or to destroy the Jewish state, and therefore a disloyal act, is ill-founded. In July 1980, the Knesset amended the "Terror Act – 1948" to severely punish persons who publicly show identification with a terrorist organization (i.e., the PLO). Later in December, the government, using this law and the Defense (Emergency) Regulations of 1945, outlawed a Congress of Arab leaders on the grounds of presumed identification with and support of the PLO (*Haaretz*, December 2, 1980).

Ideological position in the conflict is also associated with voting (Table 6.7). Israeli Arabs who subscribe to the Labor position on the conflict report about 95% turnout for the mainstream Zionist parties or their client Arab lists in the 1977 national elections. Furthermore, 50% of those accepting Rakah ideology and 36% of those agreeing with the Sons of the Village ideology also reportedly voted for the mainstream Zionist and affiliated-Arab lists. These figures are even higher for voting intentions in the 1981 Knesset elections – 57% and 48%, respectively. They illustrate the effective hold the Zionist establishment has over Arab political behavior.

Table 6.7 Arabs' Ideological Positions on the Israeli-Arab Conflict by Voting

	Tehiya	Likud	Labor	Shelli	Rakah	Sons of the Village Movement
Voted in the 1977 Knesset elections for						
Likud, Shlomzion, religious parties	*	*	22.7	18.4	6.6	18.2
Labor, affiliated Arab lists	*	*	57.3	57.9	40.9	13.6
Democratic Movement for Change,						
CRM, Independent Liberals	*	*	14.7	7.9	2.9	4.5
Shelli	*	*	0.0	2.6	1.7	4.5
DFPE (Rakah)	*	*	5.3	13.2	47.8	59.1
Number of Cases	(0)	(6)	(75)	(38)	(347)	(22)
Intend to vote in the 1981 Knesset elections for						
Tehiya	*	*	0.0	0.0	0.0	0.0
Likud, religious parties	*	*	6.7	8.8	2.9	12.0
Labor, affiliated Arab lists	*	*	80.0	67.6	50.6	36.0
Democratic Movement, Change, CRM,						
Independent Liberals	*	*	6.7	2.9	3.5	0.0
Shelli	*	*	1.7	11.8	2.9	4.0
DFPE (Rakah)	*	*	5.0	8.8	40.0	48.0
Number of cases	(0)	(5)	(60)	(34)	(310)	(25)

* Insufficient number of cases.

Table 6.8 Jews' Ideological Positions on the Israeli-Arab Conflict by Voting

	Tehiya	Likud	Labor	Shelli	Rakah	PLO
Voted in the 1977 Knesset elections for						
Likud, Shlomzion, religious parties	68.6	78.1	39.5	35.8	*	*
Labor	20.8	18.0	39.1	18.7	*	*
Democratic Movement for Change,						
CRM, Independent Liberals	10.6	3.9	19.5	18.5	*	*
Shelli	0.0	0.0	1.9	27.0	*	*
DFPE (Rakah)	0.0	0.0	0.0	0.0	*	*
Number of Cases	(62)	(258)	(460)	(15)	(5)	(0)
Intend to vote in the 1981 Knesset elections for						
Tehiya	14.6	4.9	0.0	0.0	*	*
Likud, religious parties	52.3	57.7	20.0	18.9	*	*
Labor	29.1	36.8	77.0	74.3	*	*
Democratic Movement, Change, CRM,						
Independent Liberals	4.0	0.3	2.0	0.0	*	*
Shelli	0.0	0.4	1.0	6.8	*	*
DFPE (Rakah)	0.0	0.0	0.0	0.0	*	*
Number of cases	(65)	(222)	(373)	(11)	(5)	(0)

* Insufficient number of cases.

Similar patterns prevail among the Jews. Briefly, ideological position is associated with the choice of a political body that offers the best solution to the conflict (r = 0.47), voting in 1977 (r = 0.32), and voting intention (r = 0.41). There are significant discrepancies, however. Some 26% to 29% of the Jews classified as Tehiya and Likud adherents choose Labor and Shelli solutions to the conflict, while 26% of those classified as Labor select Tehiya and Likud solutions and 73% of the Jews classified as Shelli fail to choose Shelli or PLO solutions (Table 6.6). Indeed, 18% of Jews who are Likud in their position on the conflict voted in 1977 for Labor and 37% intended to vote Labor in 1981, whereas 39.5% of those who take a Labor stand on the conflict voted Likud or religious parties in 1977 and 20% of them intended to do so in 1981 (Table 6.8 above).

The Conflict as a Barrier to Arab-Jewish Equality

From the prevailing perspective of most Israeli Jews, the above Israeli Arab views on the conflict constitute prima facie evidence of potential disloyalty or subversion. Many Jews in Israel ponder: how can Arabs be trusted if they wish Israel to withdraw to its indefensible pre-1967 borders and to establish a Soviet client, Palestinian state that will antagonize Israel? Does not their support of the PLO imply a tacit acceptance of the Palestinian National Charter, the PLO's constitution, to destroy the Jewish state? This rationale dominates the thinking of most Jews in Israel. Only a few of the Jews do reason that under Israeli democracy Arabs are entitled to a right of dissent, that dissent does not necessarily mean disloyalty to the state, and that Israeli Arab stands on the conflict correspond with a growing international consensus that includes many nations friendly to Israel. Since the area of dissent involves national security, most Jews feel that they cannot afford "tolerance" of the Israeli Arab position.

Survey data indeed show that national security looms large in Jewish attitudes toward the Arab minority. Actually 41% of the Jews regard Arabs as a real danger to national security, 43% a certain danger, and only 16.5% see no danger. In addition, 66% feel that it is impossible to trust Arabs in Israel and 65% advocate an increase in surveillance over them. When asked if security restrictions should be imposed on Arabs as long as the Israeli-Arab conflict persists, 68% are in favor, 25% are for some limitations, and 7% are against (Table 14.5 in Chapter 14).

According to the Van Leer survey taken in January 1980, 31% of the Jews believe that only a few Arabs are engaged in espionage against Israel, 51% charge that some of them are involved, and as many as 18% accuse most or all Arabs of spying. As many as 41% justify preventive arrests of Arabs for security reasons even without evidence against them, 20% are indifferent, and only 39% are opposed. A large majority, 77%, maintain that national security legitimizes restrictions over Arabs compared to only a minority who think the same about other possible justifications, e.g., the fact that Arabs differ from Jews in religion and have a very high natural population increase, and the belief that Jews hate Arabs and Arabs hate Jews.

Given these Jewish attitudes, it is not surprising that the Israeli-Arab conflict actually provides a ready-made credible ideology for imposing restrictions over Arabs, marking them off from the Jews and depriving them of various resources. Since at least three other major factors, namely, the Jewish-Zionist character of the state, Jewish vested interests, and Jewish ethnocentrism, also contribute to Arab-Jewish inequality, it is hard to disentangle and assess the relative impact of the Israeli-Arab conflict. It is precisely the pervasiveness of this fatal and protracted dispute that can make it a cover for less socially acceptable motives.

The conflict impairs the basic status of Arabs as loyal citizens. Being viewed as part of the enemy has two related consequences: treatment as a potential fifth column and exclusion from the national security establishment. The state takes various countermeasures to deter the Arab security hazard. During the years 1948 to 1966, Arab regions were officially placed under military government, and the Arabs were subject to restrictions of movement and organization. The Defense (Emergency) Regulations of 1945 are left essentially intact to permit selective or total restoration of military government, if necessary. The security functions of the military government have been consigned to special departments for internal Arab affairs in the General Security Service (Shabac), the police (Latam), and the Arab section of the Information Center (Merkaz Hasbara-Agaf Aravi). The latter keeps dossiers on Arab public personalities, blacklists Arab troublemakers, helps in issuing security clearances, and in general serves as a liaison between the bureau of the Prime Minister's Adviser on Arab Affairs (where it is located) and the security agencies. All these bodies, which are assisted by civil servants in other Arab departments in the government, Histadrut, political parties, as well as by a large network of paid informants, are engaged in extensive surveillance activities and have established over the years a record of efficiency.

Arab exclusion from the national security establishment has several consequences. With the minor exception of the Druzes who are subject to the draft and Bedouin who may volunteer to the army, Arabs are exempted from military duty. They are barred from employment in the border police and the military-industrial complex (Taas) which employs about one quarter of the total Jewish industrial labor force. They are also prevented from serving in the Civil Guard (Mishmar Ezrahi – armed citizens who patrol residential quarters to prevent terrorism and crime) and Civil Defense (Haga, which is part of Israel Defense Forces) during wartime.

Army exemption results in certain liabilities. It is, on the one hand, advantageous not to serve in the army for three years and not to be part of the army reserves for over thirty years. On the other hand, absence of veteran status means disqualification from many white-collar jobs in the public and private sectors. Additionally, certain benefits such as supplementary social security payments and housing loans are unavailable. Many plants and businesses that supply goods to the army refuse to hire Arabs.

National security has been widely used by the authorities to justify other related restrictions. Most important are land expropriations, relocation of some Arabs from border areas to the interior, refusal to let internal refugees return to their abandoned villages, a ban on certain nationalist political organizations, and administrative detentions. Court appeals by Arabs are rejected when security considerations are invoked by the state without further need of specification or substantiation (Jiryis, 1976).

Arabs as a Party to the Conflict

The Israeli-Arab conflict is multilateral, involving Israel, the Palestinians, the Arab countries, and the superpowers as active participants. The question arises whether the Arab minority is or is becoming another party to the conflict. It can play one of three roles in the dispute: a fifth column, a bridge to peace, or a pressure group. As yet, it has not been a party to the conflict in any one of these capacities, although it is now attempting to become a political pressure group.

As indicated above, four fifths of the Arabs ideologically reject the Jewish consensus on the conflict. Furthermore, they sympathize emotionally with Israel's enemies. When the June 1967 war broke out, two thirds of those surveyed in 1967-68 expected the Arab countries to win (Peres, 1971: Table 20). Half the Arab respondents in 1980 observe that at least some of the Arabs in Israel rejoice at Israel's suffering and three fifths either justify or rejoice when Jewish fellow citizens are killed in Fedayeen actions.

The fact is, however, that Arabs have not turned into a fifth column, but rather have been passive and have refrained from hostilities during and between all Israeli-Arab all-out wars. This remains true despite some cooperation with infiltration in the early fifties and the conviction of about 400 Arabs in collaborative offenses since 1949.

Arab neutrality may be explained by the combined effect of three restraints. First, till the early 1970's, Arabs were put under a machinery of control which virtually stripped them of any resistance capability (Lustick, 1980; Smooha, 1980). Second, by acting against the state, they are bound to suffer legal persecution, economic sanctions, mass incarcerations and other privations. And third, there is no mobilizing body. Since the Arab countries are keenly aware of Israeli Arabs' inherent weakness and precarious situation, they bombard them with anti-Israeli propaganda but stop short of seeking their active participation in the armed struggle against Israel. Until 1967, the Arab minority was even suspected of collaboration with the Zionist adversary, but thereafter the PLO spearheaded a turn toward national rehabilitation. It projected an image of Israel's Arabs as part of the Palestinian resistance, elected three ex-Israeli Arabs to its national council, and launched a drive to recruit Israeli Arabs for PLO terrorist activities that succeeded for a number of years but then failed and was discontinued.

All these countervailing forces are still effective in curbing the emergence of an Arab fifth column. Arabs continue to be under some watch. Although some possess arms, as a group they have neither training installations nor subversive organizations.[7] In case of a prolonged war in which Israel would appear to be losing, some Arabs might perpetrate sabotage acts (E. Nakhleh, 1977:31-32) which could, in turn, provoke counteractions to "thin-out" the Arab population (Minister Sharon's threat, *Haaretz*, December 2, 1980). Also, still missing is an organizing body, either within or outside the state, that is both willing and able to forge the Arabs into a belligerent power.

It is equally doubtful that the Arabs of Israel are or can be a bridge to peace in the Middle East. The bridge metaphor implies at least that Arab-Jewish coexistence in Israel is peaceful and exemplary enough to yield a demonstration effect for Israeli-Arab coexistence in the region. But this is far from being the case. It is also questionable whether Arabs can function as an impartial third party to the conflict, contributing to mediation between the protagonists. Being simultaneously part of Israel, the Palestinians, and the Arab world makes them empathic but neither neutral nor "trustworthy."[8]

Nor have Arabs so far been an effective party to the conflict within Israeli politics. They share a consensus on this question which falls outside Israel's national consensus but within the world's operative consensus. Behind the Arab consensus are the Rakah-dominated Democratic Front for Peace and Equality and the Progressive List for Peace which provide an articulate ideology, an organizational base, and a dynamic leadership. But since both parties are beyond the pale of the

---

[7]It is ironic that Arabs acquire arms legally and illegally, mostly for use in hamula feuds.

[8]While Arabs in Israel are not and will not be instrumental in bringing peace to the region, they will play an intermediary role in cementing the peace once it is achieved and will also benefit from it (Tessler, 1980: 24).

legitimate coalitionary forces in Israeli politics, they actually isolate the Arabs and delegitimize their political views.

Israeli Arabs can overcome their political inefficacy by becoming a strong, dovish faction within the Labor party, by supporting the small, dovish, Zionist parties (Citizens Rights Movement, Mapam, Shinui), or by forming a new, non-Zionist, predominantly Arab party eligible for admission into coalition governments. With the growing politicization of Israeli Arabs and the even split of Jews between the Labor and Likud political camps, one or more of these possibilities is likely to develop.

Along with achieving equality in Israel, the Palestinian problem is the Israeli Arabs' greatest concern. Its neglect is the focus of their criticism against the Israel-Egypt peace treaty. The concern stems both from their commitment to the Palestinian cause and from the relevance of the conflict-resolution to their own lives in Israel. In fact, 65% of the Arabs in the survey see the relationship between the Palestinian question and their own as strong, 20% as fair, and only 15% as nonexistent. Along with the majority favoring a Palestinian state in the West Bank and Gaza Strip, there is an overwhelming majority of four fifths who would feel better as Arab citizens of Israel if such a state were eventually to arise.

Influenced by, but not coordinated with the Palestinian resistance in the West Bank and Gaza Strip since the mid-seventies, various Israeli Arab groups have consistently taken public stands and held demonstrations with regard to the Palestinian issue. They have protested the continued military occupation, settlements in the occupied territories, strong-arm policies against the Palestinian population, the peace treaty, the autonomy plan, and so forth.

The attempt to become a party to the Israeli-Arab conflict culminated with the adoption of the so-called "June 6 document" as a platform by various Arab leaders on September 9, 1980. The gist of the declaration was recognition of the Palestinians' right to self-determination by the Israeli Arab minority as a whole and endorsement of a Palestinian state alongside Israel (*The Jerusalem Post International Edition*, November 30-December 6, 1980). It was resolved to convene in December an all-Arab congress that could claim representativeness for the Arabs of Israel and take an official stand on their behalf in the Israeli-Arab conflict and other relevant matters. As mentioned above, the government moved quickly to ban the congress, charging it with subversion and with serving as a front organization for the PLO within Israel. Underlying these moves has been the Arab desire to enter Israeli politics as a legitimate pressure group, like the Peace Now Movement or Shelli Party, and the repudiation of Arabs by a majority of Jews (it is claimed) for national security and other reasons.

The ambition of many Arabs in Israel is much greater, however. As the events surrounding the outlawed Arab congress may suggest, they aspire to internationalize their problem by tying it directly to that of the Palestinians. They want their minority status to be recognized as an integral component of the complex Palestinian question and to be dealt with in this manner. They would like to be represented in future negotiations involving the Palestinians so that their pressing needs and disagreements with the Israeli government will be properly considered. The agenda may contain Israel's acceptance of Israeli Arabs as a Palestinian national minority, international guarantees of their political and cultural rights, institutional autonomy, land disputes, compensation for property losses, relations with the new Palestinian entity, and the like. Fearful of precisely these demands, the authorities are decisive in counteracting the ongoing Arab efforts in this direction.

Conclusions

The major repercussions of the Israeli-Arab conflict for the Arab-Jewish relations in Israeli society have been explored. It is shown that on this vital issue, Israeli Arabs sharply disagree with Jews and hence constitute an ideologically dissident group.

It is also suggested that the conflict sustains the inferior position of the Arabs by generating concerns or reasons which lead to denying them equal access to jobs, housing, governmental assistance, and Jewish institutions. On the other hand, Israeli Arabs have so far proved inconsequential for the Israeli-Arab conflict because of their limited active involvement.

What are the wider implications of these findings for future peacemaking in the region? Several observations may be offered. A historical reversal in Jewish and Arab attitudes toward the Israeli-Arab dispute has been underway since the 1967 war. The dominant Jewish position during the British Mandate and the first nineteen years of statehood was of compromise with a Palestinian entity in part of the land to the West of the Jordan River. The Arab stand, in contrast, was uncompromisingly insistent on an all-Arab Palestine (Harkabi, 1970). World public opinion generally accepted Israel's right of existence in the region and supported its defensive posture.

The post-1967 war era saw a significant shift of positions of all the concerned parties. Israel has been consolidating its control over the occupied territories (except Sinai), has argued that an independent Palestinian presence would be a threat to its security and integrity, and has made greater demands on the Arabs in exchange for territorial concessions. The differences between the Likud and Labor parties on ideological positions and government policies should not overshadow the operative Jewish consensus that rejects the PLO and a separate Palestinian state between Jordan and Israel, from which only minor Jewish groups dissent. Labor partakes in this consensus, though it does not favor unrestricted settlement or retention of the present borders.

The Arab world has softened its traditional uncompromising politics and has become increasingly divided over the conflict. Egypt, the largest and strongest Arab state, signed a peace treaty with Israel and is urging the Arab world to accommodate itself to it. Some other Arab states, notably Libya and Syria cling to their rejectionist stance. States like Morocco, Jordan, and Saudi Arabia try to steer an in-between course.

The Palestinians have also become fragmented. Centrist and rejectionist factions have emerged within the PLO. The PLO mainstream and the Palestinians in the occupied territories have been undergoing a number of transformations. The idea of an independent Palestinian state in the West Bank and Gaza Strip has entered their national agenda and has started to undermine their long-standing rejectionism. This solution is most strongly accepted by the Israeli segment of the Palestinian people (the Arab citizens of Israel).

The international community moved away from Israel after the 1967 war. Most of it supports the redivision of Palestine and the creation of a Palestinian entity in the West Bank and Gaza Strip. The recognition of the PLO has been coupled with a disavowal of its rejectionist covenant and terrorism. Israel's continued hold of the territories and settlements and its denial of Palestinian self-determination have very often been censured and Israel has become politically isolated.

The differences in views between Jews and Israeli Arabs well illustrate the difficulties in the peacemaking process in the Middle East. The Jews regard the position of their fellow Arab citizens as extremist and subversive, although it coincides with the international consensus. Support of the PLO is branded as complicity with the destruction of the Jewish state. Israeli Arabs who advocate Israel's withdrawal to the pre-1967 borders and the formation of a Palestinian state are also seen in this light. Most Jews conceive of compromise with Palestinian self-determination as antithetical to national survival.

There is no basis for the belief that Israeli Arabs will constitute a real obstacle to peace. It is not clear whether they will succeed, by closing ranks with the Zionist left in persuading Jewish public opinion to accede to an independent Palestinian state alongside Israel. Yet, it is possible that they will become an effective pressure group in Israeli politics, reinforcing the peace camp and even providing the extra needed strength to turn it into a winning force.

In the case of negotiations between Israel and the Palestinians, the problem of the Arab minority will in all probability be raised. Israel may object to include it on the agenda because it sees it as an internal matter. The Palestinian delegation will probably press the issue out of a sense of responsibility for all Palestinians. It is argued (Hilf, 1979) that the resolution of the Israeli-Arab conflict will be incomplete if the Arab minority is left unheeded.

If the question of Israeli Arabs is discussed in future peace negotiations, many demands will be made. The Palestinian side will call for the recovery of some of the confiscated lands or for proper compensation, the return to villages destroyed in the 1948 War, the repatriation of relatives, the legalization of 40 makeshift Arab settlements and thousands of unlicensed buildings, the proportional appropriation of budgets, the wider official use of Arabic, and more generally, state recognition of the Arabs as a Palestinian national minority with certain collective rights.

On the other hand, the Jewish side may question the status of Arabs as Israeli citizens, in conjunction with the unsettled status of Arabs in East Jerusalem and Jewish settlers living in the territories ceded to the Palestinians. In exchange for territorial concessions and in an effort to consolidate Israel's Jewish majority, hardliners might demand disenfranchisement or even relocation of the Arab population, particularly of Arabs unwilling to serve in the army.

The turning point in the Israeli-Palestinian conflict in 1988 has made these remote options into relevant issues. The mass uprising in the occupied territories put the Palestinian question on the international agenda. In an unexpected move, Jordan dropped any claim to the West Bank and endorsed the idea of a Palestinian state, headed by the PLO, in the West Bank and Gaza Strip. The Palestinian National Council declared the independence of the State of Palestine alongside Israel. By the first anniversary of the Intifadeh the PLO moderated its position further in order to be acceptable as a negotiating partner. It moved to meet the three conditions set by the United States in 1975, namely, renunciation of terrorism, acceptance of United Nations resolutions 242 and 338, and explicit recognition of Israel's right to exist. The United States reciprocated by opening a substantive dialogue with the PLO. The official contacts between the United States and the PLO ushered in a new, positive stage toward the resolution of the Palestinian question.

These dramatic developments have found Israel paralyzed by a sharply divided population and a stalemated unity government. The inconclusive results of the November 1988 national elections and the sudden shift in the American policy toward the PLO prompted the Likud and Labor parties to form a broad government based on the old, national consensus against a retreat to the pre-1967 borders, an independent

Palestinian state, and talks with the PLO, and for a continued clampdown on the rebellious Palestinians in the occupied territories.

No matter how it may look, Israel is not intransigent on the Palestinian issue, however. Most Israeli Jews do not espouse the ideology of Greater Israel. They also insist on keeping Israel Jewish and democratic. This makes Israel's disengagement from the territories almost a necessity, especially because it will have no adverse effect for the daily life of the average Israeli. The real power of the Likud camp has so far rested on inertia, the low and invisible costs of the prolonged occupation, Palestinian rejectionism or ambiguity, inaction by the United States, and lack of viable alternatives. But with the change that swept the area during 1988, all these forces have appreciably eroded. Israel's negative national consensus is bound to shatter, no matter what the old guard of the Likud and Labor parties does to stand fast.

7

Collective Identity

The collective identity of a nondominant minority conceivably reflects its problematic status in the wider society. Accommodating minorities resign themselves to the identity imposed upon them by the dominant majority. Rising minorities often redefine their identity as part of their struggle to improve their position in the society (e.g., the shifts from Negro to Black and Mexican-American to Chicano in the United States). The minority collective identity often becomes a crucial issue on which the majority and minority, as well as groups within the minority, are divided.

The identity problem of Israel's Arabs hinges on the degree of congruence between two elements: civil (Israeli) and national (Arab, Palestinian). As Nakhleh (1975) observes, up to the 1967 war the Israeli component was dominant owing to the disorientation and isolation of Israel's Arabs in the region. The encounter with other Arabs in the occupied territories following the 1967 war made the Arab component more salient. Then, after the 1973 war, with the ascendancy of the PLO and the spread of Palestinian consciousness the world over, Arab nationalism in Israel has moved toward becoming more and more Palestinian.

The survey responses substantiate a number of tendencies. First, nationality is the most central identity among Arabs. In the 1976 survey, respondents were asked to rank five types of identity. Nationality is selected as the most important identity by 40.5% of the Arab sample, religion by 31.5%, social class by 15%, hamula by 8%, and citizenship by 4% (Table 7.1). Identity for 60% of the Arabs is, therefore, modern (i.e. nationality, class, and citizenship). Were it not for the low appeal of Israeli citizenship, there would be a far larger majority attaching the utmost importance to modern identities. The salience of national identity is further demonstrated by the feeling of 56% of the Arabs that being an Arab in Israel affects one's thinking and behavior.

Table 7.1 Centrality of National Identity

	Arab Public	Jewish Public
The most important identity		
Nationality	40.5	10.8
Religion	31.5	8.6
Socioeconomic status	15.2	8.6
Hamula	8.4	28.1
Citizenship	4.4	43.9
The extent to which thinking and behavior are considered to be affected by the fact that one is an Arab/a Jew in Israel		
To a great extent	30.1	46.1
To some extent	26.1	24.1
Little	21.0	6.4
Not at all	22.8	23.4

Source: The 1976 survey.

National identity is no less important for Jews than it is for Arabs. Although only one tenth of the Jewish respondents choose nationality above other identities, they, in fact, express their strong ties to Jewish nationalism through religion and Israeli citizenship. Hence, in reality, 63% of the Jews see their national identity as the most fundamental, as also evidenced by 70% who consider their thinking and behavior to be affected by being Jews in Israel (Table 7.1). Under normal circumstances, such a high level of national consciousness among a dominant majority would be surprising. It is more easily understood, however, in the light of the recency of Jewish dominant status and the unrelenting challenge to the legitimacy of Jewish national identity and Israeli statehood in the Middle East.

A second tendency confirmed by the data is that the Arabs are deeply divided over their self-identity. Some 53% hold that the term "Israeli" describes them well, as opposed to 47% who consider it inadequate (Table 7.2). Similarly, 55% feel the name "Palestinian" fits them well, in contrast to 45% who do not. These figures also demonstrate the relatively greater appeal of Palestinian identity. This is even more true of the Arab leaders. The Rakah-affiliated leaders who pursue the Arab mainstream feel more comfortable with a Palestinian self-description than with an Israeli one (69% vs. 44%). As expected, the Arab leaders who are affiliated with the Zionist establishment identify themselves primarily as Israeli, whereas the rejectionist Arab leaders see themselves as exclusively Palestinian.

Table 7.2 Appropriateness of Terms of National Self-Identity

	Arab Public	Estab. Affil. Arab Lead.	Rakah Affil. Arab Lead.	Rejec- tion. Arab Lead.	Jewish Public	Dovish Jewish Lead.	Jewish Arab- ists	Hawkish Jewish Lead.
Consider each of the following terms as an appropriate self-description								
Israeli	53.0	80.0	43.8	0.0	95.8	96.9	100.0	91.7
Palestinian/Jew	54.7	36.0	68.8	100.0	95.3	100.0	96.6	100.0

In sharp contrast with Arabs, the Jewish public and leaders unanimously agree that the terms "Israeli" and "Jewish" are appropriate self-descriptions (Table 7.2).

Third, unlike the Jews, for whom Jewish and Israeli identities are complementary and mutually reinforcing, the Arabs experience their civic and national identities as contradictory.[1] This contradiction is imposed on the Arabs by the broader dispute between the Palestinians and Israel, which causes Jewish negation of anything Palestinian. Hence, Arabs who feel equally Palestinian and Israeli face a dilemma of loyalty when these identities collide with each other. They also find themselves rejected by the Jews who consider the two affiliations irreconcilable. For this reason it is no wonder that most Arabs escape the dilemma by choosing either a Palestinian or Israeli identity, but the proportion of those who attempt to keep and synthesize both identities is growing quickly. In fact, Rakah and the PLP espouse and propagate the synthesis. These observations are supported by the survey findings.

Table 7.3 Arabs' Self-Identity as Chosen from Given Alternatives

	Arab Public	Establishment Affiliated Arab Leaders	Rakah Affiliated Arab Leaders	Rejectionist Arab Leaders
Define oneself (from the following seven alternatives) as				
Israeli	4.6	0.0	0.0	0.0
Israeli Arab	30.3	52.0	12.5	0.0
Arab	10.5	0.0	0.0	0.0
Israeli Palestinian	7.7	28.0	9.4	0.0
Palestinian (Palestinian Arab) in Israel	21.1	20.0	68.8	6.5
Palestinian	3.6	0.0	0.0	12.9
Palestinian Arab	22.1	0.0	9.4	80.6

[1]There is a negative correlation (r=-0.53) for the general Arab population between the responses to the adequacy of the appellations "Israeli" and "Palestinian."

Fourth, the existing internal split among the Arabs is additionally highlighted when Arabs are forced to select one of seven rival national identities that consist of the terms Israeli, Arab, Palestinian, and some of their combinations (Table 7.3). The most attractive identities are "Israeli Arab" (30%), "Palestinian Arab" (22%), and "Palestinian Arab in Israel" (21%). These compound and more informative terms are definitely preferable to them than the unitary descriptions (Israeli, Arab, and Palestinian, which together draw only 19%).

Table 7.4 Arabs' Identity by Population Groups

	Non-Pal-estinian Israeli	Israeli Palestinian	Non-Israeli Palestinian
Total	45.4	28.8	25.7
Community			
Druze	94.5	4.6	0.9
Christian	48.8	37.4	13.8
Northern Bedouin	55.6	25.9	18.5
Negev Bedouin	36.1	26.4	37.5
Non-Bedouin Moslem	36.9	30.6	32.5
Age			
18-25	39.1	33.1	27.8
26-45	48.5	25.4	26.2
46 or over	50.0	29.2	20.8
Education			
0-8	48.3	25.4	26.3
9-12	40.1	36.5	23.5
13 or more	37.6	34.4	28.0
Effect of land expropriations			
None	30.4	27.5	42.1
Some	42.9	37.2	19.9
Much	53.4	28.2	18.4
Voting in 1977			
Jewish parties	58.1	27.0	14.9
DFPE (Rakah)	22.0	41.5	36.5

It is possible to reclassify Arabs by their national self-identity. A simple dichotomy would establish a majority of 54.5% who already opt for the various Palestinian identities as opposed to 45.5% who still prefer non-Palestinian self-identifications. It is more fitting, however, to divide Arabs into three categories. At the more accommodating end of the continuum there is a distinct group of 45% identifying as "non-Palestinian Israelis" (Israelis, Israeli Arabs, Arabs), while another distinct group of 26% identifying as "non-Israeli Palestinians" (Palestinians, Palestinian Arabs) falls at the other end, and in between are found the

29% "Israeli Palestinians" (or Palestinian Arabs in Israel) who try to reconcile their Israeli and Palestinian affiliations. This categorization correlates highly with stands on many issues of Arab-Jewish relations. To illustrate, rejection of Israel's right to exist is 5%, 9%, and 24%, respectively, among Arabs in the three categories of identity. The three-way typology differentiates well according to community, effect of land expropriations and voting behavior, but poorly between age and education groups (Table 7.4).[2] Yet the typology clearly points to distinctions among the Arab leaders. Those linked with the Zionist establishment are evenly split between the non-Palestinian Israeli and Israeli Palestinian identities, those affiliated with Rakah are concentrated in the Israeli Palestinian identity, and the rejectionists are virtually all in the non-Israeli Palestinian identity.

Fifth, Israeli Arab identity is already a major controversial issue between Arabs and Jews. Whereas 54% of the Arabs define Israel's Arabs in Palestinian terms (and 54.5% identify themselves as such), less than one tenth of the Jewish public and less than one quarter of the Jewish leaders so define Arabs in these terms (Table 7.5). While the

Table 7.5 Perception of the National Identity of the Arabs in Israel

	Arab Public	Estab. Affil. Arab Lead.	Rakah Affil. Arab Lead.	Rejec-tion. Arab Lead.	Jewish Public	Dovish Jewish Lead.	Jewish Arab-ists	Hawkish Jewish Lead.
Define Arabs in Israel (from the following seven alternatives) as								
Israeli	2.4	0.0	0.0	0.0	3.4	0.0	0.0	0.0
Israeli Arab	35.4	52.0	12.5	9.7	64.9	72.7	73.3	88.0
Arab	8.2	0.0	0.0	0.0	23.4	3.0	3.3	4.0
Israeli Palestinian	8.0	24.0	3.1	0.0	1.6	6.1	6.7	4.0
Palestinian (Palestinian Arab) in Israel	21.8	24.0	78.1	12.9	1.8	9.1	3.3	0.0
Palestinian	3.5	0.0	0.0	12.9	1.6	0.0	0.0	0.0
Palestinian Arab	20.7	0.0	6.3	64.5	3.3	9.1	13.3	4.0

overwhelming majority of Jews do not consider Arabs in Israel to be Palestinians, they fully realize that Arabs see themselves as such (85% of the Jews in a representative sample of the urban population in April 1979 thought that the majority of Arabs regarded themselves as Palestinians;

---

[2]Although civic and national identities are not contradictory for Jews, their relative importance is as meaningful for the Jews as it is for the Arabs. Surveys of identity among Jewish youth show that those identifying primarily as Israeli tend to be more secular, democratic and tolerant than those identifying primarily as Jewish.

Peled, 1979). Whereas Palestinian identity has already gained currency among the Arabs, Jews unequivocally still regard it as threatening and illegitimate and withhold it from Israeli Arabs.

Sixth and last, Arabs are simultaneously Israelis and Palestinians in many respects. They speak Arabic and Hebrew and shuttle between both cultures; they feel solidarity with the Palestinian people and act on their behalf, but realize that their fate, life chances, and loyalty are tied to Israel.

Arabs' compound identity is well manifested in the relative position they occupy between Israeli Jews and non-Israeli Palestinians. Only 28% of Israeli Arabs have relatives in the territories or abroad (Table 7.6). Some 49% pay social or business visits to the West Bank and Gaza Strip but only 12% do so often or regularly. On the other hand, 77% hold frequent contacts with Jews, 66% have Jewish friends, and 38.5% have visited Jewish friends in the past two years (Table 7.7). These figures show that the Israeli dimension in the Arab identity is even stronger than the Palestinian one.

Table 7.6 Arabs' Ties with Arabs outside Israel Proper

	Arab Public	Establishment Affiliated Arab Leaders	Rakah Affiliated Arab Leaders	Rejectionist Arab Leaders
Ties with relatives living across the Green Line or in Arab countries				
Have relatives there and maintain ties with them	28.2	48.0	46.9	16.7
Have relatives there but do not maintain ties with them	29.3	12.0	25.0	30.0
Do not have relatives there	42.4	40.0	28.1	53.3
Frequency of social or business visits to the West Bank and Gaza Strip in the past year				
Once or more a month	12.4	24.0	19.3	24.1
Several times a year	36.4	60.0	38.7	20.7
None	51.2	16.0	41.9	55.2

This duality is also well reflected in feelings toward Palestinians and Israelis. When asked whom they more resemble in style of life and daily behavior, most Arabs recognize both influences and their status as a truly distinct cultural group (Table 7.8).[3] While Arabs feel a bit culturally nearer to Israeli Jews by a ratio of 24% to 17%, they feel generally nearer to Palestinians in the territories by a ratio of 39% to 20% (Table 7.9). Their

[3]Only the rejectionist Arab leaders take exception, of whom 71% observe that Israel's Arabs are culturally closer to the Palestinians than they are to Israeli Jews.

"heart" is no doubt with their own people, yet they actually maintain more ramified connections with Israeli Jews.

Table 7.7 Interethnic Contact

	Arab Public	Jewish Public
Frequency of interethnic contact		
Daily	34.0	14.7
Very often	11.4	10.9
Often	31.3	20.1
Almost never	23.3	54.3
Friendship and visiting terms with Jews/Arabs over the past two years		
Have Jewish/Arab friends and have visited them	38.5	11.6
Have Jewish/Arab friends but have not visited them	27.9	10.9
Have no Jewish/Arab friends	33.6	77.5

Table 7.8 Cultural Resemblance

	Arab Public	Estab. Affil. Arab Lead.	Rakah Affil. Arab Lead.	Rejec- tion. Arab Lead.	Jewish Public	Dovish Jewish Lead.	Jewish Arab- ists	Hawkish Jewish Lead.
Compared to Arabs in the West Bank and Gaza Strip and Jews in Israel, Israeli Arabs more resemble in style of life and daily behavior								
Arabs in the West Bank and Gaza Strip	17.7	0.0	25.0	71.0	37.6	16.1	30.0	20.8
Jews in Israel	24.1	16.0	15.6	3.2	27.6	12.9	30.0	8.3
Both	31.1	40.0	37.5	9.7	25.5	58.1	36.7	58.3
Neither	27.0	44.0	21.9	16.1	9.4	12.9	3.3	12.5

Table 7.9 The Feeling of Closeness

	Arab Public	Establishment Affiliated Arab Leaders	Rakah Affiliated Arab Leaders	Rejectionist Arab Leaders
Feel closer to				
Arabs in the West Bank and Gaza Strip	39.1	13.6	58.1	93.5
Jews in Israel	19.8	18.2	3.2	0.0
No difference	41.0	68.2	38.7	6.5

Furthermore, the acquisition of various Palestinian identifications is manifested mostly in feelings of solidarity but not in a desire to dissociate oneself from Israel and to join any Palestinian entity. The overwhelming majority of the Arabs would be relieved by a settlement of the Palestinian problem, and in particular, 80% would feel better as Israeli citizens if a Palestinian state were to be established in the West Bank and Gaza Strip (Table 7.10). Yet, only 8% of them (and virtually none of the leaders, including the rejectionists) are willing to consider a move to such a state (Table 7.11). For practical and ideological reasons Arabs feel firmly attached to their homes and places of residence and would not leave Israel under this circumstance. In fact, fewer Arabs than Jews left the country since 1949, despite the enormous pressure, wars, economic hardships, and discrimination. Arabs are, indeed, a permanent minority in Israel.

Table 7.10 Arabs' Feeling about Israel If a Palestinian State Were to Be Established

	Arab Public	Establishment Affiliated Arab Leaders	Rakah Affiliated Arab Leaders	Rejectionist Arab Leaders
Would feel better as an Arab citizen of Israel if a Palestinian state were to be established in the West Bank and Gaza Strip				
Yes	57.1	52.0	93.8	6.5
Possible	23.1	32.0	6.3	29.0
Doubtful	10.9	8.0	0.0	16.1
No	8.9	8.0	0.0	48.4

Table 7.11 Arabs' Willingness to Move to a Palestinian State

	Arab Public	Establishment Affiliated Arab Leaders	Rakah Affiliated Arab Leaders	Rejectionist Arab Leaders
Willingness to move to a Palestinian state, if it were established alongside Israel				
Yes	8.3	0.0	0.0	0.0
Perhaps	18.1	8.0	0.0	3.2
No	73.6	92.0	100.0	96.8

In conclusion, the dilemma of collective identity which strains intergroup relations in many societies is also evident in Israel. Arabs are asserting themselves as Palestinians while keeping their Israeli identity. Their national identity, being defied by Jews, has become a critical issue. However, economic, social, cultural, and even emotional ties, which have been established with Israeli Jews since 1948, appreciably modify the meaning of Palestinization in a way that makes it more compatible with Israeli identity and life in Israel. As a result, a new synthesis, "Israeli Palestinian identity," is emerging and spreading out among the Arabs.

8

Institutional Separation

In general, institutional separation between ethnic groups characterizes their often tense relations in deeply divided societies. It becomes controversial when the subordinate group is or feels itself to be the victim of involuntary segregation, imposed assimilation, or both. It is particularly difficult to strike a balance between ethnic separation and integration in industrial sharply fragmented societies where the potential for social and geographical mobility and for the mixing of populations is substantial.

The problem is potentially contentious in Israel because considerable separation is built into the country's basic values and major social institutions. Jews and Arabs are legally endogamous and nonassimilating sectors that can only seek coexistence in terms of integration rather than amalgamation. They are almost completely isolated in residential quarters, schools, certain public bureaucracies which maintain special Arab departments, and the army.

Arab integration presents a dilemma for Jews and Arabs. For the Jews, to permit integration is to demonstrate goodwill. It is also a device calculated to coopt and contain the Arab minority. Yet it runs counter to Israel's Jewish-Zionist mission of preventing Jewish assimilation by positive and negative reinforcements. For the Arabs, integration is a forceful means to achieve equality of opportunities and resources, but also a threat to their separate existence and identity.

Is institutional separation between the two communities a disputatious issue? Since separation is the rule in Israel, it is more relevant to assess the proportion of the population that takes exception to it. It is clear that by and large only a minority in both sectors object to the status quo of isolation in the schools, neighborhoods, political parties, and public offices (Table 8.1). These integrationist minorities are sizable, however, ranging from 33% to 49% among the Arabs and 22% to 39%

among the Jews. Apart from the issue of schools, Arab and Jewish leaders wish more integration than their rank and file. A large majority of Arab leaders also advocate the liquidation of the separate Arab departments in government, Histadrut, and political parties. They view them as vehicles of institutional discrimination against Arabs.

Table 6.1 Institutional Separation

	Arab Public	Estab. Affil. Arab Lead.	Rakah Affil. Arab Lead.	Rejec- tion. Arab Lead.	Jewish Public	Dovish Jewish Lead.	Jewish Arab- ists	Hawkish Jewish Lead.
Schools should be separate for Arabs and Jews								
Yes	48.0	56.0	62.5	74.2	61.8	61.8	62.1	69.2
Not Certain	16.8	24.0	15.6	12.9	14.0	11.8	17.2	7.7
No	35.3	20.0	21.9	12.9	24.2	26.5	20.7	23.1
Neighborhoods should be separate for Arabs and Jews								
Yes	42.2	52.0	37.5	45.2	60.0	34.4	42.9	32.0
Not Certain	17.8	28.0	3.1	9.7	17.1	37.5	14.3	28.0
No	40.0	20.0	59.4	45.2	22.9	28.1	42.9	40.0
Political parties should be separate for Arabs and Jews								
Yes	30.4	16.0	9.4	32.3	42.6	6.5	16.7	16.7
Not Certain	20.9	8.0	15.6	12.9	18.5	6.5	10.0	12.5
No	48.7	76.0	75.0	54.8	38.9	87.1	73.3	70.8
The present special Arab departments should be abolished								
Against	47.7	4.0	3.1	6.7	50.2	36.4	37.9	42.3
Have reservations	18.9	12.0	6.3	0.0	27.8	9.1	20.7	19.2
In favor	33.4	84.0	90.6	93.3	22.1	54.5	41.4	38.5

It is worth stressing the agreement among all leaders that political parties should not be separate. It is actually congruent with the present situation where Arab political activity is confined to the Arab-Jewish Rakah and Progressive List for Peace, or within the Jewish parties.[1] Behind this consensus, however, are divergent motivations and considerations; Arab political integration is a mechanism of control by Jewish leaders, a means of access to power by accommodationist Arab

[1] The new Arab Democratic Party (DAP) is the only exception. Although it is more moderate than Rakah and the PLO, the DAP was deliberately founded in 1988 as an Arab party and it has been criticized for this reason too. In defending its exclusive Arab composition, Knesset Member Darawshe who leads it argues that for the time being an Arab party is needed to promote the political representation and special interests of Israeli Arabs.

leaders, both a protection against suppression and a lever by oppositionist Rakah Arab leaders for reaching out to the Jewish majority, and lip-service to the secular-democratic state slogan espoused by the rejectionist Arab leaders.

As for the army, both sides also agree to maintain the current exemption of the Arabs from compulsory military service (Table 8.2). Only 18% of the Jews feel that Arabs should serve in the army. This dissenting view is held by 22% of the Druzes who have been subject to the draft since 1956, 12% of the Bedouin who may volunteer to the professional army only, and 3% of the Christians and non-Bedouin Moslems who are barred from the army (on the question of Arabs in Israel Defence Forces, see Katzenell, 1987).

Table 8.2 Imposition of Military and Civil Service Duty on Arabs

	Arab Public	Estab. Affil. Arab Lead.	Rakah Affil. Arab Lead.	Rejec-tion. Arab Lead.	Jewish Public	Dovish Jewish Lead.	Jewish Arab-ists	Hawkish Jewish Lead.
Imposition of compulsory military service on Arabs in Israel[a]								
Against	83.7				73.7			
Not Certain	10.0				8.0			
In favor	6.2				18.2			
Imposition of civil service duty on Arabs in Israel in lieu of military service								
Against	58.4	20.0	59.4	96.8	35.8	15.2	23.3	19.2
Only under certain circumstances	27.5	60.0	37.5	3.2	24.3	36.4	13.3	26.9
In favor	14.2	20.0	3.1	0.0	39.8	48.5	63.3	53.8

[a] The 1976 survey.

For some time the Jewish Arabists have proposed the idea of instituting mandatory national service for Arabs in lieu of the military draft. While this possibility was deliberated in 1979 by the Knesset Committee on Foreign and Security Affairs, it has never been seriously considered. In light of the past experience with national service by religious Jewish women, such a plan might call for a one-year assignment of Arab youths to community development projects or services in Arab localities. The survey shows that Jews as a whole are disposed toward imposing civil service on Arabs, while most Arabs are opposed or reserved. Jews who tend to accuse Arabs of evading basic duties, such as military service and payment of taxes, would like Arabs to do more. On the other hand, Arab reluctance reflects not only an obvious interest in keeping a dubious benefit of segregation but also a fundamental fear of being further manipulated by the authorities.

Several conclusions can be drawn from the data. First, most Arabs and Jews condone the status quo of substantial separation. Second, beyond this basic consensus there is some asymmetry; namely, Arabs covet more integration than Jews and more integration than is available to them today. And third, separation appears rather voluntary and uncontroversial. By and large, the Arabs constitute a nonassimilating minority mostly out of collective choice and only partly because of forced segregation.

Although this last conclusion is in line with the centuries-old millet system (i.e., the legal separation in marriage and personal status between religious communities) which is still the practice in the Arab world and Israel, it should be qualified. To demonstrate it beyond reasonable doubt, there is need for evidence relating to Arab and Jewish response under real circumstances of free choice between separation and integration. Since Israel is not an open society where Arabs and Jews can legitimately select either option, the question whether Arab-Jewish separation is involuntary remains, in the final analysis, moot.

9

National Autonomy

One possible distinct response of a disaffected, nonassimilating minority is to seek ethnic autonomy, i.e., to exercise a measure of self-determination within or even outside the state's boundaries (Hall, 1979). The world today abounds in national minorities with separatist inclinations or demands for community control, and in some cases full sovereignty (Horowitz, 1985). Governmental efforts to maintain stability range from fostering all-inclusive loyalties, through concessions, to outright suppression. Although the causes for the emergence of ethno-nationalism are diverse and unclear (McCord and McCord, 1979; Smith, 1979), national autonomy is highly controversial in societies containing nonassimilating minorities.

Israeli authorities have always considered Arab national autonomy a threat to Jewish domination and to the state's political stability and have adopted diverse countermeasures to avert it. These include depriving Arabs of control over their own institutions, preventing them from forming independent organizations, endeavoring to dismantle their majority status in certain regions, coopting their leaders, encouraging traditional internal divisions, and treating them as an ethnic rather than national group. These policies coupled with other restraints comprise the machinery of political control over the Arab minority.

Despite all the constraints, Arabs still exhibit various features that facilitate separatist tendencies. They have their own genuine culture (i.e. language, religion, nationality, and traditions), communal institutions, a territorial base (the Western-central Galilee and the Triangle), a predominantly Palestinized national identity, and numerous overt grievances. The crucial question then is whether Arabs actually harbor genuine separatist sentiments and whether Jews support the state's policies and practices vis-à-vis the Arab minority. Attitudes toward Arab national autonomy will be discussed in terms of a sense of nationalist consciousness, community control, representative leadership, regional self-rule, and irredentism.

One component in the Israeli government's policy of preventing Arabs from developing into an autonomous national minority is to strengthen the internal communal splits along sectarian and kinship lines. This weakens the common national ties. More positively, the government hopes that "Arabs" will become a mixture of even smaller minorities, such as Moslems, Christians, Druzes, Bedouin, Ahmedians, and so forth cut off from the broader Palestinian population and acquiring a new Israeli minority consciousness. While the Jewish public's perception of the Arabs as divided is fashioned by these policies, the Arabs themselves emphasize unity at the ideological level (Table 9.1). The large majority of Arabs view hamula and religious loyalties as obstacles to social development. They also think that Arabs of all religions hold common goals. This stress on the commonality of fate corresponds with the centrality of nationality in the set of Arab identities (Table 7.1).

Table 9.1 Perception of Internal Divisions among Arabs in Israel

	Arab Public	Jewish Public
Moslems, Christians and Druzes in Israel have little in common and differ in their goals		
Agree	24.7	69.8
Have reservations	21.4	15.5
Disagree	53.9	14.7
Hamula and sectarian loyalties inhibit social development among Arabs in Israel		
Agree	77.5	*
Agree to some extent	14.6	*
Disagree	7.8	*

* Not asked.

Source: The 1976 survey.

Although Arabs are allowed separate community institutions, the institutions are denied autonomy. The Arabs neither dominate their separate institutions nor are they permitted to set up certain types of organizations. The authorities fear that separate Arab bodies might become independent bases of power and resistance. The most central Arab institution under Jewish rule is education.[1] Whereas both sides

[1]In 1987 an Arab career bureaucrat was appointed as a head of the Arab education branch in the Ministry of Education and Culture. Although Arabs are still denied control of their education, this gesture indicates a piecemeal growth of Arab institutional autonomy.

agree to leave Arab education separate (Table 8.1), they disagree on whether it should be autonomous (Table 9.2). Majorities ranging from 63% to 93.5% of the Arab public and leaders desire Arab control over Arab education, an idea about which majorities of 53%-72% of the Jewish public and leaders feel reserved or opposed. It is significant that the Arab-Jewish disagreement is greater at the leadership level where the stakes involved are better understood. These conflicting views probably hold for other policy areas, especially with regard to the expansion of the authority of local governments, religious bodies, and economic development.

Table 9.2 Arab Control of Arab Education

	Arab Public	Estab. Affil. Arab Lead.	Rakah Affil. Arab Lead.	Rejec- tion. Arab Lead.	Jewish Public	Dovish Jewish Lead.	Jewish Arab- ists	Hawkish Jewish Lead.
Arabs should control and manage their own system of education								
In favor	63.3	68.0	90.0	93.5	42.0	46.7	42.9	28.0
Have reservations	21.2	24.0	10.0	0.0	25.3	33.3	39.3	20.0
Against	15.5	8.0	0.0	6.5	32.7	20.0	17.9	52.0

The formation of new, independent Arab institutions is even more disputatious. There is no Arab university, Arab trade union, or Arab radio and television station which is independent of the Zionist establishment. Although one finds an Arab press of some impact, notably the Communist *Al-Ittihad* and the commercialized *Al-Sinara*, there is no non-partisan, Arabic news daily covering the Israeli Arab sector. Under these circumstances, it is no wonder that a clear Arab majority, ranging from 63% to 72%, are in favor of establishing independent Arab institutions (Table 9.3). An equally clear Jewish majority, ranging from 78% to 83%, object to them or have reservations. The accommodating Arab leaders side with the Jewish leaders and do not favor such autonomous institutions.

Rakah-affiliated and rejectionist Arab leaders differ on this issue. On the one hand, they concur on the need for an Arab university and Arab mass media. In fact, a special organization was founded to struggle for an Arab university ("Al-Tzawt"). In 1980, it elected a steering committee and pressed its claim in the Knesset Committee on Education and Culture, which, as could be predicted, totally rejected the idea. On the other hand, Rakah-affiliated Arab leaders oppose the creation of an Arab trade union, while rejectionist Arab leaders and the Arab public endorse it. Their objection has less to do with a Communist-inspired belief in the class solidarity of Arab and Jewish workers than with a calculated fear that separate Arab unions might inflict a loss of protection and benefits presently extended to Arab members by the giant Histadrut labor federation. In contrast, the rejectionist leaders wish to see a breakaway Arab trade union because they share the revolutionary Matzpen (Israeli Socialist Organization) criticism of the Histadrut as an accomplice in class and national exploitation.

Table 9.3 Formation of Independent Arab Organizations

	Arab Public	Estab. Affil. Arab Lead.	Rakah Affil. Arab Lead.	Rejec- tion. Arab Lead.	Jewish Public	Dovish Jewish Lead.	Jewish Arab- ists	Hawkish Jewish Lead.
Unreservedly in favor of forming each of the following as an independent Arab organization								
University	71.0	40.0	83.9	96.7	22.1	21.9	3.3	7.7
Mass media	71.9	28.0	73.3	90.3	17.1	23.5	3.3	8.0
Trade union	63.1	16.0	31.3	83.9	19.0	8.8	0.0	3.8

The question of separate Arab politics is obviously central to Arab national autonomy. The five major options are non-autonomous integration into the Jewish parties, coalitionary Arab parties, oppositionist Arab-Jewish parties like Rakah, nationalist Arab parties, and non-participation. Different people would perceive differently the last two options: nationalist parties may be viewed as militant or rejectionist, and non-participation may be seen as avoidance of confrontation or active boycott of the Israeli political system.

The division between Arabs and Jews and among the Arabs themselves is clear from the data. The most favored option by the Jewish public and Jewish leadership in particular is integration into the Jewish parties; coalitionary Arab parties is the second best choice; and Arab non-participation emerges as the third least evil for the Jewish public (Table 9.4). In Jewish eyes, these three options imply minimal political autonomy for Arabs. Another position is expressed by the Arab leaders who are affiliated with Jewish parties. They are divided between integration and coalitionary Arab parties, aspiring for greater political leeway and clout than they enjoy today.

On the other hand, the Arab public is attracted primarily to oppositionist Arab-Jewish parties (31%) and coalitionary Arab parties (29%), and secondarily to nationalist Arab parties (18%) and integration into Jewish parties (15%). Although Arabs view nationalist Arab parties (only 23% oppose them) positively, they are realistic enough not to prefer this type of autonomous Arab politics to more moderate alternatives.

Most importantly, only 7% of the Arabs favor non-participation, showing their great desire to be an integral part of Israeli politics.

Table 9.4 Independent Arab Political Parties

	Arab Public	Estab. Affil. Arab Lead.	Rakah Affil. Arab Lead.	Rejec- tion. Arab Lead.	Jewish Public	Dovish Jewish Lead.	Jewish Arab- ists	Hawkish Jewish Lead.
The most desirable type of political organization for Arabs today is								
To join existing Jewish parties as individuals with equal status	15.1	54.2	0.0	0.0	33.7	80.6	73.3	56.0
To form Arab parties that can reach agreement or cooperate with the existing Jewish parties	28.6	41.7	15.6	3.4	32.7	19.4	23.3	32.0
To belong to non-Zionist parties composed of Arabs and Jews	31.4	4.2	68.8	48.3	5.6	0.0	3.3	0.0
To establish independent nationalist Arab parties	18.1	0.0	12.5	24.1	3.7	0.0	0.0	4.0
No political party organization at all	6.7	0.0	3.1	24.1	24.3	0.0	0.0	8.0
Formation of an independent nationalist Arab party								
In favor	48.2	40.0	37.5	35.5	13.1	26.7	10.0	12.5
Have reservations	28.5	20.0	25.0	16.1	20.2	6.7	6.7	8.3
Against	23.3	40.0	37.5	48.4	66.7	66.7	83.3	79.2

Over two thirds of the Arab leaders who are affiliated with Rakah endorse non-Zionist parties composed of Arabs and Jews and options represented by Rakah itself, while the rest are divided between coalitionary (16%) and nationalist (12.5%) parties.

It is worth noting the failure of even the majority of Arabs active in the Sons of the Village Movement to endorse nationalist Arab parties (only 24% of them elect this alternative). It springs from their reluctance to recognize Israel's right to exist, on the one hand, and ironically from the certainty of being banned by the authorities if they embark on this course, on the other.

A further element of national autonomy is the rise of an authentic, representative, statewide Arab leadership that the Israeli government uncompromisingly opposes. Indeed, all types of Jewish leaders deny official recognition to any Arab public body as representative of all Arabs in Israel (Table 9.5). The Jewish public is, however, evenly divided on this issue. Its lack of decisive disapproval probably stems from misunderstanding rather than genuine liberalism, especially when considered in the light of its rejection of autonomous Arab organizations. With the understandable exception of the Arab leaders who are affiliated with the Zionist establishment, the Arab public and other Arab leaders want Israel to recognize a representative Arab leadership. In fact, such a demand was made in 1976 by the Committee of Heads of Arab Local Councils. Rabin, then the Prime Minister, utterly dismissed the plea, declaring that Arabs are merely a cultural and not a national minority and, hence, not entitled to representative leadership (*Maariv*, June 20, 1976).

Table 9.5 Recognition of Representative Arab Leadership

	Arab Public	Estab. Affil. Arab Lead.	Rakah Affil. Arab Lead.	Rejec- tion. Arab Lead.	Jewish Public	Dovish Jewish Lead.	Jewish Arab- ists	Hawkish Jewish Lead.
The Israeli government should recognize an Arab public body as the authoritative representative of Arabs in Israel								
Agree	68.2	47.6	70.0	64.2	50.0	33.3	26.7	12.0
Disagree	31.8	52.4	30.0	35.7	50.0	66.7	73.4	88.0

The authorities are particularly anxious about possible Arab claims for autonomy in the Western-central Galilee and Triangle. Originally, these two areas were excluded from the Jewish state in the 1947 UN Partition resolution. The Arab Galilee was occupied by Israel in the 1948 war and the Triangle was ceded by Jordan to Israel in the ceasefire agreement of April 1949. Israeli efforts to settle the Western-central Galilee and parts of the Triangle with Jews have not been sufficient to blur their Arab character and majority.

In view of the history and demography of these regions, separatist sentiment may prevail among some Arabs there. For instance, on occasion one hears Arabs shouting, in a way of protest, slogans calling for the Arab liberation of the Galilee. On the other hand, it must be emphasized that since 1967 there has been no Israeli Arab political group demanding secession of these regions from Israel or Arab autonomy there.[2]

Arab assertion of self-determination in the Galilee and Triangle could take the form of regional self-rule or irredentism if a Palestinian state were established in the West Bank and Gaza Strip. There is, however, a

---

[2]Till the late fifties, Maki (Israeli Communist Party) recognized the right to self-determination of the Arabs of the Galilee and Triangle because it advocated the full implementation of the 1947 UN Partition plan. In the aftermath of the 1967 war the 1947 Partition borders vanished even for Rakah which subsequently stands for a Palestinian state in the West Bank and Gaza Strip, excluding the Galilee and Triangle.

Jewish national consensus against both, as evidenced by the positions of all Zionist political parties and movements (including Shelli and Peace Now). When asked about the possibility of granting self-government to Arabs in the Galilee and Triangle, Jews are strongly opposed (Table 9.6). If questioned about allowing Arab secessionism, they would certainly be also opposed.

Table 9.6 Regional Autonomy

	Arab Public	Estab. Affil. Arab Lead.	Rakah Affil. Arab Lead.	Rejec- tion. Arab Lead.	Jewish Public	Dovish Jewish Lead.	Jewish Arab- ists	Hawkish Jewish Lead.
Arab self-rule in the Galilee and Triangle								
In favor	33.1	4.0	12.9	64.3	8.4	5.9	0.0	4.0
Have reservations	30.9	36.0	48.4	10.7	17.9	14.7	6.9	0.0
Against	36.1	60.0	38.7	25.0	73.7	79.4	93.1	96.0

On the other hand, a sizeable minority of the Arab public and one segment of Arab leadership are attracted to both autonomy options. The Arab population is nearly equally divided into proponents, reserved, and opponents of the regional self-administration idea (Table 9.6). They are almost evenly split on an irredentist policy for the Galilee and Triangle (Table 9.7). The 46% of Arabs who reject retention of the Galilee and Triangle squares with the 38% of Arabs who condition their acceptance of a peace settlement on Israel's withdrawal to the 1947 partition borders or on its dissolution and replacement by a new Palestinian state (Table 6.2).

Table 9.7 Irredentism

	Jewish Public	Dovish Jewish Leaders	Jewish Arabists	Hawkish Jewish Leaders
If a Palestinian state were to be established in the West Bank and Gaza Strip, then the Galilee and Triangle should remain integral parts of Israel				
Definitely agree	16.9	45.8	34.4	0.0
Agree	37.6	45.8	56.3	3.4
Disagree	29.9	4.2	3.1	37.9
Definitely disagree	15.7	4.2	6.3	58.6

The disagreement among the Arab leaders closely conformed to the positions of the political bodies to which they are attached. The accommodating leaders, who are tied to the Zionist establishment, predictably oppose both alternatives and thereby fall into the Jewish consensus. Likewise, the leaders affiliated with Rakah adhere to the

Rakah's platform of not sanctioning either claim. In contrast, the strong dissidence of the activists in the Sons of the Village Movement is unmistakably mirrored in their reluctant endorsement of regional autonomy and irredentism (the latter alternative is contingent on the formation of a Palestinian state contrary to their will).

In concluding this section, several comments are in order concerning the notion of "a national minority" status which commonly dominates discussions of Arab national autonomy in Israel. This basic concept gained currency in post-WWI Europe when rampant minority problems emerged from the dissolution of the Austro-Hungarian and Ottoman empires. One way of handling the situation was to grant ethnic minorities the status of national minorities. It meant they had the right to use their language, to maintain separate cultural institutions, and in some cases they were assured a quota of political representatives. When these rights were infringed upon by the dominant majority, the minorities then appealed to the League of Nations. This was to little avail. The League of Nations was unable to act and reluctant to intervene in the internal affairs of its constituent countries (Claude, 1955).

When the United Nations was established, the concept of national minority rights fell into disrepute. Instead of protecting the rights of ethnic collectivities, the UN moved toward the protection of individual rights. In this way minorities were not recognized as such, while the rights of their members were protected, as were those of majorities.

This shift in policy regarding national minority rights did not eliminate their existence nor the diverse arrangements all over the world to accommodate them. Minorities who differ in nationality from a country's dominant group vary considerably in the degree they are accorded national minority status. For example, in the Soviet Union some minorities are denied any such status and are forced to assimilate, others are granted certain rights as "national minorities," and still others are acknowledged as full-fledged "nationalities" and provided with statehood (the Soviet Republics).

So far Israel has pursued a policy of minimizing the national character of its Arab minority. The Arabs are considered a linguistic and religious minority only, granted institutional separation in these areas, while at the same time denied any form of national autonomy. The vehement Jewish opposition to any kind of national autonomy by the Arab minority, as reflected in the survey findings, shows that the Israeli authorities enjoy wide support from the Jewish public in their sustained effort to control the Arab minority. This firm Jewish consensus rests on fears that Arab autonomy would threaten state security by nourishing disloyal and irredentist sentiments, undermine Israel's Jewish-Zionist identity by turning it into a binational state, and weaken Jewish class dominance by forcing a redistribution of national resources and power.

Arabs hope, on the other hand, to gain more equality, more expression of national feelings, and more control of their destiny by obtaining concessions for autonomy from the Jews. They want national minority status. The specific contents of this demand are still ambiguous, but it invariably includes some autonomy. For instance, the Rakah party platform calls on the Israeli government to treat Arabs as a national minority. Seen in this perspective, lands are not expropriated from individual landowners who happen to be Arab but from an Arab national group that loses its territorial and economic base in the process. Hence, Rakah's demand to stop the confiscation of Arab lands extends beyond concern for personal civil rights to a defence of landlords in the name of collective national rights. This national minority viewpoint is, therefore, instrumental in expanding the scope of the autonomy issue. In its 1985 Congress, Rakah stepped up its call for a state recognition of the Arabs' right to national minority status, full legal equality, and protection against any national discrimination and land confiscations in particular (Israeli Communist Party, 1985:88-90). These demands have remained ambiguous, however. It is, rather, Rakah's failure to demand any separate legal status for Arabs as a national minority and its stand against regional self-rule and irredentism, that strongly restrain Arab aspirations for autonomy.

While the Israeli government is reluctant to consider conferring even limited national rights to the Arab minority, it is more willing to do so with regard to the Palestinian people. In fact, the Likud autonomy plan offers the Palestinians in the occupied territories a diluted national minority status, but explicitly excludes Israel's Arabs. In contrast, some observers of the Israeli-Arab dispute contend that the Palestinian problem should be resolved by the formation of a Palestinian state alongside Israel and by granting Arabs within Israel a national minority status entitling them to an officially recognized representative leadership, regional self-jurisdiction, and special legal rights and privileges (Hilf, 1979; for a more limited proposal, see Klein, 1987). It appears that as Israeli Arabs are becoming a pressure group, they will increasingly press for such autonomy formulas for themselves and for a separate state for Palestinians.

10

Group Goals

Disagreement on the collective goals of minorities and majorities toward each other can often become critical issues. In fact, it is regarded by specialists as so central to the pattern of intergroup relations that it provides a common basis for general classifications of ethnic groups. To cite only a few typologies, Wirth (1945), in his classic essay on the ghetto, adopted eventual minority goals as a device to distinguish among assimilationist, pluralistic, secessionist and "militant" (i.e., dominance seeking) minorities. Simpson and Yinger (1972) discern six types of majority policies toward minorities: assimilation, pluralism, legal protection, population transfer, continued subjugation, and extermination. A fourfold typology which stresses congruence-incongruence in minority-majority goals is advanced by Schermerhorn (1970): voluntary assimilation, voluntary separation, imposed assimilation, and imposed separation.

Given the wide range of potential group goals, it is better to present respondents with a choice between competing alternatives than to ascertain their opinions on each goal separately. For example, the selection of "separation" out of several possibilities is a better measure of the most desired group goal than approval or disapproval of "separation" as a goal.

Two survey questions constituted the major source of information on collective goals. One read: "What policy should Israel adopt today toward the Arabs in Israel?" The five options offered range from the status quo, through equality and integration, to an independent national minority status within the state. The other question called for selecting the most desired of four "compromise solutions to the problem of Arabs in Israel." Altogether Arabs and Jews were presented with alternatives involving integration and separation (or exclusion). The answers to these questions were first analyzed in terms of different options, which were then combined to develop an overall classification system of group goals.

One potential alternative is the retention or exacerbation of the status quo. Following three years of unexpected benign neglect, during the last year of the first term of the Likud government, and at the time of data-collection in the summer of 1980, the status quo meant the reinforcement of long-standing dominance patterns. There was also a widespread feeling among Jews that the Israeli Arabs were "getting out of control." The Arabs, on the other hand, actually felt the government's additional strong-arm tactics. Given these circumstances, it is extremely significant to find that 73.5% of the Jewish public opposed to only 6.5% of the Arab public opt for either the status quo or intensified domination ("increase in surveillance over Arabs") (Table 10.1). Over three quarters of the hawkish Jewish leaders (who were then part of the ruling government coalition) follow suit, whereas the dovish Jewish leaders, most of whom are affiliated with the opposition, disapprove of this hardline policy. It is important to note that the Jewish Arabists, who are traditionally Labor supporters, disassociate themselves from the Likud policies they are charged with implementing. It is clear, therefore, that the Arab public and leadership totally reject the status quo, whereas a large majority of the Jewish public and the governing elite wish to retain or augment it.

Table 10.1 Advocated Policy toward Arabs in Israel

	Arab Public	Estab. Affil. Arab Lead.	Rakah Affil. Arab Lead.	Rejec- tion. Arab Lead.	Jewish Public	Dovish Jewish Lead.	Jewish Arab- ists	Hawkish Jewish Lead.
Policy that the state should adopt today toward Arabs in Israel								
Increase in surveillance over Arabs	1.2	0.0	0.0	0.0	42.7	0.0	13.3	25.0
Continuation of the present policy	5.3	0.0	0.0	0.0	30.8	18.2	23.3	41.7
Achievement of equality and integration with Jews	59.7	72.0	50.0	36.4	21.2	75.8	60.0	33.3
Allowing Arabs to organize independently and become partners in state institutions	22.5	28.0	46.9	18.2	3.7	3.0	3.3	0.0
Granting Arabs separate legal status like the autonomy offered to the Arabs in the West Bank and Gaza Strip	11.3	0.0	3.1	45.5	1.6	3.0	0.0	0.0

Another potential group goal is equal opportunities for Arabs. It would require considerable openness by Israeli society "to achieve Arab equality and integration with Jews." Since Arabs are a nonassimilating minority, this option consists of integration without assimilation. This is indeed the official policy of the state toward the Arabs. A majority of the Arab public (60%), the establishment-affiliated Arab leaders (72%), the dovish Jewish leaders (76%), and Jewish Arabists (60%) favor this collective goal in Arab-Jewish relations (Table 10.1). At the same time, this goal does not seem to be liberal enough for other Arab leaders, and it seems too liberal for the Jewish public and hardline leaders.

Another alternative is a limited amount of Arab national autonomy. A milder formula "allows Arabs to get organized independently and become partners in state institutions" and a stronger objective is "granting Arabs a separate legal status like the autonomy offered to Arabs in the West Bank and Gaza Strip." It is the official policy and actual practice of the state to deny Arabs any national autonomy because it is believed that such power would be misused and undermine Israel's national security and Jewish-Zionist character. The figures are unequivocal in demonstrating the outright opposition of the Jewish public and leadership to any Arab autonomous status (Table 10.1). Even when Jews were asked about the possibility of independent Arab organizations, like those of Israel's Orthodox Jews, whose purpose is to advance their particular interests, the majority of Jews were not receptive (Table 10.2). Only the dovish Jewish leaders were open to this idea, apparently because they perceive even independent Arab organizations as cooptable into the existing system.

Table 10.2 Jews' View of Independent Arab Organizing

	Jewish Public	Dovish Jewish Leaders	Jewish Arabists	Hawkish Jewish Leaders
Arabs in Israel should organize independently, like Orthodox Jews, in order to advance their vital interests				
In favor	16.6	57.1	17.2	16.0
Have reservations	29.3	25.0	37.9	32.0
Against	54.1	17.9	44.8	52.0

Given staunch Jewish objections, most Arabs are restrained in articulating their collective desires. Only 34% of the Arab public, 28% of the Arab leaders attached to the establishment, 50% of the Rakah-affiliated Arab leaders, and 64% of the rejectionist Arab leaders select the two ethnic autonomy options as prime goals (Table 10.1).

A radical resolution of the problem is a total physical disengagement between Arabs and Jews. Some Jews may be interested in a voluntary or forced removal of Arabs because it allows Israel to dispose of its Arab minority while keeping its territorial integrity. Some Arabs, on the other hand, may desire secession of their regions, i.e., the Galilee and Triangle, to an adjacent Arab state. Such Arab irredentism is indeed feared by most Jews, who would take it as a serious development that might destabilize relations between Israel and a future Palestinian state in the West Bank and Gaza Strip (Plascov, 1981:45-46) Despite his sympathy with the idea of an independent Palestinian state alongside Israel, Heller maintains that "the threat of secessionism is in fact one of the gravest implications for Israel of a Palestinian state" (1983:106).

After all, these two Arab regions were intended to be part of the Palestinian state designed by the 1947 UN Partition plan before they were annexed by Israel in 1949. The data show that 16% of the Arabs pursue secession (Table 10.3) and a comparable 15% of the Jews seek exclusion of the Arab minority as a primary goal (Table 10.4). Although these figures are clear in indicating a lack of mass support for these drastic options, the small segments on both sides who are disposed to them might become politically significant if they effectively organize.

Table 10.3 Arabs' Solution to the Arab Minority Problem

	Arab Public	Establishment Affiliated Arab Leaders	Rakah Affiliated Arab Leaders	Rejectionist Arab Leaders
The solution to the Arab minority problem that one is willing to reconcile oneself with				
Arabs will live in Israel as a people with equal rights	64.6	100.0	96.9	0.0
Arabs will move to a Palestinian state to be established in the West Bank and Gaza Strip	4.0	0.0	0.0	0.0
Arabs will be part of a Palestinian state to be established in the West Bank, Gaza Strip, the Galilee, and Triangle	15.8	0.0	0.0	9.7
Arabs will live in a secular-democratic state to be established in all of Palestine in place of Israel	15.6	0.0	3.1	90.3

Finally, a still more radical option is a Palestinian secular-democratic state. It is an anathema to nearly all Jews who see it as a means to destroy the Jewish state. It would be more attractive to many Arabs because it was the official goal of the PLO during the 1970's and because it is intended to make them equal to the Jews. The Jews, as expected, oppose the possibility that "Arabs will live as an equal people in Israel as a non-Jewish state" (Table 10.4). On the other hand, 90% of the rejectionist Arab leaders who openly espouse the Rejection Front ideology prefer that "Arabs will live in a secular-democratic state to be established in all of

Palestine in place of Israel" (Table 10.3). But only 16% of the Arab public take this position.

Table 10.4 Jews' Solution to the Arab Minority Problem

	Jewish Public	Dovish Jewish Leaders	Jewish Arabists	Hawkish Jewish Leaders
The solution to the Arab minority problem that one is willing to reconcile oneself with				
Arabs will live as an equal people in Israel as a non-Jewish state	3.4	0.0	0.0	0.0
Arabs will live in Israel as a national minority with equal rights	34.5	78.8	46.7	25.0
Arabs will live in Israel only if they are resigned to their minority status in a state designed for Jews	47.3	21.2	53.3	70.8
Arabs will be forced to live outside Israel	14.9	0.0	0.0	4.2

The two major questions have been combined in order to construct a comprehensive typology of group goals. Since the answers are not identical in wording or meaning for Arabs and Jews, the following definitions differ to some extent between the two communities:

1. *Exclusion.* This option is obviously limited to Jews only. Jews who uncompromisingly insist on an Arab departure from the state as the only solution to the Arab problem have been placed in this category.

2. *Continued domination.* Some Arabs may condone continued government domination for the short-run as a way to prevent a disastrous confrontation. Arabs who advocate increased surveillance of their own community fall into this category. For Jews, continued domination constitutes endorsement of the status quo. Jews who will only accept Arabs if they reconcile themselves to minority status in a Jewish state and who, at the same time, object to Arabs independently organizing fall into this category.

3. *Equal opportunity.* This category includes Arabs who favor a policy of equality and integration without assimilation and Jews who consent to conferring national minority status with equal rights on Arabs, without allowing them to independently organize.

4. *Consociationalism.* Arabs who favor the participation of independent organizations in state institutions, or seek separate legal status within Israel, are so classified. Jews qualify if they agree to grant Arabs national minority status with equal rights and also allow them to independently organize.

5. *Secession.* Secessionists are Arabs who demand separate legal status outside of Israeli territory and sovereignty. On the other hand,

Jewish supporters of Arab secession are Jews who agree to both a separate legal status to Arabs within Israel and to Arab self-rule in the Galilee and Triangle.

6. *Non-sectarianism.* Arabs and Jews who endorse a secular-democratic state in all of Mandatory Palestine in lieu of Israel and who see this new state as the only acceptable solution to the Israeli-Arab conflict are non-sectarian. Non-sectarianism does not actually mean the same thing to both sides. For Arabs it probably marks an end to their subordinate status, whereas for Jews it signifies Arab domination.

The overall distribution of Arabs and Jews into these six categories yields a number of conclusions (Table 10.5). First, group goals certainly emerge as a critical issue for a majority of the Arabs: 63% demand an official policy of equal opportunity, that is, equality and integration without assimilation. A majority of the Jews, 63%, either insist on continued domination or on the summary exclusion of Arabs from the state. Second, from a Jewish viewpoint, 36% of the Arab public, 50% of the Rakah-affiliated Arab leaders, 94% of the Arab leaders of the Sons of the Village Movement and Progressive National Movement pursue dissident goals of consociationalism, secession, and non-sectarianism. And third, only 12% of the Arabs are hardcore rejectionists, those who favor secession or a new non-sectarian state. This tenth would settle for no less than redrawing the political boundaries and reversing the pattern of national domination. While this Arab segment is by no means insignificant, especially with leadership and ideological bases both within and outside of Israel, it is a far cry from the widespread Jewish suspicions and apprehensions of massive subversion.

Table 10.5 Classification and Distribution of Group Goals

	Arab Public	Estab. Affil. Arab Lead.	Rakah Affil. Arab Lead.	Rejec- tion. Arab Lead.	Jewish Public	Dovish Jewish Lead.	Jewish Arab- ists	Hawkish Jewish Lead.
Goals pursued toward the Arab minority								
Exclusion	0.0	0.0	0.0	0.0	14.6	0.0	0.0	4.2
Continued domination	1.1	0.0	0.0	0.0	48.0	23.5	53.3	70.8
Equal opportunity	63.0	72.0	50.0	6.5	25.3	32.4	33.3	20.8
Consociationalism	24.0	28.0	50.0	9.7	10.9	41.2	13.3	4.2
Secession	5.1	0.0	0.0	0.0	1.0	2.9	0.0	0.0
Non-sectarianism	6.9	0.0	0.0	83.9	0.1	0.0	0.0	0.0

Finally, most Arabs and most Jews do conceive of a future that tie them together. Apart from the small proportion of Arab secessionists or non-sectarianists and Jewish exclusionists, they all seek solutions to their troubled relations inside, rather than outside, Israel.

11

Leadership Credibility

An important feature of all deeply divided societies is their fractured leadership. The nondominant groups are forced to generate potential leadership of their own because the national leadership does not properly respond to their special needs. To be effective, the nondominant leadership must be recognized by both the minority and majority. It is, however, hard to gain wide acceptance because of the factionalism within the minority and the counteractions adopted by the majority's leadership. Hence, minority leadership credibility is likely to emerge as an issue, especially in societies where control of disgruntled minorities is difficult to sustain.

The 1970's in Israel was a period of considerable decline of cooptation of Arab leadership and emergence and differentiation of non-accommodating leaders. The accommodating leaders, including traditional hamula elders and modern politicians who are affiliated with the Israeli establishment, became a target of stiff criticism from rising, militant leaders. Rakah grew during the decade to a dominant position in the Arab sector. In order to win mass support it penetrated broadly based leadership groups, particularly the Committee of Heads of Arab Local Councils, the Committee for Defense of Arab Lands, and the National Committee of Arab University Students, all of which were established in the mid-1970's. The rejectionist leadership of the Sons of the Village Movement and Progressive National Movement, which also emerged during this period, did much to publicly expose the middle-of-the-road posture of Rakah and the public figures associated with it.

The reactions of Arabs and Jews to the shifts in Arab leadership during the seventies are diverse and conflicting. The survey data make it possible, however, to draw several conclusions. First, the Arabs feel a dire need for genuine, representative leadership. Doubting the capability of the Israeli government to serve their interests, they wish to have representative leadership of their own and want it to be recognized by the state.

Second, the real issue which divides most Arabs and Jews is the style of Arab leadership. Having great stakes in continued dominance, Jews are only willing to recognize accommodating Arab leadership, though this leadership is overwhelmingly rejected by the Arab population. A majority of 55% of the Jews, in contrast to only 15% of the Arabs, regard Arab election lists affiliated with the Labor Party as truly representative of Israeli Arabs (Table 11.1) On the other hand, all the non-accommodating Arab leadership groups enjoy much less credibility among Jews than among Arabs. This Jewish denial of recognition is even more striking at the leadership than mass level. For instance, 12.5% to 25% of the Jewish leaders as opposed to 41% of the Jewish public recognize the Committee for Defense of Arab Lands.

Table 11.1 Leadership Credibility

	Arab Public	Estab. Affil. Arab Lead.	Rakah Affil. Arab Lead.	Rejec- tion. Arab Lead.	Jewish Public	Dovish Jewish Lead.	Jewish Arab- ists	Hawkish Jewish Lead.
Consider each of the following bodies to be truly representative of the interests of the Arabs in Israel								
Arab lists affiliated with the Labor Party[a]	14.6				55.4			
Committee of Heads or Arab Local Councils	55.3	66.6	93.7	12.9	41.9	33.3	13.3	22.7
Committee for Defense of Arab Lands	58.9	56.5	100.0	16.2	41.3	25.0	14.3	12.5
Rakah (Israeli Communist Party)	34.6	12.0	87.5	0.0	28.4	9.1	16.7	12.0
Sons of the Village Movement and Progressive National Movement	40.2	4.5	16.2	96.8	*	*	*	*
Palestine Liberation Organization	48.5	0.0	25.9	96.8	20.6	2.9	10.3	12.0

* Not asked.

[a] The 1976 survey did not include leaders.

Third, Arab political factionalism is easily seen in attitudes toward Arab leadership. The distinctions among leaders affiliated with the Zionist establishment, with Rakah, or oriented toward the Rejection Front are confirmed by the different stands taken by the Arab public.[1] The establishment-affiliated leadership is only approved by a small minority. In contrast, the Rakah-affiliated leadership already surpasses

[1]A factor analysis of the 1976 survey attitudes toward the representativeness of six Arab leadership groups yields three distinct factors, clearly referring to these three approaches.

the 50% credibility mark. This has been facilitated by a shift of the accommodating leaders away from the Zionist establishment. The broad base of the Committee of Heads of Arab Local Councils and the Committee for Defense of Arab Lands is made clear by the endorsement of these committees by 76% and 56.5%, respectively, of the establishment-tied Arab leaders and by virtually all the Rakah-affiliated Arab leaders.

It is worth noting, however, that Rakah itself enjoys the trust of only 35% of the Arab public. Rakah's credibility is equal to its electoral support. In the 1981 national elections it amounted to 38% of the Arab vote. This is due to widespread ambivalence toward Rakah among Israeli Arabs. On the one hand, Rakah champions the Arab cause both within and outside Israel. Many Arabs, on the other hand, have reservations about its Communist, pro-Soviet, class-oriented, mixed Jewish-Arab, anti-religious, and anti-traditional orientations. The fact that Rakah fails to win the confidence of an Arab majority prompts it to form front organizations or to penetrate other groups in order to widen its popular support.

The growing popularity of the PLO among the Arab public in Israel is marked indeed. Nearly half of the respondents recognize the PLO as a representative of Israeli Arabs. This is an exceedingly high proportion given the complete illegality of the PLO in Israel and Rakah's claim that the PLO represents the Palestinians outside Israel but not the Arab citizens of Israel. The acceptance of the PLO by Israel's Arabs, like recognition by the United Nations and many other states, indicates a recognition of the Palestinians' right to self-determination but not necessarily an endorsement of its National Charter and terrorist tactics. This is reflected in the smaller support for the rejectionist Sons of the Village Movement and the Progressive National Movement than for the PLO itself.

Fourth and finally, Arabs fall short of their clear desire for a publicly recognized, independent, national leadership. Only the Committee of Heads of Arab Local Councils is moving in this direction. The Committee for Defense of Arab Lands provides merely a single-issue leadership. The limitations of Rakah in becoming a nationalist Arab party are all the more clear. Not only is it a Jewish-Arab body, but its attempt and that of its sympathizers to organize a representative, mass-based, nationalistic Arab congress was declared illegal by the Israeli government on December 1, 1980.

It seems that attitudes toward Arab independent status in Israeli society form a consistent pattern. The majority of Israeli Arabs desire some degree of autonomy and a credible nationalist leadership, although they have little of each. The majority of Jews regard these aspirations as hazardous and the Israeli government has so far succeeded in averting them.

12

Educational Goals

Education in culturally and nationally pluralistic societies is a critical problem area. On the one hand, it tends to reflect existing patterns of minority-majority relations. Where these societies attempt to build a common culture, a unitary system of education is the vehicle. In consociational democracies, where strong cultural minorities exist, there is nationally autonomous education. In pluralistic societies with a dominant majority, the education of subordinate minorities tends to become a means of ensuring dominance. On the other hand, education is expected to promote new patterns of minority-majority relations by providing disadvantaged minorities with opportunities for social mobility, acculturation, and assimilation into the mainstream in place of the assertion of national minority identity.

In Israel, the Arabs have a separate and dependent educational system. It carefully reflects the controlled conditions under which they live. To quote the late Mar'i, an Arab educational psychologist: "The Arab minority in Israel has always been treated as an object, as a periphery... The authorities endeavor to manipulate the peripheral Arab minority through education in such a way that the central Jewish majority can maintain its interest" (1978:54).

Given the fact that Israel is a political democracy which cannot officially institutionalize dominance, the formulation of official educational goals for the Arab minority is exceedingly difficult. For this reason, Arab education has so far been omitted from official government goals. Kopilevitch, the director of the Arab Education Department, admits that Arab schools "have been functioning without a defined goal" (1973:326). This does not exclude an unofficial operative, implicit goals, which underlie the activities of the Arab Department of Education.

Two Israeli government committees were formed in the 1970's to develop Arab educational goals. One, the Yadlin committee, recommended the adoption of the values of peace and loyalty to the state and the goals of economic and social integration and the improvement of women's status (Ministry of Education and Culture, 1972). While Westernization is also advocated, Arab nationalism is ignored. As Mar'i states in his critique: "It seems that the Yadlin Document does not only try to deemphasize and blur the national identity of Arabs in Israel, but it also tries to cancel out their culture by imposing morals and values accepted by the predominantly Jewish Israeli society upon them through a government controlled educational system" (1978:53).

The issue of educational goals for both Arabs and Jews was dealt with by a special sub-committee on educational goals for the 1980's. It formulated the goals into sixteen clauses, thirteen of which apply to all Israelis, two of which are exclusive to Jewish education, and one to Arab education.

Exclusive goals for Arab education were adopted mainly from the Peled Committee, formed as part of the Planning Project of Education for the Eighties. Its report reads as follows (Ministry of Education and Culture, 1976:38):

> The goal of state education in the Arab sector is to be based on the foundations of Arab culture; on the achievements of science; on the aspirations of peace between Israel and its neighbors; on the love of the homeland common to all the citizens of the state, and on loyalty to the State of Israel – while emphasizing the shared interests and promoting the uniqueness of Israel's Arabs; and on knowledge of the Jewish culture.

In comparison, the goals recommended exclusively for Jewish education are as follows:

> To help the young form a full personality as a Jew who identifies himself with the heritage and destiny of his nation; is keenly aware of his uniqueness as a Jew; is keenly aware of the ties between the People of Israel and the Land of Israel, between the People of Israel in their State and the Jewish People in the Diaspora; and has a sense of common fate and responsibility for his nation.

> To inculcate the values of Jewish culture by the practical and academic acquisition of this heritage, as it was crystallized in all the ethnic groups of the People of Israel until recent generations in their homeland and in the Diaspora. At the same time they should be exposed to the best cultural heritages of other nations and become familiar with the culture of the Arab minority.

These suggested official goals for Arabs and Jews can be compared by using three criteria. One criterion is the dilemma of either to retain the distinct cultural heritages and consequently their uniqueness, or to melt them down into one mold. Another criterion is whether biculturalism should be encouraged in each group without necessarily blurring their own distinct cultures. The last criterion refers to the type of national identity proposed by the Peled Committee for each group.

A comparison of the above goals shows symmetry between Arab and Jewish education with regard to cultural heritage and biculturalism, but asymmetry in nationalism. Parallel to the inculcation of the "values of Jewish culture" and the "uniqueness" of the Jews in Jewish education, one finds the "Arab culture" and "uniqueness of Israel's Arabs" as the basis for Arab education. Familiarity with "the culture of the Arab minority" by Jews is a sought equivalent to "the knowledge of the Jewish culture" by Arabs.

These similarities contrast strikingly with the dissimilarity of the nationalist goals of education. Jewish education purports to intensify Jewish identity and Zionism, as indicated in the aim of strengthening the "ties between the People of Israel and the Land of Israel, between the People of Israel in their State and the Jewish People in the Diaspora." These nationalist elements are conspicuously absent from the goals proposed for Arab education, i.e., there is no reference to the Arab or to the Palestinian nations. Instead, "love of the homeland common to all citizens of the state and loyalty to the State of Israel" and "shared interests" are underscored in Arab education, but they are absent from Jewish education.

These contrasts did not escape the attention of Arab critics. Mar'i, although part of the Peled Committee, comments: "The fact that Arabs in Israel are an inseparable part of the Palestinian nation has been consistently overlooked not only in the statement of educational goals itself, but also in the rationale preceding and in the discussion following such a statement (1978:54). Nakhleh finds in the new goals "no recognition, implicit or explicit, of the Arabs in Israel as constituting a national minority, whose political, historical and symbolic sentiments are uncompromisingly Palestinian." He goes on to say: "The guiding concerns in the process of so-called re-definition in summary are: (1) How to portray Zionism and the State of Israel in the best light; (2) How to minimize animosity to the state; and (3) How to deal with Arab nationalism without producing nationalist students" (1977:35).

The goals recommended for Arab and Jewish education in the Planning Project of Education for the Eighties have not yet been officially accepted. What do exist are the implicit goals. Comparative studies of the curricula demonstrate that they are even more divergent for Arabs and Jews than the proposed, formal goals (Peres, Ehrlich, and Yuval-Davis, 1970; Mi'ari, 1975; Mar'i, 1978:71-89).

With regard to cultural heritage, there is much ambivalence in both Arab and Jewish education. On the one hand, separate Arab schools are maintained, Arabic is used as the medium of instruction, Arab holidays and traditions are celebrated, and religion and Arabic literature are taught. On the other hand, this cultural heritage, as transmitted, is diluted through secularization (i.e., the separation of religious from non-religious schools, which exist in Jewish education does not exist in Arab education) and denationalization (for example, classical Arabic literature and history are taught to a greater degree than modern national literature and history). In contrast, whereas the national character of the Jewish cultural heritage is emphasized in Jewish schools, much ambivalence still remains as to the degree of secularization in its presentation.

Biculturalism is a norm in Arab education but almost non-existent in Jewish education. Arab students are instructed extensively in the Hebrew language and literature, Jewish history, the Bible, Mishna and Agada, and other Jewish traditions. Jewish students, however, are scarcely exposed to the Arab cultural heritage. The apparent purpose is that through one-way biculturalism Arabs will be better equipped to cope with Israeli society and be more readily coopted into it.

Nationalism is the stickiest question of all. While Jewish nationalism is intensively inculcated in Jewish education, it is left in abeyance in Arab education. Arabs are taught to be loyal citizens of Israel and are infused with Israeli Arab or Druze consciousness. In a complementary fashion, they are denied exposure to Arab or Palestinian nationalism in the schools.

These practical goals of Arab education: the ambivalence toward the Arab cultural heritage, the stress of Arab biculturalism, and the denial of Arab or Palestinian national identity are highlighted in a comparative study of Israeli school curricula (Peres, Ehrlich, and Yuval-Davis, 1970:161):

> The Israeli-Arab school curriculum has not achieved a balance between 'Arab nationalism consciousness' and 'loyalty to the state'... Instead, it has fallen victim to a tendency to blur Arab nationality and to educate the Arab student into self-disparagement vis-a-vis the Jewish majority. These tendencies are revealed in the main in two ways: (a) The goals of various subjects are formulated with a disregard of the nationalist elements in the Arab pupils' consciousness; (b) a wide and profound knowledge of purely Jewish subjects (for example, Jewish history, Bible) is demanded of the Arab students at the expense of their own culture. This tendency is even more conspicuous against the background of an almost total absence of the Arabic language and culture in the Jewish pupils' education.

Given these official, but implicit goals, it is interesting to examine the educational preferences of the Arab and Jewish publics. In the 1976 survey, Arab and Jewish respondents were asked ten questions regarding goals for Arab and Jewish education. These ten questions tapped the three issues: traditional heritage, biculturalism, and nationalism.

Traditional heritage emerges as a divisive issue, not between Arabs and Jews, but rather within each group (Table 12.1). Only a minority in both camps wish to dispose of traditional values for either Arab or Jewish education. The large majorities, which desire to keep their traditional heritages, are split into those interested in maximal versus partial retention.

Table 12.1 Traditional Heritage as an Educational Goal

	Arab Public	Jewish Public
The most desirable goal for Arab education		
Retain traditional values as much as possible	43.1	52.2
Retain part of the traditional values	41.7	33.3
Dispose of traditional values	15.2	14.5
The most desirable goal for Jewish education		
Retain traditional values as much as possible	30.4	65.7
Retain part of the traditional values	47.5	30.1
Dispose of traditional values	22.0	4.2

Source: The 1976 survey.

In a Jewish state where Arab culture is not incorporated into the national culture, but where Arabs are undergoing intense Westernization, one would expect Arabs to express in a way of self-protection very strong attachment to their heritage. In fact, they want less cultural retention than Jews (43% vs. 52% for Arab education, 30% vs. 65% for Jewish education). This lower preference by Arabs should be understood in light of the problematic status of cultural heritage in Arab education today. For some Arabs it carries a stigma of backwardness, constitutes a hindrance to Westernization, and arouses opposition because it is not taught in a nationalist perspective.[1]

Their attitude toward bilingualism and biculturalism is rather complex. On the one hand, bilingualism is widely accepted. Arabs and

[1]There is a certain tendency for the more nationalistic Arabs to reject traditional heritage as a desirable goal for Arab education. For instance, those who wish to dispose of traditional values entirely constitute 12% of those identifying themselves as Israelis, Israeli Arabs, or Arabs, 17% of those identifying themselves as Israeli Palestinians, and 21% of those identifying themselves as Palestinian Arabs or Palestinians.

Jews concur that they should both be bilingual (Table 4.10) and accordingly agree that both Arab and Jewish schools should teach both languages (Table 12.2). On the other hand, both sides are rather guarded toward biculturalism despite their partial endorsement of it. They both consider appreciable biculturalism a threat to their cultural integrity. Since Arabs, as a cultural minority, carry the bulk of the burden of biculturalism they probably wish Jews to be biculturally educated in order to even out the current bicultural imbalance in the two educational systems. They also may hope that reciprocal biculturalism would dilute Israel's Jewish-Zionist character.

Table 12.2 Bilingualism and Biculturalism as Educational Goals

	Arab Public	Jewish Public
In favor of retaining or extending Hebrew instruction in Arab schools	91.9	85.8
Hold that Arab education should transmit Jewish culture (language, lifestyles, practices) in addition to Arab culture		
Yes	30.2	40.3
To a certain degree	47.5	37.4
No	22.3	22.3
Unreservedly in favor of compulsory instruction of Arabic in Jewish schools	82.7	74.5
Hold that Jewish education should transmit Arab culture (language, lifestyles, practices) in addition to Jewish culture		
Yes	62.1	42.1
To a certain degree	28.8	33.6
No	9.1	24.3

Source: The 1976 survey.

With regard to the nationalist goals of education, all respondents in the 1980 survey were asked two questions. The one concerning Arab education offered three options: to be a loyal minority member in a Jewish state; to love Israel as the common homeland of its two people, Arab and Jewish; and to be a member of the Palestinian people. These alternatives are neither comprehensive nor mutually exclusive. They comprise, however, the major educational possibilities envisaged or practiced in Israel today. The "loyal minority" option is the implicit goal of Arab education. The "common homeland" theme is the corrected version suggested by the Peled Committee. As noted above, the phrasing of this option in the report of the Planning Project of Education for the Eighties refers to the "love of the homeland common to all the citizens of the state," and not the "love of Israel as the common homeland of its two peoples, Arab and Jewish," which was presented to respondents in the survey. Our wording, which may imply a desire to make Israel binational, would be as appealing to those Arabs as it is unappealing to those Jews who understand it this way. The third alternative of "Palestinian education" clearly breaks away from the status quo. In whatever manner this concept is understood by the respondents, its very divergence from present practice is *ipso facto* an undisputed indication of militancy.

A parallel question on the nationalist goals of Jewish education was also presented. The options given were to be a loyal citizen, to love Israel as the common homeland of its two peoples, Arab and Jewish, and to be a member of the Jewish people. The similarity to the nationalist goals of Arab education is only partial, however. Unlike the contradiction between the comparable first and third alternatives in the question on Arab education, the first and third options for Jewish education are compatible, underscoring the complementary natures of Israeli and Jewish identities. Yet the "common homeland" objective is a major departure from the present Jewish-Zionist mission of Jewish education.

Arabs and Jews sharply disagree on the nationalist goals of both Arab and Jewish education (Table 12.3). First, only 6% of the Arab public, as opposed to 54% of the Jewish public, endorse the status quo of educating Arabs to be a loyal minority in a Jewish state. The contrast in the views of leaders is even more pronounced. As few as 0% to 8% of the Arab leaders (including those attached to the Zionist establishment) as compared with 60% to 81% of the Jewish leaders (including the dovish ones) opt for the existing situation.

Second, while the majority of Jews prefer the status quo, in which Arabs must learn to adjust to Israel as it is, with a minimum of Arab nationalism, the majority of Arabs want a truly "binational" Arab education. This is probably not true for many of the 42% of the Jews who support the "common homeland" goal for Arab education. They apparently do not mean to endorse binationalism for Israel but rather to express a need to make the Jewish state more palatable to Israeli Arabs.

Third, a sizable minority, 29.5% of the Arabs vs. 4% of the Jews, desire "Palestinian" Arab education. The significance of this preference under the existing circumstances can be best appreciated by contrasting its total rejection by the establishment-affiliated Arab leaders with its total acceptance by the rejectionist Arab leaders (0% and 93%, respectively, favor it).

And fourth, most Arabs would like to de-Judaize and de-Zionize Jewish education and render it binational, whereas most Jews repudiate binationalism and insist on nationalist Jewish education, with a stress on Israeli rather than Jewish identity. Although Arabs are consistent in advocating and Jews are consistent in rejecting binationalism for the two educational systems, Arabs advocate it more for Jewish education, and

Jews reject it less for Arab education. Each side hopes to gain by denationalizing the other.

Table 12.3 Alternative National Goals for Arab and Jewish Education

	Arab Public	Estab. Affil. Arab Lead.	Rakah Affil. Arab Lead.	Rejection. Arab Lead.	Jewish Public	Dovish Jewish Lead.	Jewish Arab-ists	Hawkish Jewish Lead.
The most desirable goal for Arab education								
To be a loyal minority member in a Jewish state	5.7	8.0	0.0	0.0	53.8	60.0	76.7	80.8
To love Israel as the common homeland of its two peoples, Arab and Jewish	64.8	92.0	71.9	6.7	42.0	33.3	23.3	15.4
To be a member of the Palestinian people	29.5	0.0	28.1	93.3	4.2	6.7	0.0	3.8
The most desirable goal for Jewish education								
To be a loyal citizen	11.9	8.0	0.0	0.0	56.9	60.0	50.0	82.6
To love Israel as the common homeland of its two peoples, Arab and Jewish	78.1	92.0	93.8	79.2	23.1	26.7	36.7	4.3
To be a member of the Jewish people	10.0	0.0	6.3	20.8	20.0	13.3	13.3	13.0

Table 12.4 Instruction of History in Schools

	Arab Public	Jewish Public
Hold that instruction of Jewish history in Arab schools should be		
Abolished	11.3	9.6
Reduced	39.8	12.5
Retained as is	33.7	37.5
Extended	15.3	40.4
Hold that instruction of Arab history in Jewish schools should be		
Abolished	3.3	9.3
Reduced	0.9	17.1
Retained as is	21.5	50.0
Extended	74.3	23.6

Source: The 1976 survey.

General Arab-Jewish disagreements on the nationalist goals of education are exemplified in the questions on the instruction of history. At present, Arab and Jewish students are taught little modern Arab history and much Jewish history. This, of course, creates an imbalance. While half of the Arabs wish to abolish or reduce the teaching of Jewish history in Arab schools, four fifths of Jews wish, in contrast, to preserve or even extend it (Table 12.4 above). By the same token, three quarters of the Arabs wish to expand the teaching of Arab history in Jewish schools, with the intention of bringing it up to par with the extensive teaching of Jewish history in Arab schools, while only one quarter of the Jews favor the idea.

In conclusion, it appears that most Israeli Arabs and Jews concur that both Arab and Jewish education should continue as an agent of cultural retention, modernization, bilingualism, and biculturalism. On the other hand, they disagree on the nationalist goals of Arab and Jewish education, with Arabs favoring the reconstitution of both educational systems along binational lines. It may be that the underlying rationale for most Arabs is to weaken Israel's Jewish-Zionist identity; for Jews it may be, rather, a feeling of self-preservation.

13

Strategies for Change

The question of strategies for ethnic change is a critical one for minorities. The means available depend on the nature of the political system in which they find themselves. In societies, like South Africa, where democracy is officially denied to the nondominant groups, there is minimal opportunity for legal protest. In contrast, a wide choice is available to minorities in political democracies. In between fall societies like Israel, where both a political democracy and controls prevail. These countervailing forces in Israel provide Arabs with diverse methods for effecting change, but with varying degrees of legitimacy and success.

Israeli Arabs can use three general methods to improve their situation:

1. *Parliamentary politics.* In the survey, this was represented by the standard democratic procedures of propaganda and political pressures.

2. *Extra-parliamentary politics.* A mild extra-parliamentary democratic tactic, which enjoys great legitimacy in Israeli society, is licensed demonstrations. On the other hand, general strikes, protest actions abroad, and boycotts of institutions or plants are firm democratic ways which gain less public support. Questions about these four measures were raised in the survey.

3. *Extra-legal politics.* Inquiries about two illegal steps were included in the survey: unlicensed demonstrations and resistance with force.

Since the legitimacy of parliamentary politics is seldom problematic, respondents were asked about how effective this moderate approach is in promoting Arab interests in Israel (Table 13.1). A small proportion believe these methods were of no avail, while a solid across the board majority regard Israeli democracy as a vehicle to improve Arab conditions. There is some disagreement, however, on the degree of its effectiveness. The Arab public surprisingly has more trust in the conventional procedures than does the Jewish public (56% and 37%, respectively, feel that considerable change may be effected). Similarly, leaders understandably place more confidence in these political processes than do the rank and file. The notable exception is the Arab rejectionist leaders; only one quarter of them, in contrast to two fifths or more of the other groups, expect appreciable gains from ordinary political strategies.

Table 13.1 Parliamentary Politics as a Strategy for Change

	Arab Public	Estab. Affil. Arab Lead.	Rakah Affil. Arab Lead.	Rejec- tion. Arab Lead.	Jewish Public	Dovish Jewish Lead.	Jewish Arab- ists	Hawkish Jewish Lead.
The extent to which it is possible to improve the Arab situation by acceptable democratic means, such as persuasion and political pressure								
To a great extent	25.9	28.0	43.8	12.9	11.7	17.6	23.3	23.8
To a substantial extent	30.0	36.0	21.9	12.9	25.1	32.4	53.3	42.9
To a certain extent	26.6	36.0	28.1	54.8	44.3	44.1	23.3	33.3
To almost no extent	17.6	0.0	6.3	19.4	18.9	5.9	0.0	0.0

The agreement between Arabs and Jews on the effectiveness of parliamentary tactics for Arab improvement is significantly reduced in the case of the Arab use of licensed demonstrations. The undisputed legitimacy of this measure is demonstrated by its endorsement by 82% to 88% of the Jewish leaders as well as by 80% to 100% of the Arab leaders (Table 13.2). But only 44% of the Jewish public, as compared to 75.5% of the Arab public, have no reservation about the exercise of the Israeli Arabs' legal right to hold demonstrations. A majority of Jews view Israeli Arabs as opposed to the regime, and hence wish to deprive them of the right to demonstrate peacefully. This is borne out by responses to two other questions, according to which only 41% of the Jews would oppose a governmental ban on critics of the regime to hold peaceful demonstrations, and only 27% would oppose it if the critics were Arabs.

Table 13.2 Extra-Parliamentary Politics as a Strategy for Change

	Arab Public	Estab. Affil. Arab Lead.	Rakah Affil. Arab Lead.	Rejec- tion. Arab Lead.	Jewish Public	Dovish Jewish Lead.	Jewish Arab- ists	Hawkish Jewish Lead.
In favor, without reservations, of each of the following means to improve the situation of the Arabs in Israel								
Licensed demonstrations	75.5	80.0	100.0	100.0	44.2	88.2	82.1	83.3
General strikes	54.6	20.0	78.1	100.0	5.9	20.6	10.3	12.5
Protest actions abroad	51.9	28.0	90.6	100.0	8.8	8.8	10.3	4.2
Boycotts of institutions or plants	47.0	12.0	28.1	96.8	4.5	12.1	3.6	0.0

The real dividing issue is nevertheless the use of extra-parliamentary politics. Since Israeli Arabs seek more comprehensive change than Jews would allow, they advocate stronger means than Jews would tolerate. Between 47% to 55% of the Arab public, 28% to 91% of the Rakah-affiliated Arab leaders, and virtually all rejectionist Arab leaders favor, without reservation, such methods like general strikes, protest action abroad, and boycotts (Table 13.2). In contrast, the establishment-affiliated Arab leaders object to these tactics which are utterly rejected by the Jewish population and leadership. The Jews, of whom 65% desire even stricter surveillance over Arabs, oppose extra-parliamentary measures because they are alarmed by the growing erosion of the current machinery of Jewish control. Working through regular political channels, and not challenging the Jews by mass politics, is also the very rationale of Arab leaders who are attached to the Jewish establishment.

The large proportion of Arabs in favor of extra-parliamentary legal politics shrinks to a small minority in the case of extra-legal politics. Illegal means are of course dismissed by the Jews. Arabs opting for these strategies usually want a radical change. Less than one tenth of the Arab public endorse without reservation unlicensed demonstrations and resistance with force and over one fifth are reserved but not opposed (Table 13.3). Most revealing is the unqualified approval of illegal means by 61% to 68% of the rejectionist Arab leaders.

Table 13.3 Extra-Legal Politics as a Strategy for Change

	Arab Public	Estab. Affil. Arab Lead.	Rakah Affil. Arab Lead.	Rejec- tion. Arab Lead.	Jewish Public	Dovish Jewish Lead.	Jewish Arab- ists	Hawkish Jewish Lead.
Unlicensed demonstrations as a means to improve the situation of the Arabs in Israel								
In favor	7.0	0.0	18.8	67.7	2.0	3.0	0.0	0.0
Have reservations	23.0	4.0	40.6	22.6	10.6	27.3	14.3	4.2
Against	70.0	96.0	40.6	9.7	87.3	69.7	85.7	95.8
Resistance with force as a means to improve the situation of the Arabs in Israel								
In favor	7.5	0.0	6.5	61.3	1.4	0.0	0.0	0.0
Have reservations	21.9	8.0	25.8	29.0	8.3	6.3	11.1	0.0
Against	70.5	92.0	67.7	9.7	90.3	93.8	88.9	100.0

The question arises with regard to how this small segment of under one tenth of Israeli Arabs, who support extra-legal politics, should be regarded. They face the disapproval of the overwhelming majority of Arabs who are law-abiding, self-restrained, and keenly aware of the prohibitive cost to themselves of Arab-Jewish confrontation. Nevertheless, it is significant that there is a small minority, comprising scores of thousands of disillusioned Arabs who are in the most active age group (16-45 years) and are prepared to go to extremes in order to effect change. They also have the backing of a dissident ideology and leadership (the Sons of the Village Movement and the Progressive National Movement). For unrest to occur, they supply more than enough of the necessary dissenters.

The actual involvement of Israeli Arabs in protest is significant and has risen considerably during the seventies. Some 40% took part in the 1976 general Arab strike, and 12% participated in one or more demonstrations protesting the treatment of Arabs in Israel (Table 13.4). These figures are as high as 60% and 32%, respectively, among men, aged 18-25, who have high school or college education.

Table 13.4 Arabs' Participation in Protest Actions

	Arab Public	Establishment Affiliated Arab Leaders	Rakah Affiliated Arab Leaders	Rejectionist Arab Leaders
Participation in the 1976 Land Day strike[a]				
Willingly did not participate	50.9	57.9	11.5	0.0
Unwillingly did not participate	9.5	5.3	0.0	7.4
Unwillingly participated	10.6	5.3	11.5	3.7
Willingly participated	29.0	31.6	76.9	88.9
Participated over the past two years in one or more demonstrations protesting the treatment of Arabs in Israel	11.6	36.0	83.4	96.8

[a] Excluding Arabs for whom participation was irrelevant (unemployed, retired, housewives, the sick, etc.).

The personal costs of protest are also appreciable. The Arabs in the survey were asked if they endured or expected privations as a result of expressing opinions or taking actions to improve the present conditions of the Arab minority. In fact, 14% say that they endured and 43% expected political harassment or economic suffering perpetrated by the Israeli authorities in retaliation for protest activities (Table 13.5). The majority of the Arabs neither experience nor anticipate privations because they are either uninvolved or involved in relatively moderate protest. Privations are much greater for protesters, especially those who use extra-parliamentary or illegal tactics. Some 34% of the Arabs who observed the 1976 Land Day strike and 57% of those who participated in demonstrations over the past two years endured economic or political privations. The marked differentiation between the three types of Arab leaders shows that the probability of privation rises dramatically with the intensity and radicalism of the struggle: 25% of the leaders affiliated to the establishment, 77% of the leaders affiliated with Rakah, and 93% of the activists in the Sons of the Village Movement report actual privations.

Table 13.5 Arab Experience and Expectation of Privations

	Endured Privations				Expected Privations			
	Arab Public	Estab. Affil. Arab Lead.	Rakah Affil. Arab Lead.	Rejection. Arab Lead.	Arab Public	Estab. Affil. Arab Lead.	Rakah Affil. Arab- Lead.	Rejection. Arab Lead.
Privations endured or expected as a result of expressing opinions or taking actions to effect the present conditions of Arabs in Israel								
Political harassment and economic suffering	3.9	8.3	40.0	56.7	28.8	20.0	36.7	54.8
Political harassment but no economic suffering	5.7	16.7	36.7	33.3	8.8	20.0	23.3	16.1
Economic suffering but no political harassment	4.5	0.0	0.0	3.3	5.8	0.0	0.0	0.0
Neither economic suffering nor political harassment	85.8	75.0	23.3	6.7	56.6	60.0	40.0	29.0

The data on strategies for change clarify the views on Israel as a political democracy. On the one hand, Israeli citizens, Jews and Arabs, clearly reject the conception of Israel as a *de facto Herrenvolk* democracy; namely, a state in which democratic procedures are practically reserved for Jews only. They believe, rather, that Israeli democracy is open for all, and it can provide Arabs with at least some change. This belief is shared even by Arab communists who ideologically reject bourgeois democracy and oppose Israel as a Jewish-Zionist state, and by Arab rejectionists who seek to dismantle Israel as a state.

On the other hand, Israeli Arabs are quite realistic about the limits of Israeli democracy. More than three decades of experience have taught them that persuasion, voting, and other regular channels can at most bring about concessions and piecemeal change. Hence, a sizable proportion of them endorse extra-parliamentary politics which are militant yet democratic. Opposed to these means, Jews are alarmed lest the increasing application of such stiff steps undermine the Arab-Jewish status quo, or even democracy itself. By applying firm democratic measures, Arabs test the limits of Israeli democracy and are more readily branded extremists than Jewish groups that employ similar tactics. The fact that some Israeli Arabs favor the use of extra-legal means and even occasionally resort to them reinforces the widespread Jewish stereotype of Arabs as a subversive element in Israeli society.

14

Ethnocentrism

Sumner (1906), in a classic essay, considers ethnocentrism as a universal syndrome of attitudes and behavior. The "ingroup" sees itself as virtuous and superior and the "outgroup" as contemptible and inferior, sanctions association with its own members and dissociation with others, loves and trusts insiders and hates and distrusts outsiders, and so forth (LeVine and Campbell, 1972). Ethnocentrism is essential for the survival of the group and for keeping its distinct identity, culture, solidarity, and ability to compete successfully with other groups. Although they simplify and distort reality, group preconceptions and prejudices provide the individual with a sense of direction and belonging. This perspective regards ethnocentrism as a permanent, functional, positive, and universal group feature. It stands in contrast with the more common and critical approach which conceives of ethnocentrism as an antonym for cultural relativism and human equality, and identifies it with intolerance, chauvinism, and racism.

These competing conceptions emphasize different components of ethnocentrism, where a simple test of proportion and plausibility would produce more balanced and realistic appraisals. To be ethnocentric, attitudes must contain an excessive or unjustified element of superiority, rejection, or hostility toward an outgroup. For instance, mistrust is not ethnocentric if it is firmly grounded in facts; objection to intermarriage is not prejudicial if minority and majority agree on separation. Judiciousness is therefore necessary for establishing a case of ethnocentrism. The task of examining each case is rather complex because ethnocentrism may manifest itself on individual and institutional levels. Spontaneous, personal ethnocentrism consists of an aggregate set of individual attitudes and behaviors, whereas organized, ideological ethnocentrism refers to public policies and institutional practices (Lanternari, 1980). Both forms should be explored. One should also look into ethnocentrism on both sides of the ethnic divide. It is a long-standing tradition in the literature of intergroup relations to concentrate solely on the ethnocentrism of the dominant group because it is more freely expressed, entrenched, and consequential. There is little ground, however, to expect less ethnocentrism from nondominant groups.

Turning to ethnocentrism in Israel, it draws its most virulent expressions from the division between Israeli Arabs and Jews. Israeli Arabs are a restive minority, on the rise demographically, as well as in the socioeconomic and political spheres. The Arab resurgence causes widespread apprehension among the Jewish majority. Jews are alarmed by the Israeli Arabs' Palestinian identity, support for the PLO, voting for anti-Zionist parties, general strikes, nationalistically motivated murders of Jews, and the like.

The growing Jewish fears of the mounting Arab militancy were exploited to form the first quasi-fascist movement in Israel, Rabbi Kahane's Kach, which calls for the voluntary or forced removal of all Arabs from the country. Kahane won 25,907 votes (1.2% of the total) in the 1984 national elections and was expected to get 2.5% of the total vote in the 1988 elections from which he was barred. He attracts the underclass, the youth, and the ultra-nationalistic fringe groups, whose combined power in Israeli society is far from being negligible. Kahane's quasi-fascist politics, along with the 1975 UN resolution equating Zionism with racism, have brought the question of ethnocentrism in Israel to national and international attention.

For a number of reasons, a significant degree of ethnocentrism should be expected in the relations between the Arab minority and Jewish majority. First, the Israeli-Arab conflict places Arabs in the position of a distrustful, hostile minority. Second, the cultural differences in language, nationality, religion, and lifestyle between Arabs and Jews make for a sense of estrangement and disdain. Third, interethnic contacts are hindered by the agreement on both sides that assimilation is undesirable. Fourth, the appreciable ethnic stratification adds a class barrier to ethnic separation. Fifth, the Jewish-Zionist character of the state nurtures reluctance to share privileges and rights with non-Jews and non-Zionists. And sixth, feelings of dominance, mistrust, and mutual rejection are bound to stem from the ongoing application of controls over Arabs. These conditions combine to make ethnocentrism an independent force and a distinct issue in Arab-Jewish relations.

Discussion of ethnocentrism in Israel is usually based either on social psychological studies of stereotypes and social distance (Peres, 1971; Robins, 1972; Amir, 1979; Hofman, 1982) or on general statements about intolerance and racism (e.g., Lam, 1983). None of the attitude studies was based on a representative sample of the adult Arab or Jewish population.

Furthermore, no serious attempt was made to arrive at a realistic assessment of ethnocentrism by integrating the individual and institutional levels. These two failings are corrected here.

Results from the 1980 Van Leer survey of Jews will supplement our findings from the main 1980 survey. All the questionnaire items relevant to ethnocentrism in both surveys are attitudinal. They are classified into four areas: stereotyping, mistrust, avoidance, and differential treatment. They will be first discussed in this order and then evaluated for their implications concerning the prevalence of ethnocentrism in Israel.

Stereotyping

Arabs and Jews should not be expected to share similar stereotypes because they differ markedly in their status vis-à-vis each other. Arabs would stereotype Jews as a modern group in control of another group whereas Jews would stereotype Arabs as a backward and potentially violent group (Peres and Levy, 1969).

Stereotypes of Jews by Arabs are in fact widespread. A majority of Arabs regard most Jews as mindless of self-respect and family honor, exploitive, and racist (Table 14.1). These negative Jewish images are even sharper among the rejectionist Arab leaders, while shared only by a sizable minority of the other Arab leaders. Arabs probably have the Ashkenazic Jews in mind as a prototype of the Israeli Jew whom they perceive as modern and devoid of human decency. These Israeli Arab beliefs draw extra significance from their consistency with the Arab world's vision of Israel as racist; namely, Jewish individuals, the Government, and Zionism are all condemned to be racist.

Table 14.1 Arabs' Stereotypes of Jews in Israel

	Arab Public	Establishment Affiliated Arab Leaders	Rakah Affiliated Arab Leaders	Rejectionist Arab Leaders
Agree that most Jews in Israel				
Do not value self-respect and family honor	75. 2	45.8	37.9	83.3
Are exploitive	69.5	32.0	32.1	80.6
Are racist	69.1	36.0	40.7	90.3

Stereotypes of Arabs by Jews are well established but less common than one would expect. Around two fifths of the Jews envision most Arabs as primitive or incapable of reaching the Jewish level of development, but only a few Jewish leaders hold this image (Table 14.2). The adverse portrait of the Arabs stood out in contrast with that of the "Israeli Jew" and "American." While 44% of the Jewish respondents stereotype Israeli Arabs as primitive, only 5.5% so envisage Israeli Jews and only 3% so perceive Americans (Table 14.3). The Jewish public is quite discriminating. Its self-image is dimmer than that of the Americans (probably constituting a positive reference group). Between 22% to 44% of the Israeli Jews regard Israeli Arabs as primitive, violent, dirty, inefficient, and lazy, but the majority either take a neutral view (between 34% to 49.5%), or even have a positive picture (between 19% to 42%).

Table 14.2 Jews' Stereotypes of Arabs

	Jewish Public	Dovish Jewish Leaders	Jewish Arabists	Hawkish Jewish Leaders
Agree that most Arabs in Israel				
Will never reach the level of development Jews				
have reached	43.6	11.8	10.0	17.4
Are primitive	38.2	2.9	0.0	4.0

Table 14.3 Jews' Stereotypes of Israeli Arabs, Israeli Jews, and Americans

	Israeli Arab	Israeli Jew	American
Progress			
Primitive	43.8	5.5	2.8
Developed	22.1	76.8	89.2
Neither	34.2	17.7	8.0
Violence			
Violent	38.7	22.2	12.4
Non-violent	21.7	34.7	51.9
Neither	39.6	43.1	35.6
Cleanliness			
Dirty	31.7	8.1	8.5
Clean	18.7	46.7	55.1
Neither	49.5	45.1	36.4
Efficiency			
Inefficient	30.2	8.7	2.9
Efficient	34.5	58.5	81.5
Neither	35.3	32.8	15.6
Industrious			
Lazy	21.6	28.3	11.4
Industrious	41.9	27.8	64.3
Neither	36.5	43.9	24.3

Source: The Van Leer survey.

Mistrust

Mutual mistrust is a graver problem than stereotyping. Two thirds of the Arabs in the study feel that it is impossible to trust most Israeli Jews, a distrust that is shared by a quarter to a third of the Arab leaders who are affiliated with the establishment and Rakah and by virtually all of the rejectionist leaders (Table 14.4). That Arabs are quite discerning in their distrust of Jews is demonstrated by the fact that a majority (59%) of them trust official or Jewish media more than other sources of information (including Rakah newspapers and non-Israeli sources).

Table 14.4 Arabs' Mistrust of Jews in Israel

	Arab Public	Establishment Affiliated Arab Leaders	Rakah Affiliated Arab Leaders	Rejectionist Arab Leaders
Agree that it is impossible to trust most Jews	66.2	24.0	31.0	89.7
Hold that the most trustworthy newspapers and broadcasts are				
Official, non-partisan Israeli newspapers and broadcasts	59.0	70.8	25.8	10.0
Israeli newspapers of the Jewish left	5.8	29.2	6.5	10.0
Rakah newspapers	8.1	0.0	61.3	15.0
Non-Israeli newspapers and broadcasts from the occupied territories, Arab States or Europe	27.1	0.0	6.5	65.0

Why do Arabs mistrust Jews but not the Jewish media? The Israeli Jewish media, catering to Jews, are known for their high professional standards, and hence are seen as superior to the propagandistic and less informative Arab sources (e.g. the Rakah newspaper). They are credible because, unlike the Jewish public, Zionism, and the Government, they are not associated in the Arab Israeli mind with manipulation, control, and exploitation. The Arab cannot confide in his fellow Jew whom he believes to be racist and cannot fearlessly share with him his dissenting views and hostile sentiments.

Jewish mistrust hinges on Arab threats to Israel's survival and spreads to other areas. A majority of both the Jewish public and leadership regard the Arab minority as presenting at least a certain danger to national security (Table 14.5). This apprehension leads two thirds of the Jewish public to believe that it is impossible to trust most Arabs, like the two thirds of the Arab public who cannot trust most Jews. In consequence, the Jewish population desires an increase in surveillance over Arabs, justifies security restrictions on Arabs, endorses a dismissal from the civil service and universities of Arabs who publicly support the PLO, and generally approves of a strong-arm policy to contain the Arab minority (Table 14.5). The Jewish leaders hold more differentiating stands – they see only a minority of Arabs as untrustworthy and a target for a closer watch. They differ, nonetheless, on how widely security restrictions should be imposed and on how Arab dissenters must be handled. On this point the hawkish Jewish leaders take a hardline stance similar to that of the public at large.

Table 14.5 Jews' Mistrust of Arabs in Israel

	Jewish Public	Dovish Jewish Leaders	Jewish Arabists	Hawkish Jewish Leaders
Consider Arabs in Israel as a danger to national security				
To a great degree	18.4	0.0	0.0	12.0
To a considerable degree	22.5	6.3	20.0	0.0
To a certain degree	42.5	50.0	40.0	44.0
No	16.5	43.8	40.0	44.0
Agree that it is impossible to trust most Arabs in Israel	66.0	15.2	10.7	31.8
Favor an increase in surveillance over most Arabs in Israel	65.4	0.0	27.6	35.0
Consider as justified security restrictions on Arabs in Israel as long as the Israeli-Arab conflict persists				
Yes	67.6	29.4	48.3	72.0
To some extent	25.4	47.1	41.4	24.0
No	6.9	23.5	10.3	4.0
Endorse a law to dismiss a civil servant or a university student who publicly declares support for the PLO	79.3	39.4	58.6	96.0
Strong-arm policy toward the Arabs in Israel				
In favor	46.5	0.0	26.9	42.9
Have reservations	33.7	37.5	46.2	47.6
Against	19.8	62.5	26.9	9.5

Mistrust raises the question of Arab loyalty to the state. Since Arabs are suspected of undermining the state, loyalty would mean, first of all, acceptance of Israel's presence as well as undivided allegiance and compliance with the law. Our figures clearly show that Arab loyalty is indeed a critical issue in Arab-Jewish relations.

Arabs and Jews disagree sharply on their assessment of the Israeli Arab acquiescence to Israel. A majority of 68% of the Arabs agree that most or almost all Israeli Arabs have already reconciled themselves to Israel's existence (Table 14.6). This proportion is even higher than the 59% of Arabs who recognize Israel's right to exist without reservation (Table 5.1 above). Most important, even among the rejectionist Arab leaders, of whom none unreservedly acknowledge Israel's right to exist, 59% feel that Arabs are already resigned to Israel's existence. A large majority (72%) of the Jews disbelieve this across the board Arab consensus on the Arab acceptance of the state.

Table 14.6 Perceived Loyalty of Arabs in Israel

	Arab Public	Establish-ment-Affiliated Arab Leaders	Rakah-Affiliated Arab Leaders	Rejec-tionist Arab Leaders	Jewish Public[a]
Consider each of the following statements true for all or most Arabs in Israel					
Reconciled themselves to Israel's existence	68.2	84.0	96.9	58.6	28.2
Torn in loyalty to Israel and to their people	47.6	52.0	42.9	3.3	45.2
Loyal to Israel	47.0	87.5	65.5	0.0	16.2
Rejoice at Israel's suffering	25.4	0.0	3.3	90.0	50.7
Hate Jews	28.6	4.2	0.0	32.3	53.5
Engaged in spying against Israel	*	*	*	*	17.6

* Not asked.

[a] The Van Leer survey.

Although both sides realize that undivided allegiance to Israel on the part of the Arabs is not a realistic expectation under the present circumstances, they differ on its implications. On the one hand, the question whether Arabs are torn between loyalty to Israel and loyalty to their people deeply divides Arabs and Jews with about half in each community feeling either way. On the other hand, for the Jews, split allegiance casts a shadow on Arab loyalty to Israel, whereas for at least half of the Arab public and most of the Arab leaders (except the rejectionists) Arab loyalty to the state remains firm in the face of countervailing pressures. Furthermore, at least half of the Jews suspect that most or all Arabs hate them or rejoice at Israel's suffering, but only a small proportion of the Arabs confirm this suspicion.

No evidence is available on Jewish public beliefs concerning Arab obedience to the law. The general impression is, however, that many Jews believe that Arabs are disproportionately engaged in illegal activities, including tax evasion, squatting on state lands, construction of unlicensed buildings, and collaboration with the enemy. Responses to a question on the last point are symptomatic. Some 18% of the Jews believe that most or almost all Arabs perpetrate espionage against Israel and an additional 22% charge that some of the Arabs do so. Given the impossibility of what these imputations suggest, these exceedingly high figures demonstrate once again fundamental Jewish mistrust of Arabs.

Avoidance

Lack of readiness to maintain contact with members of the outside group may be, but is not necessarily, a sign of ethnocentrism. The degree of willingness to participate in interethnic associations usually varies with minority-majority status and the quality of relationship. Arabs and

Jews were asked about their willingness to mix with members of the opposite community in friendship and to live with them in the same neighborhood, both of which require relationships on a personal level. For being fully legitimate and less demanding, mixed friendship is found to be completely supported by both Arab and Jewish leaders (Table 14.7). The rank and file are less receptive, with 69% of the Arabs and 38.5% of the Jews expressing willingness to make friends with members of the opposite community. Less readiness is shown by both sides to living in mixed neighborhoods because they necessitate daily contact and reorganization of local facilities. Yet most of the Jewish leaders as well as over half of the Arab leaders are willing to live in a mixed neighborhood, thereby conferring legitimacy on such a type of interethnic mixing. About half of the Arabs as compared to one fifth of the Jews state their willingness to reside in mixed neighborhoods.

Table 14.7 Willingness for Interethnic Contact

	Arab Public	Estab. Affil. Arab Lead.	Rakah Affil. Arab Lead.	Rejec- tion. Arab Lead.	Jewish Public	Dovish Jewish Lead.	Jewish Arab- ists	Hawkish Jewish Lead.
Willingness to have Jews/Arabs as friends	69.4	100.0	100.0	83.9	38.5	100.0	96.6	88.0
Willingness to live in a mixed neighborhood	47.4	52.0	53.1	64.5	22.4	58.1	75.0	60.8

The Jewish public was presented with eleven contact situations ranging from the workplace to the family. A majority of 53% to 64% are willing to work with Arabs, to host them, to have Arab friends, to visit them, or even to have their children study with Arab children (Table 14.8). Actually 42% are prepared to live in a street with Arabs and 36% to live in a building with them. However, only 6.5% are inclined to have a family member marry an Arab.

Several avoidance patterns emerge from the above statistics. First, Arabs and Jews exhibit greater willingness for mixed contacts than they have at present. To illustrate, the proportion of Arabs willing to have Jewish friends (69%) (Table 14.7) is twice as much as that of Arabs being on visiting terms with Jewish friends (38.5%) (Table 7.10). A similar picture prevails among the Jews (the respective figures are 38.5% and 12%). The 47% of the Arabs and 22% of the Jews prepared to live in a mixed neighborhood is much greater than the 3% or less who presently share residential quarters.

Second, the same figures demonstrate the asymmetry in Arab and Jewish readiness for interethnic contact. The fact that Arabs desire more

contacts with Jews than the other way around is well established in
research (Hofman, 1977:94). It is best accounted for by the greater
rewards accruing to the minority members from interethnic contacts,
whereas majority members might even lose from such contacts.

Table 14.8 Jews' Willingness for Contact with Arabs

	Jewish Public
Willing to have each of the following	
Working with an Arab in the same workplace	64.4
Working with an Arab in same room	60.6
Hosting Arabs at one's home	59.1
Friendship with Arabs	58.3
Visiting Arabs	57.9
Attending social gatherings with Arabs	54.9
Living in a city with Arabs	54.0
One's children studying with Arab children	53.0
Living in a street with Arabs	42.4
Living in a building with Arabs	36.4
One's family member marrying an Arab	6.5

Source: The Van Leer survey.

And third, willingness is greater when contact is impersonal or
temporary and much less when it is personal and lasting. Whatever
appears to threaten the separate existence and identity of each group is
resisted. For this reason most Arabs and most Jews object to neighborly
relations[1] and intermarriages.

Differential Treatment

At the core of the ethnocentrism of the dominant group is its reluctance to treat the minority as an equal. Differential treatment can be
expressed in denial of civil rights and in the imposition of restrictions.

Although Arabs formally enjoy complete civil rights in Israel, the
Jewish public does not fully sanction the current situation. Only half
favor the same rights for Arabs and Jews, and three fifths favor the same
duties (Table 14.9). Interestingly enough, over one tenth of the Jews
would impose the same duties on Arabs without granting them the same
rights.

More revealing are the Jewish responses to the question as to
whether Israel should treat both groups equally or differentially. While
91% of the Arab respondents predictably endorse "equal treatment," an

[1]A majority of 64% of the Arabs in the 1976 survey are not willing to have a Jew
as one of two immediate neighbors and 64% of the Jews in the Van Leer survey
are not willing to live in a building with Arabs.

overwhelming majority, 84% of the Jews, are for giving Jews "preference," consisting of 68% opting for "considerable preference" and 16% for "some preference" (Table 14.10). In addition, 28.5% of the dovish Jewish leaders, 50% of the Jewish Arabists, and 55% of the hawkish Jewish leaders favor preference of the Jews by the state (a possibility which is opposed by all Arab leaders).

Table 14.9 Jews' Attitudes toward Equal Rights and Duties for Arabs

	Jewish Public
Israel should grant Arabs same rights as Jews	
In favor	47.3
Indifferent	14.8
Against	37.9
Israel should impose same duties on Arabs as Jews	
In favor	60.8
Indifferent	12.2
Against	26.9

Source: The Van Leer survey.

Table 14.10 Equal Treatment

The State of Israel should	Arab Public	Estab. Affil. Arab Lead.	Rakah Affil. Arab Lead.	Rejec-tion. Arab Lead.	Jewish Public	Dovish Jewish Lead.	Jewish Arab-ists	Hawkish Jewish Lead.
Prefer Jews to Arabs considerably	1.7	0.0	0.0	0.0	67.6	7.1	19.2	36.4
Prefer Jews to Arabs to some extent	1.7	4.2	0.0	0.0	16.3	21.4	30.8	18.2
Treat both equally	91.3	95.8	100.0	100.0	15.8	71.4	46.2	45.5
Prefer Arabs to Jews to some extent	1.4	0.0	0.0	0.0	0.3	0.0	3.8	0.0
Prefer Arabs to Jews considerably	3.9	0.0	0.0	0.0	0.1	0.0	0.0	0.0

Jewish expectations of preferential treatment are best seen in their support of specific practices which benefit them. A Jewish majority ranging from 68% to 86% endorses preference for Jews in various areas, including admission to universities, jobs, housing assistance, agricultural loans, and social security benefits (Table 14.11).

Similarly, 59% to 97% of the Jewish public are reserved about or opposed to different measures that are intended to equalize Arab and Jewish statuses (Table 14.12). To illustrate, 75% are reserved about or opposed to the extension to Arab schools of the same special aid given to disadvantaged Jewish schools, or are unfavorably disposed toward the free entry of educated Arabs into the economy. Furthermore, over 90% disapprove of innovative steps such as the allocation of lands and funds to establish new Arab towns or to modify the state's symbols, like the flag or national anthem, so that Israeli Arabs could identify with them. On most of the proposed measures, the hawkish Jewish leaders and Jewish Arabists take similar stands but the dovish Jewish leaders are generally more receptive to changes that would result in greater Arab equality.

Table 14.11 Jews' Attitudes toward Equal Treatment of Arabs in Selected Areas

	Jewish Public
Reject equal treatment of Arabs (or favor preferential treatment of Jews) in each of the following areas	
Admission to universities	72.3
Admission to private workplaces	69.2
Admission to public workplaces	74.2
Housing assistance to large families	73.5
Social security allowances	68.1
Loans for development of agriculture	70.0
Senior posts in government offices	85.9

Source: The Van Leer survey.

Table 14.12 Jews' Disapproval of Measures to Improve Arab Conditions

	Jewish Public	Dovish Jewish Leaders	Jewish Arabists	Hawkish Jewish Leaders
Jews reserved or opposed to each of the following measures to improve conditions for Arabs in Israel				
Extension to Arab localities of the same special assistance given to Jewish development towns	75.0	36.6	66.7	72.0
Extension to Arab schools of the same special assistance given to disadvantaged Jewish schools	59.0	13.3	26.7	36.0
Equal admission of Arab university graduates to private and public sectors of the economy	61.8	3.0	20.6	33.3
Doing away with benefits given to army veterans or to their relatives	84.5	76.7	90.0	96.0
Allocation of lands and funds to establish new Arab towns	89.2	48.4	80.0	80.0
Enactment of a special punitive law against discrimination in jobs, housing, etc. on religious or nationalist grounds	75.2	43.8	60.0	66.7
Modification of state symbols, like the flag and anthem, so that Arabs can identify themselves with them	97.2	94.1	100.0	100.0

The Jewish public would even condone restrictions on Arab rights and on equal status if these restrictions appear to be better safeguards against adverse developments. The Jews fear, among other things, that the Arabs might subvert Israeli political democracy, the Arab population growth might undermine the Jewish majority, and Arab land holdings might impede Jewish land settlement. To avert these undesirable possibilities, most Jews in the survey support or at least do not oppose such countermeasures as a ban on Rakah, seizure of opportunities to encourage Arabs to leave the country, and expropriation of Arab lands for Jewish development projects (Table 14.13). On the other hand, with the exception of the land issue, the majority of the dovish Jewish leaders oppose these infringements on Arab rights.

Table 14.13 Jews' Views of Restrictions on Arabs

	Jewish Public	Dovish Jewish Leaders	Jewish Arabists	Hawkish Jewish Leaders
Denial by the government of the right of Arabs to hold demonstrations				
Agree	36.0	2.9	14.8	13.0
Have reservations	37.1	32.4	48.1	26.1
Disagree	26.9	64.7	37.0	60.9
Outlaw Rakah				
Agree	51.7	0.0	10.0	16.0
Have reservations	25.9	14.7	10.0	16.0
Disagree	22.4	85.3	80.0	68.0
Restrictions on Arabs in order to prevent their increase to a majority in Israel				
Agree	56.1	10.0	22.2	31.6
Have reservations	25.8	23.3	40.7	15.8
Disagree	18.1	66.7	37.0	52.6
Israel should seek and use any opportunity to encourage Israeli Arabs to leave the state				
Agree	50.3	3.0	21.4	59.1
Have reservations	30.8	21.2	42.9	13.6
Disagree	18.9	75.8	35.7	27.3
Expropriation of Arab lands within the Green Line for Jewish development				
Agree	40.7	33.3	43.3	87.0
Have reservations	35.4	30.0	40.0	8.7
Disagree	23.9	36.7	16.7	4.3

Jewish reluctance to extend equality to the Arabs takes a noticeably ethnocentric upturn with regard to acceptance of Arabs with superior social status. Around two thirds of the Jews are unwilling to have an Israeli Arab as their own personal doctor or superior in a job, thereby confirming their overt stakes in the existing ethno-status hierarchy (Table 14.14). Probably aware of the explicit ethnocentric nature of these questions, the Jewish leaders give rather liberal answers.

Table 14.14 Jews' Willingness to Accept Arabs of Superior Status

	Jewish Public	Dovish Jewish Leaders	Jewish Arabists	Hawkish Jewish Leaders
Unwilling to have an Arab as one's own				
Personal doctor	64.9	11.8	6.6	24.0
Superior in a job	70.1	30.3	25.9	36.0

Consistency and Variation in Ethnocentrism

To what extent are stereotyping, mistrust, avoidance, and norms of differential treatment closely linked to produce a consistent syndrome of ethnocentrism? How do Arabs and Jews, and social categories within each of these groups, differ on ethnocentrism? To tackle these questions, the items that are either identical or parallel for Arabs and Jews are subjected to further analysis. These items are the following:

1.   For Arabs: agree that most Jews do not value self-respect and family honor. For Jews: agree that most Arabs in Israel will never reach the level of development Jews have reached.
2.   For Arabs: agree that most Jews are racist. For Jews: agree that most Arabs in Israel are primitive.
3.   For Arabs: agree that it is impossible to trust most Jews. For Jews: agree that it is impossible to trust most Arabs in Israel.
4.   For Arabs: unwilling to have Jews as friends. For Jews: unwilling to have Arabs as friends.
5.   For Arabs and Jews: unwilling to live in a mixed neighborhood.

The statistical analysis includes the following steps: (a) intercorrelations, (b) index construction, and (c) regression analysis. It leads to several conclusions. First, the intercorrelations between the various items are all statistically significant, averaging 0.22 for the Arab public and 0.31 for the Jewish public. They indicate moderate consistency in attitudes and justify the notion of an "ethnocentrism syndrome" for both Arabs and Jews. .

Second, a simple additive index, consisting of all the five items, shows no difference in the level of the ethnocentrism, as measured, between the Arab and Jewish public. Some 18% of the Arabs and 20% of the Jews score low on the ethnocentrism index (0-1 points), 44% vs. 42% score medium (2-3 points), and 38% vs. 38% score high (4-5 points) (Table 14.15). Assuming that the two indices are based on sufficient equivalence of the items, these figures demonstrate that ethnocentrism is equally high and scattered among Arabs and Jews. At the same time, its meaning and implications might be different for the two sides as will be suggested below.

Table 14.15 Index of Ethnocentrism

	Arab Public	Estab. Affil. Arab Lead.	Rakah Affil. Arab Lead.	Rejection. Arab Lead.	Jewish Public	Dovish Jewish Lead.	Jewish Arab-ists	Hawkish Jewish Lead.
Low								
0	5.8	20.0	24.1	3.3	7.4	41.2	51.7	40.9
1	12.5	40.0	27.6	6.7	12.7	44.1	41.4	22.7
2	17.5	16.0	20.7	13.3	19.0	11.8	3.4	13.6
3	26.5	12.0	13.8	43.3	22.6	0.0	3.4	18.2
4	20.9	12.0	13.8	16.7	20.3	2.9	0.0	4.2
5	16.7	0.0	0.0	16.7	17.9	0.0	0.0	0.0
High								

Third, most leaders score low on the ethnocentrism index and they are much less ethnocentric than the rank and file. A majority of 60% of the Arab leaders affiliated with the establishment, and 52% of the Arab leaders affiliated with Rakah as compared to only 18% of the Arab public score low on the index (Table 14.15). This divergence is even more marked among the Jews. The only exception is the rejectionist Arab leaders who are moderately to highly ethnocentric and even slightly more ethnocentric than the general public.

Fourth, the four best predictors of ethnocentrism differ for Arabs and Jews. For the Arabs they are visiting terms with Jews, effect of land expropriations, dissatisfaction with local educational services, and consent to permit single Arab girls to have a boyfriend, together

Table 14.16 A Regression Analysis of the Four Best Predictors of Ethnocentrism

	N	r	R	Beta
Arabs				
Visiting terms with Jews	1,096	−0.26	0.26	−0.22722*
Effect of land expropriations	866	−0.20	0.32	−0.16644*
Dissatisfaction with local educational services	1,097	0.16	0.34	0.13988*
Consent to permit single Arab girls to have a boyfriend	1,088	0.17	0.37	0.12971*
Jews				
Voting	928	0.33	0.33	0.22438*
Visiting terms with Arabs	1,185	−0.24	0.40	−0.20076*
Education	1,187	−0.27	0.44	−0.17998*
Hawkishness	989	−0.29	0.47	−0.17577*

*Statistically significant at 0.05 level.

accounting for 14% of the variance on ethnocentrism (R=0.37) (Table 14.16). These predictors fall into two categories: the first three and main ones concern Jews' relations with Arabs or the impact of Jewish policies on Arabs, whereas the last one reflects Arab traditionalism which is associated with suspicion and seclusion.

The four best predictors, which explain 22% (R=0.47) of the variance on Jewish ethnocentrism are of a different nature. Two of them, voting and hawkishness, indicate affiliation to a political stream which in turn determines attitudes toward the Arab world and the level of political tolerance. Visiting terms with Arabs which tend to dissipate stereotypes and distrust also emerge as the second best predictor. Despite its correlation with a political stream, education seems to reduce Jewish ethnocentrism a little further. On the other hand, religious observance and ethnic origin do not have a specific or direct contribution to Jewish ethnocentrism beyond their probable impact on voting and on hawkishness.

Evaluation of Arab Ethnocentrism

Let me turn now to the difficult task of disentangling the ethnocentric component in the Arab and Jewish views.

It appears that most Arabs in Israel today are indeed moderately to highly ethnocentric. Their images of Jews as racist, exploiters, untrustworthy and devoid of self-dignity and family honor, as well as their reservations about contact with Jews, are at least partially ethnocentric. By not espousing them, most Arab leaders, except the extreme rejectionist ones, acknowledge the ethnocentric nature of these attitudes.

This assessment confirms the findings of a study of civic values of Arab high school students conducted in 1976. It was part of an international comparative study of youth in Western countries (including the United States, France, the Netherlands, West Germany, Italy, Ireland, Finland, and New Zealand). The students were asked if each of various categories of peoples (e.g. physicians, industrialists, workers, large families, beggars, critics of the government) should be given the same, less, or more rights than the majority. The proportion of ninth-graders giving straightforward, egalitarian answers averages 80% among students in the Western countries, 70% among Jewish students in Israel, but only 50% among Arab students in Israel (Rapaport, Peled, Rimor, and Mano, 1978:122-25). On the other hand, the Israeli Arab students show greater political tolerance than the other groups in the study. To illustrate, 45% of the students in the United States, 46.5% of the Israeli Jewish students, but only 26.5% of the Israeli Arab students agree to deny equal rights to Communists and critics of the regime (ibid.:124). This is because Arab students are aware of the fact that these dissident groups happen to be the champions of Arab minority rights in Israel.

Evaluation of Jewish Ethnocentrism

The more extensive and refined data on Jews make possible a more detailed evaluation of Jewish ethnocentrism. A proper assessment should combine two considerations. One is a norm of tolerance which is built into the Judeo-Christian tradition of the Western world. The other consideration is cross-cultural, namely, to be judged realistically and fairly, the Jewish treatment of the Arab minority must be compared to that of minorities elsewhere.

In exploring adequate criteria, two common ones should be dismissed because they ignore either one of the two considerations. One of these untenable yardsticks is pure tolerance in a utopian, secular, democratic state. According to this ideal, virtually all Israeli Jews are racist. While this moralistic approach is favored by critics of Israel, the other unreasonable test is favored by staunch apologists for the Jewish state. They maintain that the relevant standard for judging how Arabs are treated in Israel is the maltreatment of minorities in the Arab world, be they Jewish (especially Syrian Jews) or non-Jewish (like the Kurds in Iraq). This outlook is not only incorrect in stressing the degree of intolerance toward minorities in the Middle East (e.g., Jewish status in Morocco is different), but it is also pointless because neither Israeli Jews nor Israeli Arabs take the Middle East as a frame of reference in this respect.

By incorporating both tolerance and comparability into the evaluative scheme, it is possible to spell out four valid criteria for assessing Jewish ethnocentrism toward the Arab minority: comparison with the treatment of hostile minorities in Western societies, comparison with the treatment of dissident minorities, comparison with the treatment of nonassimilating minorities, and comparison with the treatment of Jewish minorities.

1. *Hostile minorities.* Israeli Arabs belong to a special category of hostile or enemy-affiliated minorities. They are regarded as a security risk for being part of the belligerent Arab world (which now excludes Egypt) and Palestinians. Since Israel's right to national security is accepted, the question is whether Israeli Jews are less tolerant of Israeli Arabs than Westerners are tolerant of their own hostile minorities.

The treatment of enemy-affiliated minorities in the United States during WWII is a case in point. Japanese Americans were treated as a fifth column, their civil rights were denied, and they were driven into relocation camps. Spokesmen for the Israeli government sometimes invoke this analogy to show that Israel, a country fighting for its very survival, does better in handling its hostile Arab minority. This comparison is, however, partial and one-sided. First, it is evident, in retrospect, that the Japanese Americans fell victim to needless injustice which has been recognized by the American Congress in a special legislative act in 1988. Second, the United States did not mishandle the German and Italian minorities whose loyalty could have also been questioned. And third, the Israeli case is one of protracted conflict which necessitates policies of trust-building.

Jewish mistrust of the Arab minority is excessive. The historical record does not countenance the widespread feeling that the Arabs as a whole are a security risk and that a sizeable number of them are actually involved in spying and terror, which leads to the Jewish public's demand that the already inordinate surveillance over them should be further increased. Toledano (1974), then the Prime Minister's Advisor on Arab Affairs, is no doubt right in charging the Jewish public and private sector of hypersensitivity over national security as shown in their reluctance to employ Arabs who have passed security clearance in positions of trust.

2. *Dissident minorities.* Israeli Arabs belong to a special type of ideologically dissident minorities. They object to the Jewish consensus in two basic ways. They reject Israel's national ideology of Zionism and her *raison d'être* as a Jewish-Zionist state. They also dissent from the Jewish view of the Israeli-Arab conflict, i.e., they support the solution of an independent, PLO-headed, Palestinian state on the West Bank and Gaza Strip, which is opposed by Jews. Since Arabs are a dissident minority, it is possible to compare tolerance toward them with that toward dissident minorities in Western democracies and toward other dissident groups in Israel.

There are striking similarities between the treatment of Arab dissidence and that of Catholics in Northern Ireland (Smooha, 1980). In both cases the majorities determine unilaterally the national consensus, oppose negotiation with the minorities on the terms and limits of the consensus, and regard the rejection of the consensus by the minorities as subversion and not as a legitimate dissent.

Several studies attest to the political intolerance of Jewish youths and adults in Israel. A cross-national study of the civic culture of students in elementary and high schools shows that political tolerance is lowest in Israel. To illustrate, 47% of the Israeli Jewish youths as against 32% of youths in Western Europe and the United States would give fewer rights to persons who hold views opposed to the regime. Similarly 46% and 20%, respectively, would deny equal rights to Communists (Lewy, Rapaport, and Rimor, 1978:177). In the present survey, a third to a half of the Jewish adults deny various civil rights to "critics of the regime" and "groups opposed to Israel's Jewish-Zionist character." Another comparative study concludes that political intolerance is high in Israel, higher than in the United States, intense, and focused in its target groups (Sullivan, Shamir, Roberts, and Walsh, 1984). More specifically, it is found that 64% of Israeli Jews, in a survey undertaken in 1980, select PLO supporters and Rakah as their least liked groups (Shamir and Sullivan, 1983:918).

Since the disliked or dissenting groups happen to be overwhelmingly Arab, there is a considerable coincidence in Israel between political intolerance and intolerance of Israeli Arabs. For example, 22% of the Jews are in favor of prohibiting all critics of the regime from holding demonstrations, of whom 82% are also in favor of imposing the same ban on Israeli Arabs presumably for being also critics of the regime.

It appears, therefore, that Arab dissidence figures largely in political intolerance of Jews toward Arabs. But even if Jewish intolerance of Arabs is not excessive when compared to that toward other dissidents in Israel, this would only "explain" but not "justify" it. If political democracy means a right to dissent, then Arabs as other ideological dissidents are entitled to avail themselves of the democratic procedures to change the regime.

3. *Nonassimilating minorities.* Israeli Arabs fall in the special category of nonassimilating minorities. They wish to preserve their separate identity, culture, institutions, and communities and are assured the necessary conditions to do so. The critical question is whether Israeli Arabs are treated in the same way as nonassimilating minorities in Western democracies and as Jews in Israel.

In a comparative perspective Israeli democracy has two structural weaknesses. Israel lacks the American constitution or the British tradition that provide for the protection of individual and minority rights (Shapira, 1977). It maintains instead the 1945 Emergency Regulations which can be easily misused to crack down on dissidents and unpopular minority groups. Neither does Israel have, on the mass level, a genuine democratic political culture. These failings account for the Jewish public's support for the policy of control over Arabs in Israel and for the Arabs' failure to gain control over their separate institutions.

A more formidable obstacle to the full realization of Israeli democracy is the ethnic nature of the state. As a Jewish-Zionist state, Israel is constituted to be the country of all Jews living inside or outside Israel, and not of its citizens. It is supposed to keep a Jewish majority and to promote Jewish interests and institutions. These ideas militate against the full extension of democracy and equality to the Arab minority and to other non-Jews. Although Israel differs from Western democracies by being ethnic, i.e., identified with one of its constituent ethnic groups, it is internationally recognized and legitimized as such.[2]

---

[2]This legitimacy is reflected, among other things, in the 1947 United Nations Partition Resolution which is the legal basis for Israel's existence. This resolution, which was also supported by the Soviet bloc, provided for the creation of a Jewish state (a state for Jews) in part of Palestine.

In view of these shortcomings in Israeli democracy, there is little wonder that the Jewish majority develops ethnocentric attitudes toward the Arabs. Lam (1983) argues that Israeli Jews have a nationalistic, rather than democratic, political culture. They hold that their rights, culture, and identity are superior, and deserve better protection, than those of Israeli Arabs. They dehumanize Arabs and believe that force is the best means to deal with them.

Our findings clearly expose ethnocentric excesses among the Jews. Given the fact that Arabs and Jews share the goal of separate existence or coexistence, it is morally defensible for 93.5% of the Jews to object to intermarriage and even for a majority of them to oppose mixed schools or neighborhoods. On the other hand, the same ultimate end provides no justification for the two thirds who are unprepared to work as a subordinate to an Arab, let alone for the one third who are not ready to work with any Arab.

The most crucial point hinges, however, on the unwarranted expectation of Jews to be treated preferentially. While the idea of a Jewish-Zionist state would sanction the Law of Return, Jewish state symbols, and Jewish institutions, it would not necessarily validate the claims of half of the Jews who are indifferent or opposed to granting Arabs equal rights, 84% who endorse the principle of preferential treatment of Jews by the state, and substantial proportions who favor the denial of equal treatment to Arabs in specific areas.

4. *Jewish minorities.* Three quaters of the Jews in the world today still live as minorities in many countries, mostly in the West, but also in the Soviet Union, Latin America, and Syria. As a Jewish state, Israel sees itself responsible for them and defends their safety and rights as much as possible. The sensitivity and responsibility Israel feels toward Jewish minorities is a plausible standard for appraising its treatment of the Arab minority. As Weizman, Israel's first President, noted, Israel would be judged by its handling of the Arab minority.

Israel's Arabs do not enjoy the equal rights and opportunities afforded to the Jewish minorities in Western countries today. More indicative of Jewish ethnocentrism are, however, the data from the Van Leer survey that demonstrate that Israeli Jews apply double standards with regard to Arabs in Israel and Jews abroad. While only 13% justify the rejection from universities and work places of Russian Jews because of their anti-Soviet declarations or a wish to emigrate to Israel, 73% oppose admission to universities of Israeli Arabs who publicly declare they are dissatisfied with Israel's existence yet do not plot against it. In the same vein, only 9% of the Jews justify the historical ban on land sales to Jews in certain countries but 67% object to the selling of lands in Israel's central region to Arabs. Furthermore, while preventive detention for national security reasons is condoned by 61% of the Jews in the survey when imposed on Arabs in Israel, it is condoned by only 17% in the case of Jews in the Soviet Union, and by only 26% when applied to Jews in Egypt during the 1967 war.

Conclusion

Ethnocentrism is narrowly defined as superiority, mistrust, avoidance, and unwillingness to grant equal rights and opportunities to an ethnic group beyond what is necessary to achieve legitimate collective goals. Even if these goals are identified in Israel as separate existence and equality, and for Jews also national security and the preservation of the Jewish-Zionist character of the state, there is clear evidence for the prevalence of a significant degree of ethnocentrism among both Arabs and Jews.

Since ethnocentrism in Israel, as in most cases, is not the outgrowth of interpersonal dislikes or prejudices but rather inherent in the social background of each group and in the structure of minority-majority relations, a question arises as to what extent it is reactive or genuine. Ethnocentrism is reactive if it is mostly a response to a given situation and especially if the situation is changeable, and it is genuine when it stems from the history or "mentality" of the group or is anchored in intractable conditions. This distinction is hard to make in practice, but is invoked here as a way of offering concluding remarks on the complex question of ethnocentrism in Israel.

Israeli Arab ethnocentrism springs from two different sources, one of which is the treatment Arabs actually receive in Israel. Jewish cultural dominance, institutional discrimination, rejection, extensive control, and lack of accommodation with the Palestinians engender reactive ethnocentrism among Israeli Arabs. They overreact by stereotyping and distrusting Israeli Jews as a whole. The fact that the Arabs who are not on visiting terms with Jews, suffered from land expropriations, and are dissatisfied with local services are more ethnocentric than other Arabs testifies to the centrality and vitality of this factor.

The other source of Arab ethnocentrism, which is of a genuine nature, relates to the semi-feudal, agrarian, religious, and authoritarian origins of the Israeli Arab population. Despite extensive social change, there is still an appreciable degree of conservatism, familism, communalism, and rejection of outsiders among Israeli Arabs. These predispositions are echoed in the finding that the Arabs who endorse traditional norms tend to be more ethnocentric than others. It seems, nevertheless, that the treatment of Arabs is, overall, a greater source of Arab ethnocentrism than Arab traditionalism. Hence, Arab ethnocentrism appears to be mainly reactive and transformable.

In contrast, Jewish ethnocentrism looks both genuine and intractable. It feeds on a variety of sources, of which two can be considered situational – the Israeli-Arab conflict and the dissidence of the Arab minority. Both generate enormous mistrust among the Jews. The Arabs are perceived by Jews as a threat to the physical and normative integrity of Israeli society. But this perception is likely to change if progress could be made in the settlement of the Israeli-Arab dispute.

It seems, however, that the nature of Israel as a state is a more serious and enduring source of Jewish ethnocentrism. Two forces that are built into the very structure of the state encroach on its democratic regime: religion and Zionism. In Israel religion is not separated from the state. Orthodoxy, which is the least liberal of the three main streams in modern Judaism, is dominant. Alongside humanistic tenets, Israeli orthodoxy possesses centuries-old ethnocentric traditions, which enjoy certain legitimacy and impunity in a society where the majority and state power are Jewish. For instance, in 1986 some Rabbis, and even the man in charge of religious state schools ruled against contrived group encounters between Arab and Jewish school children. Furthermore, the religious political parties strongly opposed the enactment of a law against racism lest it run counter to certain Orthodox beliefs and practices as they interpret them.

Israeli Zionism is no doubt the strongest ethnocentric force. As a politically diverse national movement, Zionism has socialist and liberal currents, and it also enshrines democracy as an undisputed national goal. Its insistence, however, on preserving Israel as a Jewish-Zionist state and its failure to come to grips with the status of the Arab minority in such a state are a constant stimulus for Jewish ethnocentrism. The Jew in the street feels superior to his fellow Arab citizens, expects better rights and treatment, regards Arabs as untrustworthy and subversive, and wishes to keep them in "their place." He draws from Zionism, as he understands it, and from many statements by some Israeli Jewish leaders, justification and reinforcement for these beliefs and feelings. For instance, 55% of the hawkish Jewish leaders say that Israel as a state should prefer Jews to Arabs (Table 14.10).

To conclude, the question of ethnocentrism in Israel extends far beyond matters of interpersonal prejudice and discrimination and hence cannot be dealt with through the dissemination of information and the promotion of interethnic contact. It rather involves the foundations of Israeli society: Zionism, Judaism, democracy, dissidence, and the Israeli-Arab conflict. A fundamental re-evaluation of them will be required in order to combat effectively Arab and Jewish ethnocentrism.

15

Deprivation and Alienation

The stark realities in deeply divided societies are reflected in the psychological responses of the disadvantaged groups. The underprivileged react against institutionalized ethnic stratification and cultural hegemony and feel deprived and alienated. In the special case of colonial situations several thinkers such as Balandier, Memmi, and Fanon have traced a pattern consisting of adoration of the colonizer, inferiority complex, and self-estrangement, leading to eventual self-assertion and resistance. Even though minorities in non-colonial pluralistic societies feel less acutely deprived and alienated than in colonial societies, their feelings are sufficiently strong to constitute a critical issue in intergroup relations. Hence, the problem is not only to redress inequities but also to instill a sense of justice and belonging.

Arabs in Israel have firm grounds for feeling deprived and alienated. Being part of a democratic society with an increasingly growing economy, they have high aspirations for equality and social mobility. They are restrained, however, by five prime factors: the Israeli-Arab conflict, Israel as a Jewish-Zionist state, cultural hegemony, ethnic stratification, and Jewish ethnocentrism.

These five constraints place Arabs in a vulnerable position in Israeli society. As a "hostile minority," they are held suspect and are denied free access to jobs and posts of trust. As a non-Jewish and non-Zionist minority in a Jewish-Zionist state, Arabs are considered dissident outsiders who are to be treated less favorably. As a Third World minority in a Western state, Arabs are bound to be culturally alienated and less competitive. Being an underprivileged sector of a highly industrialized, middle-class population, they are socioeconomically disadvantaged and concentrated at the lower strata. These constraints combine to engender and reinforce Jewish ethnocentrism (anti-Arab attitudes), which constitutes a further impediment on its own.

151

Consequently Arabs endure numerous privations, and the evidence for many of them was discussed earlier. Two more indications of Arab deprivation may be added here. One is refugee status: 21% of the respondents are members of or originated from refugee families. These are families who during the 1948 war voluntarily or by force fled their place of residence, but not the country. As a result they became "present absentees," losing their property, required to be naturalized, and in most cases obliged to relocate. These displaced persons are the internal Arab refugees of Israel who suffered great hardships during the 1950's; most, however, have since been rehabilitated (Al-Haj, 1986).

Land expropriation is probably the most significant measure of deprivation. All estimates so far have referred to the proportion of Arab land expropriated, but not to the proportion of families affected. It is estimated that Arabs lost 40% to 60% of their land between 1948 and 1967. According to our survey, 52% of all Arab families were affected by land expropriation (Table 15.1). They constitute 65.5% of landowning families (20.5% claim no land ownership). Of those affected, two thirds report their loss as being heavy. Among the landowners, 38% of the Druzes, 64% of the Christians, 35% of Northern Bedouin, 81.5% of Negev Bedouin, and 70.5% of the non-Bedouin Moslems reportedly lost lands. These figures demonstrate the endemic spread of land expropriations, so that the matter is not only ideological or emotional but also a personally experienced privation.

Table 15.1 Land Expropriations

	All Arabs	Landowning Arabs
The extent of expropriations since 1948 of lands owned by oneself and one's brothers, parents, or sons		
Own no land	20.5	–
Own land but not expropriated	27.5	34.5
Some land expropriations	20.7	26.0
Much land expropriations	31.3	39.5

Other indications in the survey point to the gravity with which Arabs view land expropriations. As mentioned above, of all the Arab leadership groups, the highest credibility is accorded the Committee for Defense of Arab Lands (59%) (Table 11.1). The strong involvement in the Land Day strike, which was organized by this committee, confirms the concern over the issue. In the 1976 survey a majority of 64% are in favor of the strike and an additional 24.5% qualify their support. This contrasts with the solid majority (77%) of Jews opposing the strike. Furthermore, 40% of the Arabs in the 1980 survey report actual participation, a majority of them willingly. The proportion should be considered as fairly high, given the facts of this having been the first general strike, the heavy Arab dependence on Jews for a livelihood, and the intimidations made by the authorities before the strike.

As one would expect, Arabs feel strongly deprived. A great majority of them feel both personal and institutional discrimination. Contrary to the high expectations minorities usually have of their national governments, 32% of the Arabs in Israel maintain that governmental policies fail to narrow the gaps between them and the Jews, while 55% go even further to accuse official policies of having a widening effect (Table 15.2). In the particular instance of the Galilee Development Project, Arabs show absolutely no trust in government intentions of developing the region for all residents.

Table 15.2 Perceived Arab Deprivation

	Arab Public	Estab. Affil. Arab Lead.	Rakah Affil. Arab Lead.	Rejec- tion. Arab Lead.	Jewish Public	Dovish Jewish Lead.	Jewish Arab- ists	Hawkish Jewish Lead.
Hold that Israel does enough or too much for the Arabs	*	*	*	*	83.6	5.9	46.6	87.5
Hold that government policies widen the socioeconomic gap between Arabs and Jews	55.0	44.0	96.9	96.8	19.7	62.5	3.3	4.8
Hold that the Galilee Development Project would cause harm to the Arabs	85.9[a]				22.7[a]			
Hold that Arabs do not enjoy equal job opportunities or doubt if they do	79.0	92.0	100.0	93.5	50.3	73.5	75.9	60.0
Hold that Arab youth do not have reasonable chances of fulfilling their occupational aspirations	55.7	44.0	81.3	93.6	26.6	58.8	33.3	40.0

* Not asked

[a] The 1976 survey, which did not include leaders.

Seventy-nine percent of the Arabs feel that they do not enjoy equal job opportunities even when unrelated to national security. In addition, 56% maintain that Arab youth do not have reasonable chances of fulfilling their occupational aspirations in Israel. This sentiment of deprivation is even more intense among the Rakah-affiliated and rejectionist Arab leaders but less so among the establishment-affiliated leaders.

In contrast, only a minority of Jews concede that Arabs are really deprived. Whereas a half confirm that job opportunities are unequal, only one quarter see Arab youth affected by slim mobility chances (Table

15.2). Most revealing is the gut feeling of most Jews that Israel does enough or too much for Arabs, that it does not widen Arab-Jewish inequality, and that the Galilee Development Project is beneficial to both communities. These self-righteous views are most pronounced among the hardline hawkish Jewish leaders and least accepted by the liberal dovish Jewish leaders.

The discrepancy in perceptions between Arabs and Jews can be readily understood. Arabs are more aware of discriminatory acts and policies against them. Furthermore, Jews, who tend to regard Arabs as outsiders and suspects, would not perceive the treatment of Arabs as discriminatory but, rather, as expedient under the current exigencies of national security and as legitimate in light of the Jews' right to preferential treatment in a Jewish-Zionist state. It is, moreover, in the Jews' own self-interest to underestimate Arab deprivation.

Arab dissatisfaction with state institutions varies considerably (Table 15.3). One quarter or less are dissatisfied with medicine (7%), the state President (16%), and the courts (25%). These are the least politicized institutions and more or less impartial in dealing with Arabs and Jews. Between one third to two fifths are dissatisfied with education and culture (34%), Israel Defense Forces (37%), the Knesset (38%), and police (41%). But half or over are dissatisfied with democracy (51%), freedom of expression (53%), and the Prime Minister (72%). Dissatisfaction peaks with the Prime Minister, Mr. Begin at the time, because this post symbolizes Jewish effective power in Israel. It is in line with the widespread charge that the Israeli government discriminates against the Arabs in its policies. This considerable range demonstrates, nonetheless, that the Arab population holds a rather complex attitude toward state institutions and that its disaffection is possibly commensurate with the kind of treatment it is afforded by each of them. The important implication is that change of policies can effect the overall level of Arab dissatisfaction.

Dissatisfaction among Arab leaders is rather politicized and partisan. The establishment-affiliated Arab leaders report less disaffection. At the time of the survey in 1980, they were more disenchanted with the Prime Minister because they belong to the Zionist parties in opposition to the Likud government. They also voice particular dissatisfaction with the Knesset because greater Arab representation in the parliament would benefit them personally. Since the rationale of being a Rakah-affiliated Arab leader is opposition to the present state institutions and policies, dissatisfaction should be predictably high among them. Indeed most of them are dissatisfied with most institutions except medicine, the state presidency, and courts, reconfirming the fairness of these public bodies. The acute and indiscriminate dissatisfaction felt by the rejectionist Arab leaders testifies to their unconditional negation of the state and its institutions.

Table 15.3 Arabs' Dissatisfaction with State Institutions

	Arab Public	Establishment-Affiliated Arab Leaders	Rakah-Affiliated Arab Leaders	Rejectionist Arab Leaders
Dissatisfied with each of the following				
The President of the State	16.2	0.0	12.5	51.7
The Prime Minister	72.4	88.0	100.0	96.8
The Knesset	38.3	60.0	68.8	90.3
Democracy	50.9	16.0	81.3	100.0
Freedom of expression	52.9	16.0	81.2	96.8
Israel Defense Forces	36.6	20.0	75.0	96.8
Courts	25.3	0.0	32.2	93.5
Police	40.9	44.0	84.4	100.0
Medicine	7.2	0.0	0.0	22.6
Education and culture	34.4	40.0	75.1	83.9

The Arabs feel that they do not get equal opportunities and services to which they are entitled as citizens. As many as 55% feel discontent with being Israeli citizens and 65% with local education and cultural services (Table 15.4). These Arab levels of dissatisfaction can be better appreciated when contrasted with Jewish ones: 13% and 35%, respectively.

Table 15.4 Dissatisfactions

	Arab Public	Estab. Affil. Arab Lead.	Rakah Affil. Arab Lead.	Rejec- tion. Arab Lead.	Jewish Public	Dovish Jewish Jewish Lead.	Arab- ists	Hawkish Jewish Lead.
Dissatisfied with being an Israeli citizen	55.3	48.0	59.4	100.0	13.4	6.2	0.0	3.8
Dissatisfied with educational and cultural services in one's place of residence	64.9	72.0	96.9	96.8	35.2	31.3	16.7	26.8

Dissatisfaction with the state and its institutions is generalized to alienation from the state. A large majority, 76% of the Arabs would not feel more at home in Israel than in an Arab country (Table 15.5). This is despite the fact that they have never lived in Arab countries and what they know about them is quite discouraging. Besides, 70% feel at least some cultural alienation. The magnitude of Arab alienation, which is also high among the leaders, stands out against the firm Jewish attachment to the state: 82% of the Jews, compared to only 30% of the Arabs, do not feel cultural alienation.

Table 15.5 Feelings of Alienation

	Arab Public	Estab. Affil. Arab Lead.	Rakah Affil. Arab Lead.	Rejec- tion. Arab Lead.	Jewish Public	Dovish Jewish Lead.	Jewish Arab- ists	Hawkish Jewish Lead.
Feel at home								
More in an Arab country	24.1	9.5	17.9	88.9	*	*	*	*
No difference	40.3	42.9	46.4	11.1	*	*	*	*
More in Israel	35.7	47.6	35.7	0.0	*	*	*	*
Feel alien in Israel in style of life, practices, and values								
To a great degree	8.2	0.0	6.3	38.7	2.2	0.0	0.0	4.0
To a considerable degree	16.0	4.0	18.8	16.1	3.1	6.5	0.0	0.0
To some degree	45.6	52.0	53.1	32.3	12.3	9.7	3.6	8.0
Do not feel alien	30.3	44.0	21.9	12.9	82.4	83.9	96.4	88.0

* Not asked.

Mutual detachment is widespread. Since Jews oppose vehemently PLO terrorism, of which they are victims, Arabs are asked how they feel about it. A majority of 61% of the Arabs concede that they either rejoice at or justify Fedayeen actions in which Israeli Jews were killed (Table 15.6). To gain a sense of Jewish detachment, Jews are asked if they would feel relief if all casualties in a car accident were later announced to have been Arabs. Half of them indeed would feel at least some relief.

Table 15.6 Detachment

	Arab Public	Estab. Affil. Arab. Leaders	Rakah Affil. Arab Leaders	Rejec- tionist Arab Leaders	Jewish Public
Feeling about a Fedayeen action in which Israeli Jewish citizens were killed					
Rejoice and justify action	8.8	0.0	0.0	10.0	*
Rejoice but do not justify action	3.8	0.0	0.0	3.3	*
Sadden but justify action	48.7	25.0	67.9	86.7	*
Sadden and do not justify action	38.8	75.0	32.1	0.0	*
Feel relief if all casualties in a car ac- cident were later identified as Arabs in Israel	*	*	*	*	49.7[a]

* Not asked.

[a] The Van Leer survey.

To conclude, it is evident that a majority of Arabs feel strongly deprived and alienated, although a sizeable minority do not. Their grievances, which are well founded and politicized by their leaders, have become, since the mid-1970's, the basis for large-scale mobilization and struggle. However, the high levels of Arab deprivation, alienation, and protest should not be interpreted as rejection of Israel, but rather as a wish to reap the full fruits of Israeli citizenship. As noted in much of the evidence discussed earlier, there are many indicators to that effect. To mention just a few, Israeli Arabs compare their lives to other Israelis rather than to Arabs or Palestinian Arabs elsewhere, have confidence in the efficacy of Israeli democracy for advancing their cause, and consequently do no intend to move to a Palestinian state if it were established in the West Bank and Gaza Strip.

16

Issues as a Measure of Arab-Jewish Dissension

After concluding the discussion of the issues dividing Arabs and Jews, it is possible to characterize the scope and nature of the overall Arab-Jewish dissension. How deeply split are Arabs and Jews on the key issues? Two simple additive indexes are constructed to summarize the differences in opinions between and within the two sides.

The first index is designed as a summary measure of Arab dissidence and factionalism, namely, the extent to which Israeli Arabs dissent from the Jewish national consensus but also disagree among themselves on the main issues. To arrive at this index, a score of 1 is assigned to any respondent who takes a stand dissenting significantly from the Arab-Jewish status quo, and a score of 0 if he or she fails to do so.

The following seven representative stands are taken to indicate dissent from the Jewish consensus:
1. Favor the repeal of the Law of Return.
2. Agree to the establishment of a Palestinian state in the West Bank and Gaza Strip alongside Israel.
3. Define the collective identity of Israeli Arabs as Palestinian.
4. Maintain that goals of Arab education should be either Palestinian nationalism or the love of Israel as a common homeland for Arabs and Jews.
5. Hold that reduction of Arab-Jewish inequality should be an urgent state goal.
6. Support the establishment of an Arab university.
7. Approve of the use of general strikes as a means of struggle to improve conditions for Arabs.

As designed, the index indeed shows consensus among the Jews: 89% of the Jewish public and 73% to 93% of the Jewish leaders score 0 to

2 points (Table 16.1). This Jewish consensus cuts across all the major internal divisions of class, political affiliation, ethnicity, and religious observance.

Table 16.1 Arabs' Dissidence and Factionalism

	Arab Public	Estab. Affil. Arab Lead.	Rakah Affil. Arab Lead.	Rejec- tion. Arab Lead.	Jewish Public	Dovish Jewish Lead.	Jewish Arab- ists	Hawkish Jewish Lead.
Degree of acceptance-rejection of the Israeli Jewish consensus								
Fully accepting								
0	0.4	0.0	0.0	0.0	29.2	26.1	39.0	49.2
1	1.5	0.0	0.0	0.0	37.4	17.9	31.1	23.4
2	8.2	24.0	0.0	0.0	22.4	29.2	18.3	20.7
3	10.8	16.0	3.1	0.0	8.8	2.7	5.8	3.4
4	18.6	8.0	3.1	0.0	1.4	0.0	5.8	3.4
5	18.7	28.0	6.3	29.0	0.7	8.9	0.0	0.0
6	24.8	24.0	37.5	67.7	0.1	5.9	0.0	0.0
7	17.1	0.0	50.0	3.2	0.0	9.2	0.0	0.0
Totally rejecting								

Arab dissidence is evidenced by the 90% of the Arab public, 76% of the establishment-affiliated Arab leaders, 100% of the Rakah-affiliated Arab leaders, and 100% of the rejectionist Arab leaders opposing the status quo (scoring 3 or more points on the index). Arabs as a whole (including over three quarters of the establishment-affiliated leaders) do not share the Jewish views on key issues, and hence do constitute a dissident minority in Israel.

This massive dissent does not negate internal Arab factionalism, however. Arabs are scattered along the entire continuum of the index. Some 10% of them score 0-2 points, 29% 3-4, 43.5% 5-6, and 17% 7 points.

Like the Arabs, consensus among the Jews on certain issues does not preclude internal disagreement on other questions of Arab-Jewish coexistence. A measure was constructed to capture the varying degrees of rejection by Jews of the Arabs as a national Palestinian minority with equal rights.

The following seven representative stands are considered to indicate Jewish intransigence, rejection of Arabs, and reluctance to adapt Israel to Arab needs:

1. View Israel as the homeland of Jews only.
2. Feel that Israel is doing too much for Israeli Arabs.
3. Favor a strong-arm policy toward Israeli Arabs.
4. Believe that it is impossible to trust most Israeli Arabs.
5. Object to the establishment of an Arab university.

6. Object to the Israeli Arabs' use of general strikes as a means of struggle.

7. Are unwilling to have an Israeli Arab as a superior in a job.

Of course, Israeli Arabs do not identify themselves with these views.[1] Only 19% of the Jews who obtain 0-2 points are clearly receptive of Arabs, whereas the overwhelming majority exhibit varying degrees of rejection of Arabs (Table 16.2). This proportion of receptivity of Arabs is higher among Jewish leaders: 26% of the hawkish leaders, 37% of the Arabists, and 68% of the dovish leaders.

Table 16.2 Jews' Intransigence and Factionalism

	Jewish Public	Dovish Jewish Leaders	Jewish Arabists	Hawkish Jewish Leaders
Degree of acceptance-rejection of the Arabs in Israel as a national Palestinian minority with equal rights				
Fully accepting				
0	1.9	21.0	3.2	0.0
1	6.2	18.1	2.6	0.0
2	10.9	29.2	31.6	25.8
3	14.2	18.7	26.3	9.4
4	16.7	13.0	25.9	30.8
5	18.3	0.0	10.5	26.8
6	19.2	0.0	0.0	3.6
7	12.6	0.0	0.0	3.6
Totally rejecting				

Jews are, however, divided on their overall orientation toward Arabs. Along with the 19% (scoring 0-2 points) who are fully receptive of Arabs, 31% (3-4 points) are only partially receptive, 37.5% (5-6 points) are moderately rejecting, and 13% (7 points) are totally rejecting.

Together, the two summary measures show several tendencies. First, as far as Jews are concerned, most Arabs are dissident on the critical issues of Arab-Jewish coexistence. Second, as far as Arabs are concerned, most Jews are intransigent in their views concerning the Israeli Arabs' status as a Palestinian national minority in the Jewish state. Third, the Arabs' dissidence and the Jews' intransigence testify to Israel's character as a deeply divided society. And fourth, Arab-Jewish dissension is softened by the factionalism prevalent in both communities with regard to the orientation toward the other side. This question of factionalism is further examined in the next chapters.

[1]It is not possible to compute the index for Arabs because questions 3, 4, and 7 were not presented to the Arabs.

Part Two

TYPOLOGIES

17

Studying Orientation Types

Typologies can be considered as heuristic tools with three basic functions. They serve as handy descriptions by compactly summarizing numerous and diverse phenomena. They also facilitate theorizing by encouraging the search for social milieux which mold types and theories of inter-type change. The third function is a social one, to correct popular misconceptions and inform public policies.

Frequent misuse has caused typologies to fall into disrepute. Tiryakian (1968) discusses their problematic use. They distort reality by disregarding certain individual features and hence misclassifying people. The temptation to reify types is also great. Furthermore, they are often incorrectly treated as de facto explanations thereby hampering further theorizing. Another widespread misconception of types, as static, erroneously assumes that human beings are incapable of changing significantly. In time, types also undergo labeling and consequent stigmatization, even though they were originally intended to be and were in fact neutral.

Typologies have to meet several methodological criteria: the dimension on which types are differentiated should be critical to the research objectives, clearly defined, and yield a manageable number of types which are both comprehensive and mutually exclusive.

Convinced that the triple gains (i.e., succinct description, theorizing leverage, and social applicability) of a typology outweigh its potential pitfalls, I constructed a typology of orientations of the Arab minority and a typology of orientations of the Jewish majority according to the above guidelines. I will show that these typologies can serve as a useful device for the study of political factionalism among Arabs and Jews and of the relations between them.

The comparison between Arab and Jewish views on key issues of coexistence, discussed above, discloses polarization. This may be, at least in part, due to the fact that such a comparison tends to overemphasize disagreement between two sides and, as a result, to underplay the discord within each. Yet, a pronounced difference of opinion between two communities does not necessarily exclude the existence of sharp internal divisions, which must also be examined in order to reach a balanced assessment.

The two typologies, presented below, are based on the firm assumption that Israeli Arabs and Jews are nonassimilating groups; hence, persons who favor an open society, where nationality is completely privatized or neutralized and assimilation is acceptable and common, are too infrequent to be a viable type. These rare "egalitarianist" Arabs and Jews desire to transform Israel into a non-ethnic state that is neither Arab nor Jewish, and geared neither to Zionism nor to Palestinian nationalism. For this reason, the egalitarianist type is excluded from the Arab and Jewish typologies.

The methodology of the construction of the typologies used here needs some clarification. In a previous study on Arab-Jewish relations (Smooha, 1983), I applied an empiricist method. Over 60 of the questions concerning attitudes toward Arab-Jewish coexistence were subject to a factor analysis; 7-14 of these questions were selected to represent the major factors, and the chosen items scored to obtain an additive index. Finally four types, classifying the entire sample, were derived by imposing two cutting points on the continuous index. Although a careful discretion was exercised throughout, there was still appreciable arbitrariness in deciding the final types. The procedure was open to the criticism that the types might be indistinct, methodological artifacts. Doubts lingered despite the later successful testing of the validity and utility of the typology.

To overcome these weaknesses, an alternative, "substantive" method is used in this study. It is grounded on the premise that in an ideologized and politicized society like Israel, orientation types reflect the ideological and political streams prevalent in the general population. Hence each type is defined in advance according to a set of attitudes corresponding to a known ideological outlook. The predetermination of the meaning and distinctiveness of each type lends credence to the resultant typology. Its validity is further strengthened by allowing the data empirically to determine the proportion of the sample falling into the preset types and the relative frequency of each type.

It is possible, of course, to compare the results of the empiricist and substantive typologies and to generalize about the genuine differences among Arabs and Jews beyond the arbitrariness of the techniques used.

The following discussion will begin with the Arab typology and the attitudinal indicators utilized to compose it. The Arab types will then be compared on various attitudes, behaviors, and background factors. Following this analysis, a typology of Jews will be presented and analyzed. Finally, some implications will be drawn from the two typologies.

18

Arab Orientation Types

The accommodation-militancy continuum is the most important dimension on which minority responses differ (Vander Zanden, 1972:305-06). It provides a universal rationale for identifying four major orientations. An "accommodationist" orientation accepts the status quo and seeks concessions through the system. In contrast, a "rejectionist" stance negates the present situation altogether and challenges it through independent action. In between are diverse minority responses, which can be seen as either a "reservationist" or "oppositionist" posture, depending on the amount of change and independence of struggle pursued.[1]

Constructing the Typology

In line with this universal rationale and the major ideological and political currents in the Arab sector, four Arab orientation types to Arab-Jewish coexistence are spelled out and identified by survey questions as follows:

1. *The accommodationist type.* Arabs who conform in their views to the Zionist establishment are considered accommodationist. They believe that by accepting the Jewish consensus and working through the system, they can best extract concessions from the Jews.

Arabs are classified as accommodationists if they meet 4-6 of the following conditions on which Jews agree: (1) accept Israel's preservation of a Jewish majority, (2) accept Israel's right to exist as a Jewish-Zionist state, (3) oppose protest abroad as a means of struggle to improve the

---

[1]There is also a fifth, "egalitarianist orientation," which stands for full equality and elimination of dominant-subordinate statuses. As indicated in Chapter 17, this extreme orientation hardly exists among israeli Arabs who constitute a nonassimilating minority.

Arab situation in Israel, (4) oppose general strikes, (5) favor the Israel-Egypt Peace Treaty, and (6) do not endorse the Arab refugees' right of repatriation to the territory within the Green Line.

2. *The reservationist type.* Many Arabs find themselves sandwiched between the Zionist establishment and the Communist opposition. They have reservations about both but do not wish to antagonize either. They reason that change can best be effected by organizing independently and negotiating with, rather than opposing, the authorities. Since the reservationists are still not crystallized organizationally, politically, or ideologically, their views are ambivalent and ambiguous. These rising, non-partisan Arabs attempt to steer an independent middle course between the two powerful rival establishments in the Arab sector – the governing-Zionist vs. the oppositionist-anti-Zionist.

Arabs are placed in the reservationist orientation if they take 4-6 of the following moderate stands: (1) do not deny Israel's right to exist as a Jewish-Zionist state, (2) do not agree that Zionism is racism, (3) do not endorse protest abroad, (4) oppose unlicensed demonstrations, (5) do not oppose the Israel-Egypt Peace Treaty, and (6) concede or consider conceding the Arab refugees' right of repatriation for a peace settlement.

3. *The oppositionist type.* The ideology and politics of the Israeli Communist Party (Rakah) serve as a guide to this Arab type. Rakah accepts Israel as a state but opposes its Zionist character. It falls clearly outside the Jewish consensus and, hence, is not taken into consideration by the Jews as a political ally or as a potential coalition partner. Oppositionist Arabs, like Rakah supporters, are convinced that only by challenging the Zionist establishment from the outside can they alter Israeli society.

To belong to the oppositionist type, Arabs have to assent to 4-6 of the following opinions: (1) deny Israel's right to exist as a Jewish-Zionist state, (2) hold that Zionism is racism, (3) endorse protest abroad, (4) do not oppose unlicensed demonstrations (5) do not endorse the Israel-Egypt Peace Treaty, and (6) oppose or have reservations about conceding the Arab refugees' right to repatriation.

4. *The rejectionist type.* Followers of the Sons of the Village Movement and the Progressive National Movement are certainly rejectionist. These Arabs totally negate Israel and desire to replace it with a secular-democratic or a Palestinian state in all the area of Palestine. Some less radical ones reject being an Arab minority in a Jewish state and wish to include the Galilee and Triangle, where most Israeli Arabs live, in a future, independent, Palestinian state. These rejectionists Arabs are not committed to the democratic process, and they endorse partly or fully the use of extra-legal means of struggle.

Rejectionist Arabs are identified by holding 4-6 of the following views in the survey: (1) deny Israel's right to exist, (2) oppose the recognition of Israel by the PLO, (3) endorse unlicensed demonstrations, (4) endorse the use of violence, (5) favor either a Palestinian state in all of Mandatory Palestine or Israel's withdrawal to the 1947 UN partition resolution borders, and (6) favor either a secular-democratic state instead of Israel or a Palestinian state that includes the Galilee and Triangle.

Evaluating the Typology

This set of definitions managed to classify 89% (1,017 of 1,140) of the Arab sample, a high percentage in view of the inconsistency of opinions expected of rank-and-file Arabs and non-responses. The typology satisfies several reliability checks. It correlates highly (r=0.71) with an empiricist typology based on an additive index, constructed according to the technique described in the previous chapter. The two typologies yield similar incidence of types and more or less identical findings with regard to inter-type differentiation and prediction.

The typology also passes initial tests of validity. The distribution into 11% accommodationists, 44% reservationists, 38% oppositionists, and 6.5% rejectionists is meaningful. The split between the 55% "moderates" and 45% "militants" in the typology is similar to the division between the 49% Arabs who voted in the 1981 Knesset elections for Jewish parties or Arab affiliated lists and the 51% who voted for the Rakah-dominated Democratic Front for Peace and Equality (DFPE).

The distribution into types is also significant in other respects. Each of the two accommodationist and rejectionist types amounts to only about a tenth of the Arab population. Of course, espousal of certain accommodating and rejecting opinions far exceeds 10%, but there is insufficient convergence to increase the two consistent, extreme types. The real division, therefore, is in the broad middle between the reservationists and the oppositionists, who are otherwise unequal in political power and ideological sophistication. While the reservationists lack an ideological and organizational base, the oppositionists behave as if they were the Arabs' exclusive establishment. The future has much in store for the politically untapped reservationist segment in the Arab sector. The Democratic Arab Party, which was established by Knesset Member Darawshe in 1988, may in time fill this gap.

Most important, the typology passes the critical validity test of distinguishing very well among the three Arab leadership groups included in the survey. Despite the internal heterogenity in views usually found among leaders belonging to the same political stream, 96% of the Arab leaders affiliated with the Zionist establishment fall into the accommodationist and reservationist types, 77% of those affiliated to

Rakah are classified as oppositionists, and 87% of the activists in the Sons of the Village Movement and the Progressive National Movement fit the rejectionist category (Table 18.1). This close fit shows that these types are real, authentic, political types rather than straw men.

Table 18.1 Arab Orientation Types

	Arab Public	Establishment Affiliated Arab Leaders	Rakah Affiliated Arab Leaders	Rejectionist Arab Leaders
Orientation type				
Accommodationist	11.3	24.0	3.3	0.0
Reservationist	43.9	72.0	20.0	0.0
Oppositionist	38.3	4.0	76.7	12.9
Rejectionist	6.5	0.0	0.0	87.1
Total	100.0	100.0	100.0	100.0
Number of cases	1,017	25	30	31

Test of significance for leaders only: Chi-square = 113.61175 , d.f = 6, p<0.000.

Differences in Views and Identity

The typology's most fundamental contribution lies in its parsimonious depiction of views with regard to the major issues in Arab-Jewish relations. This is particularly true for the views used to construct the typology. It must be emphasized that the ability of the typology to distinguish between the types on these views is not a methodological artifact because each of the types is constructed independently employing criteria that only partially overlap.

Table 18.2 reproduces the political views used in building the typology of the four Arab types. The differences among them are sharp indeed. For instance, Arabs opposing the resort to general strikes constitute 79% of the accommodationists, 20% of the reservationists, 4% of the oppositionists, and none of the rejectionists (Table 18.2). On the other hand, those denying Israel's right to exist as a Jewish-Zionist state are 18%, 31%, 87%, and 91%, respectively.

Disagreement among the four Arab types prevails in other issues related to Arab-Jewish coexistence (Table 18.3). To illustrate from the civic area, 15% of the accommodationists, 39% of the reservationists, 45% of the oppositionists, and 73% of the rejectionists reject Jews as a comparison group for assessing their own socioeconomic achievements; 9%, 42.5%, 79%, and 95.5%, respectively, feel dissatisfied with being Israeli citizens; and 34%, 48%, 73%, and 85%, respectively, oppose compulsory military or civil service for Arabs.

If orientation types are valid as comprehensive characterizations of Arab attitudes toward their minority status and the state, then they

Table 18.2 Arab Orientation Types by Constituent Components

	Accommoda-tionists	Reserva-tionists	Oppositionists	Rejection-ists
Total	11.3	43.8	38.3	6.5
Accommodationist orientation				
Accept Israel's preservation of a Jewish majority	79.6	17.8	4.5	1.5
Accept Israel's right to exist as a Jewish-Zionist state	58.4	13.2	2.6	0.0
Oppose protest abroad	77.4	22.8	4.9	6.2
Oppose general strikes	79.1	20.3	4.1	0.0
Favor Israel-Egypt Peace Treaty	94.9	64.0	16.0	7.7
Do not endorse the Arab refugees' right of repatriation	67.5	29.8	6.2	6.0
Reservationist orientation				
Do not deny Israel's right to exist as a Jewish-Zionist state	82.3	68.7	12.7	9.1
Do not agree that Zionism is racism	72.0	64.4	11.1	10.8
Do not endorse protest abroad	92.2	72.0	15.9	9.3
Oppose unlicensed demonstrations	91.3	86.2	46.5	27.7
Do not oppose Israel-Egypt Peace Treaty	97.4	96.4	54.9	24.6
Concede or consider conceding the Arab refugees' right of repatriation for a peace settlement	84.2	85.1	43.0	44.6
Oppositionist orientation				
Deny Israel's right to exist as a Jewish-Zionist state	17.7	31.3	87.4	90.9
Hold that Zionism is racism	27.9	35.6	88.8	89.2
Endorse protest abroad	7.8	28.0	84.1	90.6
Do not endorse Israel-Egypt Peace Treaty	5.2	36.0	84.0	92.3
Oppose or have reservations about conceding the Arab refugees' right to repatriation	49.0	61.4	90.1	86.2
Rejectionist orientation				
Deny Israel's right to exist	0.0	4.1	11.9	72.3
Oppose the recognition of Israel by the PLO	2.7	5.8	10.7	81.8
Endorse unlicensed demonstrations	0.0	1.0	8.3	60.0
Endorse the use of violence	2.6	2.7	7.5	58.5
Favor a Palestinian state in all of Mandatory Palestine or Israel's withdrawal to the 1947 UN partition resolution borders	14.0	26.6	47.7	93.6
Favor a secular-democratic state in place of Israel or a Palestinian state that includes the Galilee and Triangle	5.4	14.6	45.0	96.9

Table 18.3 Arab Orientation Types by Selected Attitudes

	Accommoda- tionists	Reserva- tionists	Opposi- tionists	Rejection- ists
Total	11.3	43.8	38.3	6.5
Reject Jews as a comparison group for assessing own socioeconmic achievements	15.2	38.6	45.0	73.0
Think that Arabs cannot be equal citizens of Israel as a Jewish-Zionist state and cannot identify themselves with the state	23.7	34.2	74.1	87.7
The most preferred solution to the Israeli-Arab conflict is proposed by				
Tehiya, Likud	12.6	9.2	1.0	1.6
Labor	65.5	43.6	9.3	3.2
Shelli, Rakah	13.8	31.8	41.2	9.7
PLO	8.0	15.4	48.5	85.5
Feel closer to Arabs in the West Bank and Gaza Strip than to Jews in Israel	3.6	20.3	60.7	90.8
Agree that neighborhoods should be separate for Arabs and Jews	28.7	31.0	51.8	66.7
Oppose compulsory military or civil service for Arabs	33.9	48.4	72.9	84.8
Hold that the best political organization for Arabs is the formation of independent Arab nationalist parties	2.7	7.4	30.0	58.1
Favor Arab self-rule in the Galilee and Triangle	14.5	24.2	42.0	64.6
Unwilling to leave the Galilee and Triangle as parts of Israel if a Palestinian state were to be established	36.7	31.8	55.6	90.1
Consider the PLO as truly representative of the Arabs in Israel	7.6	34.0	69.2	88.9
Hold that Arab education should be Palestinian in its goal	1.8	14.0	47.8	83.1
Feel that it is impossible to trust most Jews in Israel	37.2	54.3	79.7	95.5
Believe that most Jews in Israel are racist	41.2	58.7	82.5	97.0
Believe that most or all Israeli Arabs hate Jews	14.9	21.7	34.5	69.3
Believe that most or all Israeli Arabs are loyal to the state	63.7	53.7	39.5	23.4
Unwilling to live in a mixed neighborhood	38.2	44.9	62.5	75.8
Hold that Arab youth do not have reasonable chances of fulfilling their occupational aspirations in Israel	30.4	43.9	73.9	77.3
Feel dissatisfied with Israeli democracy	18.5	34.1	74.4	89.4
Feel dissatisfied with being an Israeli citizen	8.6	42.5	79.3	95.5
Would feel more at home in an Arab country than in Israel	2.7	11.5	36.8	70.7
Would rejoice or justify Fedayeen actions in which Israeli Jews were killed	20.9	51.1	80.3	95.2

should differ significantly in their national self-identity. Since orientation is conceptualized very broadly to refer to degree of acceptance of the existing political and social position of Arabs in Israeli society, it is expected to encompass national self-identity as an integral part. In fact, there is a strong relationship between orientation and identity: the more militant the orientation, the more Palestinian (or less Israeli) is self-identity.

This is precisely what is found. To illustrate, 94% of the accommodationists consider the term "Israeli" as an appropriate self-description but only 16% so perceive the term "Palestinian" (Table 18.4). The rejectionists feel exactly the opposite – 6% and 94%, respectively. That Palestinization of self-identity has become a reliable expression of orientation is evident in the differences in choice by types of the most fitting self-description. The correlations between orientation and the chosen self-identity is 0.53. As many as 88% of the accommodationists opt for non-Palestinian identities (Israelis, Israeli Arabs, Arabs); the reservationists are divided between 61% who define themselves as non-Palestinians and 26% as Israeli Palestinians (or Palestinians in Israel); the oppositionists are evenly split between 38% who see themselves as Israeli Palestinians and 40% as non-Israeli Palestinians (Palestinians, Palestinian Arabs) as against 82% of the rejectionists who regard themselves as non-Israeli Palestinians. More generally, although the Israeli and Palestinian components of national identity are accepted by the Arabs, the types differ markedly on which of the two components is more emphasized.

Table 18.4 Arab Orientation Types by National Self-Identity

	Accommodationists	Reservationists	Oppositionists	Rejectionists
Consider the term "Israeli" as an appropriate self-description	93.9	71.5	27.5	6.0
Consider the term "Palestinian" as an appropriate self-description	16.0	27.5	76.7	93.9
Define oneself as				
Israeli, Israeli Arab, Arab	87.8	61.0	22.2	6.1
Israeli Palestinian, Palestinian in Israel	10.4	25.9	37.7	12.1
Palestinian, Palestinian Arab	1.7	13.1	40.1	81.8

Differences in Behaviors

These divergences in the political views and national self-identity between Arab orientation types demonstrate the great utility of the typology as a summarizing descriptive tool. It has further uses, however. One of them pertains to behaviors. Since the typology is designed to consist of attitudes only, it would be more useful if it can also differentiate among behaviors. Table 18.5 shows how Arab types differ in certain behaviors, namely, newspapers read, contacts, politics, and protest activities.

Table 18.5 Arab Orientation Types by Selected Behaviors

	Accommoda-tionists	Reserva-tionists	Opposi-tionists	Rejection-ists
Newspapers read				
An Arabic newspaper	36.3	49.1	67.1	61.4
Al-Ittihad or a West Bank newspaper	7.5	20.9	53.7	49.1
Contacts				
Have Jewish friends	76.5	67.6	65.9	47.0
Have visited the West Bank or Gaza Strip				
during the past two years	37.7	40.7	60.0	60.0
Maintain ties with relatives in West Bank, Gaza				
Strip or Arab countries	13.9	24.4	35.3	36.4
Party membership				
Member of a Jewish political party	18.1	13.6	5.6	1.9
Member of Rakah	0.0	1.5	9.7	3.6
Voting in the 1977 elections				
Jewish parties or affiliated Arab lists	93.4	83.0	35.2	26.1
DFPE (Rakah)	6.6	17.0	64.8	73.9
Voting intention in the 1981 elections				
Jewish parties, affiliated Arab lists	17.0	32.9	15.4	2.9
Independent coalitionable Arab party if				
established	73.6	40.0	9.5	2.9
DFPE (Rakah)	1.9	10.3	42.9	31.4
Independent nationalist Arab party if				
established	7.5	16.8	31.9	62.9
Protest activities				
Participated in the 1976 Land Day strike	8.0	28.8	57.3	58.5
Have demonstrated in recent years in protest				
of treatment of Arabs	0.9	6.2	21.3	21.3
Have suffered privations (economic loss or				
political harassment) resulting from protest				
on behalf of Arabs	0.9	8.3	24.0	28.1

The more militant Arab types are more likely to read a newspaper in Arabic, and particularly the Communist *Al-Ittihad* or a West Bank daily, which tend to be critical of the government. For instance, while 7.5% of the accommodationists and 21% of the reservationists read one of these anti-government newspapers, 54% of the oppositionists, and 49% of the rejectionists do so. These figures would suggest that the more militant types attend probably more to foreign broadcasts, including PLO stations, which reinforce their critical views.

Type of contact also highlights differences in orientation. The rejectionists, as one would expect, have fewer Jewish friends than the accommodationists (76.5% vs. 47%). On the other hand, these two polar types differ at a ratio of 60% to 38% in paying visits to the West Bank and Gaza Strip and at a ratio of 36% to 14% in maintaining ties with relatives across the Green Line (including Arab countries).

Most directly pertinent, however, are differences in political behavior. Only 15% of the Arabs report party affiliation – 11% to Jewish parties and 4% to Rakah. By and large the accommodationists and reservationists belong to the Jewish parties whereas the oppositionists belong to Rakah and the rejectionists to neither. A similar division obtains with regard to voting in the 1977 national elections. When asked about their voting intentions in the next Knesset elections, the accommodationists and reservationists would vote for the Jewish parties or Arab parties affiliated or cooperating with them, the oppositionists would vote more for Rakah but also for nationalist Arab parties if established, and the rejectionists would vote for nationalist Arab parties. In a way, these differences in the politics of the types directly validate the whole typology which aims primarily to capture the ideological-political divisions within the Arab population.

Arab types clearly differ in the degree of engagement in the rising Arab protest activities. To illustrate, 8% of the accommodationists, 29% of the reservationists, 57% of the oppositionists, and 58.5% of the rejectionists report participation in the 1976 Land Day strike to protest impending land expropriations. Given the official censoring and intimidation, participation in this landmark strike is a clearcut measure of politicization and militancy. The more militant types also report more participation in public demonstrations and pay more personally in political harassment and economic loss as a result of their involvement in protest.

Determinants

Determinants are factors that shape orientation. They are background or behaviors which predispose or reinforce the degree of militancy. Most of them are solely causes, but some are themselves affected by the orientation through reciprocal causation.

The classification of determinants into four sets of predictors, each accompanied by a rationale, follows:

1.   *Susceptibility.* The literature and public opinion commonly hold that certain background characteristics, of which youth and education are prime examples, expose Arabs to radicalization pressures (Peres, 1970). These in turn activate other radicalizing processes such as Westernization and relative deprivation to be discussed shortly.

2.   *Westernization.* Theory and research, starting to appear in the 1970's, have established modernization (industrialization, urbanization,

secularization, Westernization) as correlates of ethnic mobilization and militancy (See and Wilson, 1988). As Esman maintains, "under conditions of modernization, latent communal identities become manifest and are mobilized politically along communal, not national, lines. Aspirations and expectations tend to increase more rapidly than resources, and the competitive struggle for scarce political, status and economic values become more intense and thus more communally divisive" (1973:69). Accordingly Israeli Arabs are expected to radicalize as they Westernize because of the gradual replacement of traditional identities by non-Israeli national identity and because of the widening gap between their growing needs and achievements. Arab Westernization is measured by endorsing certain modern views: the idea that modern values and practices should prevail in Israel, abolition of the traditional value of hamula loyalty, and the adoption of the norm of small family size.

3. *Contact.* Social psychologists (e.g., Amir, 1976) stress that not contact per se but its quality, determines its effect on intergroup relations. Accordingly friendly relations with Jews, especially if they extend to visiting terms, are predicted to increase Arab accommodation by facilitating communication, understanding, equality, and social integration. They also encourage compromise and reconciliation by multiplying cross-pressures among Arabs. On the other hand, frequent contacts with Palestinians in the West Bank and Gaza Strip as well as continuous ties with relatives there or in Arab countries are supposed to have a radicalizing impact by exposing Arabs to militant perspectives and pressures.

4. *Deprivation.* Both absolute and relative deprivation are expected to radicalize Arabs. Deprivation is best indexed by the following three measures. First is community status, viz., the higher ranking and greater favor granted to Druzes as compared to other Arabs. Second is the extent of loss suffered through land expropriations. Third is satisfaction with local services.[2] It follows, therefore, that Arabs who are Druze, unaffected by land expropriation, or satisfied with local services are more likely to be more accommodating.

In testing the above four hypothesized sets of predictors, three variables are selected for each set. A multiple stepwise regression analysis is first conducted for each set separately and then for all the 12 predictors together.

---

[2]There is a low inverse correlation between satisfaction with and actual level of local services. As compared to less urbanized areas, residents in more urbanized areas experience greater relative deprivation and hence greater dissatisfaction because expectations rise faster than the level of services.

Both tests of regression analysis show the superior effectiveness of deprivation and contact variables to the other sets of factors. Deprivation accounts for 20% of the variance on the typology, contact 7%, susceptibility 5%, and Westernization less than 2% (Table 18.6). In order of predictive power, the five best predictors rank as follows:

1. Dissatisfaction with local educational and cultural services
2. Community status
3. Effect of land expropriations
4. Visiting terms with Jews
5. Visits to the West Bank and Gaza Strip

All of these predictors are measures of deprivation and contact.

Table 18.6 A Regression Analysis of Predictors of Arab Orientation Types

	N	r	R	Beta
Susceptibility				
Size of locality	1,017	–0.18	0.18	–0.16755*
Education	1,016	0.13	0.21	0.07645*
Age	1,017	–0.10	0.22	–0.06621*
Westernization				
Objection to the traditional value of hamula				
loyalty	1,010	0.09	0.09	0.10920*
Desirable family size	1,001	0.07	0.12	0.07169*
Endorsement of modern values	1,013	0.04	0.13	0.03580*
Contact				
Ties with relatives across the Green Line	997	–0.20	–0.20	–0.16866*
Visiting terms with Jews	1,013	0.14	–0.24	–0.14051*
Visits to the West Bank and Gaza Strip	1,001	0.17	0.27	0.12899*
Deprivation				
Dissatisfaction with local educational and				
cultural services	1,015	0.37	0.37	0.32152*
Effect of land expropriations	789	–0.29	0.43	–0.21981*
Community status (Druze/other)	1,017	0.15	0.45	0.11276*
Five best predictors				
Dissatisfaction with local educational and				
cultural services	1,015	0.37	0.37	0.30154*
Community status (Druze/other)	1,017	0.30	0.45	0.21802*
Effect of land expropriations	789	–0.29	0.49	–0.17795*
Visiting terms with Jews	1,013	–0.14	0.50	–0.13091*
Visits to the West Bank and Gaza Strip	1,001	0.17	0.52	0.12333*

*Statistically significant at least at 0.01 level.

With the notable exception of community, types are not well distinguished by their social background. Accommodation is highest among the Druzes (though only 41% of them fall into the accommodationist type), medium among Bedouin and Christians, and comparatively lowest among non-Bedouin Moslems (Table 18.7). The young, college-educated and urbanized Arabs are only slightly more militant than the average.

Table 18.7 Arab Orientation Types by Social Background

	Total	Accommoda-tionists	Reserva-tionists	Opposi-tionists	Rejection-ists
Total	100.0	11.3	43.8	38.3	6.5
Age					
18-25	100.0	7.2	41.3	41.0	10.5
26-35	100.0	14.6	42.1	38.2	5.0
36-45	100.0	15.2	44.6	37.5	2.7
46-55	100.0	9.7	57.3	30.1	2.9
56+	100.0	11.2	42.7	39.3	6.7
Education					
0-8	100.0	13.4	46.5	34.5	5.6
9-12	100.0	6.0	41.9	44.4	7.7
13+	100.0	8.9	30.0	51.1	10.0
Size of Locality					
15,000 persons or more	100.0	5.8	39.4	49.7	5.1
10,000-14,999	100.0	4.6	33.0	49.5	12.8
5,000-9,999	100.0	7.3	55.5	32.0	4.4
Under 5,000	100.0	17.3	45.7	30.5	6.5
Community					
Druze	100.0	40.6	49.5	9.9	0.0
Bedouin	100.0	14.7	49.1	31.0	5.2
Christian	100.0	7.5	52.9	36.4	3.2
Non-Bedouin Moslem	100.0	7.0	39.2	45.0	8.8

How can the failure of susceptibility variables be explained? The most promising among them is education which also correlates with age. But contrary to popular and certain scientific expectations, education proves to have a limited effect on orientation. The view that exposure to dissident nationalism and relative deprivation increase with education is not supported by the data. While such radicalizing pressures exist, countervailing forces operate to accommodate the educated by enhancing their stake in the system (e.g., by making them more dependent on the majority for employment and by providing more opportunities for interethnic contact).

Compared to our study, Peres' study (Peres and Yuval-Davis, 1969), which establishes education as an important factor, is based on a less representative sample and uses a less comprehensive measure of orientation. Our negative results are also in line with other studies. Benjamin and Peleg (1977:141), contrary to their own expectations, find that Israeli Arab students on first entering a university are more militant than on graduating. Tessler, on the basis of a survey conducted in the Northern region in 1974, concludes that "higher levels of education do not appear to be associated with a rejection of Israeliness" (1977:322). Nakhleh (1979) finds moderate orientation among Arab university students and graduates, attributing to them conservative, petit bourgeois mentality.

The widespread misconception of the educated as radical is an overgeneralization of the greater militancy of Arab university students. It is understandable in view of the coalescence of the rebellious age of youth with the relative impunity of student status in this transitional period of life. The false radical image of the educated Arab has much to do with the activity of student leaders. They attract a great deal of public attention because of their outspoken dissidence. The leadership of the Arab student committees has been the scene of a bitter struggle between oppositionists (Rakah supporters) and rejectionists (activists in the Sons of the Village Movement or the Progressive National Movement).

The explanatory power of deprivation and contact as against the poor performance of susceptibility have a wider implication. It suggests that orientation is to a large extent a product of the treatment afforded to Arabs in Israeli society. Militancy is a reaction to the unfavorable treatment certain communities receive (such as Moslem vs. Druze), unsatisfactory local services, scarcity of friendly or visiting relations with Jews, and land expropriations. These are all subject to Jewish intervention rather than inevitable objective misfortunes. The affecting factors tend to be of a kind amenable to policy making while those found to be of limited effect, such as age and education, tend to be of an intractable nature. This demonstrates the great importance of policy toward Arabs in Israel.

19

Jewish Orientation Types

Majorities differ a great deal in their attitudes toward their minorities. Simpson and Yinger (1972) distinguish among six majority policies: assimilation, pluralism, legal protection, population transfer, continued subjugation, and extermination. Although these are the modal policies, they are neither exhaustive nor mutually exclusive.

By drawing on this and other classifications, it is possible to suggest four analytically discernible orientation types among dominant majority members in societies where assimilation is neither desirable nor feasible: conciliationists, pragmatists, hardliners, and exclusionists. Conciliationists accept minority members as equals and are ready to make certain changes in the social structure to promote ethnic equality. Pragmatists support relations of dominance but would make certain concessions necessary for keeping this relationship. Hardliners seek to reinforce their dominant position without making concessions to the minority. Exclusionists desire to do away with minority-majority statuses through the total removal of the minority from the country.

In societies where assimilation is a legitimate option, however, a fifth "egalitarianist type" usually exists. Egalitarianists stand for opening up society by free mixing, doing away with relations of dominance, and striving for complete equality between the subordinate and dominant groups.

Whether these five orientation types all exist in a given society and how widespread they are depend upon the main ideological and political forces operating in the country. In a highly ideologized and politicized society like Israel, the Jewish political parties shape and nurture all five types in the Jewish population. Although most Jewish political parties lack a clear policy toward the Arab minority and although no one-to-one correspondence between the political parties and orientations toward

Israeli Arabs can be assumed, there does exist a rough fit that may serve as a rationale for constructing a typology for Israeli Jews.

Overall, four party clusters correspond to four orientations: the small Zionist, liberal (or "leftist" as they are known in the Israeli political spectrum) parties propagate a conciliationist orientation; the Labor Party promotes a pragmatist orientation; the Likud camp assumes a hardline orientation; and the Kach Party disseminates an exclusionist orientation.

This crude correspondence is grounded both in the historical origin of the parties and in their current positions on the central issues of Israeli politics; i.e., the Israeli-Arab conflict, democracy, and religion. The contrast between Herut and Mapam well illustrates this point. Herut's hardline orientation toward Israeli Arabs is in line with its pre-state Revisionist supremacist ideology with regard to the Arab question (Gorny, 1987); its post-state, neo-Revisionist commitment to Greater Israel (Peleg, 1987; Avineri, 1986); its dilution of the democratic ethos by nationalist excesses; and its strong sympathy for Jewish Orthodoxy, the Israeli version of which is intolerant of Arabs. In contradistinction, Mapam's conciliationist orientation toward the Arab minority conforms to its advocacy of a binational state with a Jewish majority before 1948, its championing of civil rights since 1948, its pushing an aggressive land-for-peace policy, and its frowning on religion.

There is no Jewish political party (or an ideological movement of significance) that advocates an egalitarianist orientation, because Israeli Jews are as nonassimilating as are Israeli Arabs. Egalitarianism would imply de-Judaization and de-Zionization of Israel and its recasting into either a secular-democratic state, in which Arab and Jewish statuses will be privatized, or a binational state, where Arab and Jewish parity will be instituted without the guarantee of a Jewish majority. Only Rakah, the Communist Party, espouses egalitarianism; but as an anti-Zionist party, it receives little support from Jews.[1] In fact, none of the Jewish leaders in the survey endorses the possibility that "Arabs will live as an equal people in Israel as a non-Jewish state" (Table 10.4). It also turns out that the 3% of the Jewish public who favor this radical alternative are actually inconsistent or confused on the issue.

For these reasons, the fourfold typology of the Jewish general public to be described below excludes the egalitarianist as a distinct type.

---

[1]Before 1948 a small intellectual group known as Brit Shalom, advocated the idea of a binational state even without a Jewish majority, but it was too weak to have an effect (Flapan, 1979:163-89). While insisting on a Jewish majority, Hashomer Hatzair (an important left-wing party) also supported this solution during the British Mandate. After the proclamation of the state, the egalitarianist position ceases, however, to be a viable option among the Jews.

Constructing the Typology

In accordance with the above rationale and for the purpose of this study, four Jewish orientation types are spelled out as follows:

1. *The conciliationist type.* The most liberal Zionist Jews in Israel insist on guaranteeing for Arabs full civil rights, equality, and integration into Israeli society, while keeping the state both Jewish and Zionist. They do not see any contradiction between Zionism and democracy, but would prefer democracy in most cases when a contradiction did develop. They criticize Israel's policies toward Israeli Arabs and advocate new policies that aim at compensating for past injustices and advancing Arab-Jewish equality and integration without assimilation. The conciliationists are close in outlook to the small leftist political parties: Shelli, Citizens Rights Movement, Mapam, Shinui (Change), and Independent Liberals. In addition to their conciliatory orientation toward Israeli Arabs, the conciliationists belong to the so-called Israeli "peace camp" – Peace Now and other dovish Zionist circles – which prides itself on its willingness to exchange peace for territory.

Jews in the survey who subscribe to 4-6 of the following views are classified as conciliationist: (1) see Israel as a common homeland for Arabs and Jews, (2) hold that the state should not prefer Jews to Arabs, (3) endorse the love of Israel as the common homeland of Arabs and Jews to be the goal of Jewish education, (4) consider the closing of the socioeconomic gap between Arabs and Jews to be an urgent, important state goal, (5) feel that the state does too little for the Arabs in Israel, and (6) oppose the idea that Israel should seek and use any opportunity to encourage Arabs to leave the country.

2. *The pragmatist type.* At the heart of the pragmatist orientation is the Labor Party's position vis-à-vis Israeli Arabs. During the first three decades of statehood, the governing Labor Party instituted a policy of control over Arabs while extending them civil rights, development funds, jobs outside their places of residence, and incorporation into Jewish institutions (e.g., the Histadrut). It still acts on the assumption that if a proper mix of inducements and sanctions were applied, Arabs would maintain law and order and contribute to the well-being of the state, even if they did not identify with it. Another belief is that as long as the Israeli-Arab conflict persists, there will be no solution to the Arab problem; hence practical arrangements should be made to reconcile the promise of equality and integration with the pressing needs of national security and continued construction of the Jewish state.

To be placed in the category of the pragmatist type, Jews in the survey have to endorse 4-6 of the following stands: (1) advocate the present policy toward the Arab minority or a policy of greater equality and integration between Arabs and Jews, (2) do not endorse a strong-arm policy toward the Arabs in Israel, (3) consider the closing of the socioeconomic gap between Arabs and Jews to be an important – but not necessarily urgent – state goal, (4) do not feel that the state does too much for the Arabs in Israel, (5) believe that it is possible to improve the Arab situation to a great or substantial degree by such acceptable democratic means as persuasion and political pressure, and (6) do not endorse the outlawing of Rakah.

3. *The hardliner type.* The hardline orientation toward Israeli Arabs approximates the positions taken by the Likud, the religious parties, and to some extent Tehiya and other hawkish Zionist circles. According to this viewpoint, the Arabs should be granted rights and opportunities to the extent that they demonstrate resignation to minority status in a Jewish-Zionist state and discharge all their civil duties. At present, they are denied full equality because they identify with the hostile Arab world, neither serve in the army nor render civil service, and behave in ways that raise doubts about their loyalty to the state. For this reason, surveillance and restrictions over the Arab population must be continued and even increased.

The hardliners are identified by supporting 4-6 of the following opinions: (1) prefer the Jewish-Zionist character of the state to democracy if the two conflict, (2) advocate a strong-arm policy toward the Arabs in Israel, (3) feel that it is impossible to trust most Arabs in Israel, (4) consider Arabs in Israel to be a certain or substantial danger to national security, (5) consider the closing of the socioeconomic gap between Arabs and Jews as neither an urgent nor important state goal, and (6) advocate the outlawing of Rakah.

4. *The exclusionist type.* Jews who believe that the Arabs should either unreservedly submit to Jewish rule or leave the country fit the exclusionist type. They perceive the very presence of Arabs in the Jewish state to be Israel's defect and liability. They feel that Jews have exclusive right to the land, the state, institutions, resources, and opportunities, and that the existence of an Arab minority, especially one that is not loyal, impairs Israel's exclusivity, mission, and integrity. These views are reminiscent of Kahane's but they fall short of his stand because of their failure to call openly for the Arabs' organized emigration, disenfranchisement, subordination, and forced segregation and for the establishment of a Jewish theocracy.

The questionnaire does not include enough questions for adequate identification of the exclusionist type. It is necessary, therefore, to resort to just three items for making this categorization. Jews are categorized as exclusionist if they accept all of the following views: (1) advocate the idea that Israel should seek and use any opportunity to encourage Arabs to leave the state, (2) totally oppose having an Arab as their superior in a job, and (3) feel that the state does too much for the Arabs in Israel.

Evaluating the Typology

Analysis of the questionnaire responses shows that 85% (1,082 of 1,267) of the Jews in the survey fall into one of the four orientation types, thus demonstrating the relevance and comprehensiveness of the typology. This achievement in classifying the overwhelming majority of rank-and-file Jews leaves only 15% unclassified because of their holding other sets of views, inconsistency, or non-response.

The theoretically conceived, predetermined typology further proves its reliability through its strong association (r=0.72) with another kind of typology, which is constructed by applying cutoff points to an empirical, additive index. The two typologies also correspond to each other in their distribution of and differentiation among the four types.

The validity of the typology is evident in the close fit between the division into types and political divisions in the Jewish public. The distribution of types into 8% conciliationists, 33.5% pragmatists, 35% hardliners, and 23% exclusionists is very significant. It yields a split of 41.5% "liberals" and 58% "illiberals" on the Israeli Arab question that corresponds to the bifurcation of the Jewish public into 43% who voted for the Labor camp in the 1981 national elections and 57% who voted for the Likud camp.[2] The typology is also in line with the well-known asymmetry between the Jewish extreme types: the proportion of exclusionists is nearly three times that of conciliationists.

The typology is further validated by its potency in distinguishing between dovish and hawkish Jewish leaders. It succeeds well in classifying 50% of the dovish leaders compared to only 4% of the hawkish leaders as conciliationists, 0% and 29%, respectively, as hardliners, and none as exclusionists (Table 19.1). On the other hand, it is less satisfactory in placing 67% of the hawkish vs. 50% of the dovish leaders as pragmatists. The disproportionate categorization of hawkish leaders into the pragmatist type is probably due in part to the genuinely moderating impact of the ascendancy to power of Likud leaders and affiliates and in part to the fact that the group of hawkish leaders in the sample also includes some hawkish leaders from the Labor camp.

---

[2]The 43:57 Labor camp/Likud camp ratio in 1981 was computed only for Jewish voters; excluded were the Arab votes for these camps, the votes for the Democratic Front for Peace and Equality, and the votes cast for election lists that failed to win a seat in the Knesset.

Table 19.1 Jewish Orientation Types

	Jewish Public	Dovish Jewish Leaders	Jewish Arabists	Hawkish Jewish Leaders
Orientation type				
Conciliationist	7.6	50.0	26.7	4.2
Pragmatist	33.5	50.0	56.7	66.7
Hardliner	36.2	0.0	16.7	29.2
Exclusionist	22.7	0.0	0.0	0.0
Total	100.0	100.0	100.0	100.0
Number of Cases	1,082	34	30	24

Test of significance for leaders only: Chi-square = 19.90210, d.f. = 6, p<0.0005.

All these methodological tests that the fourfold typology has passed show that it yields a rather useful, meaningful, and realistic set of types among the Jewish population.

Differences in Views

All Jews, irrespective of their particular orientation, share in common certain attitudes toward Israeli Arabs. They agree that Arabs should be allowed to keep their distinctive cultural heritage and separate institutions and do not expect them to assimilate culturally and socially.

There is also a consensus among Jews on Israel as a Jewish-Zionist state. Jews concur that Israel should retain a Jewish majority, the Law of Return, a commitment to Jewish immigration, a preference of Jews to Arabs, and the Jewish symbols of the state. Arabs are expected to reconcile themselves to these parameters of Israeli society, despite the unequalizing effects on their status.

In addition, Jews are united in rejecting certain views on the Israeli-Arab conflict. While they approve of the Israel-Egypt Peace Treaty, they oppose Israel's return to the pre-1967 borders, recognition of the PLO, formation of a separate Palestinian state in the West Bank and Gaza Strip, redivision of Jerusalem, and granting the right of repatriation to the Arab refugees. Jews are aware that Israeli Arabs do not share these beliefs, but they expect the latter not to act upon a contradictory set of opinions.

Beyond this fundamental Jewish consensus, the typology reveals that Jews disagree on the treatment of and tolerance toward Israeli Arabs. As expected, the four Jewish types are well distributed on all the views that were incorporated as components of the typology itself. For example, 90% of the conciliationists, 36% of the pragmatists, 15% of the hardliners, and 5% of the exclusionists see Israel as a common homeland for Arabs and Jews (Table 19.2). On the other hand, 7%, 28%, 54%, and 100%, respectively, endorse the idea that Israel should encourage Israeli Arabs to leave the country.

Table 19.2 Jewish Orientation Types by Constituent Components

	Concilia-tionists	Pragma-tists	Hard-liners	Exclu-sionists
Total	7.6	33.5	36.2	22.7
Conciliationist orientation				
See Israel as a common homeland of Arabs and Jews	90.1	36.0	15.4	4.7
Hold that the state should not prefer Jews to Arabs	71.1	19.7	8.9	0.0
Endorse the love of Israel as a common homeland of Arabs and Jews as a goal of Jewish education	74.0	25.1	19.6	11.0
Consider the closing of the socioeconomic gap between Arabs and Jews as an urgent, important state goal	69.0	21.0	7.6	2.6
Feel that the state does too little for the Arabs in Israel	87.4	22.2	8.8	0.0
Oppose the idea that Israel should seek and use any opportunity to encourage Arabs to leave the state	73.1	25.4	14.1	0.0
Pragmatist orientation				
Advocate the present policy or a policy of greater equality and integration between Arabs and Jews	79.5	86.9	41.2	17.7
Do not endorse a strong-arm policy toward the Arabs in Israel	82.0	91.8	32.4	16.2
Consider the closing of the socioeconomic gap between Arabs and Jews as an important (but not necessarily urgent) state goal	92.9	77.6	23.3	14.3
Do not feel that the state does too much for the Arabs in Israel	96.9	92.0	71.8	0.0
Believe that it is possible to improve to a great or substantial degree the Arab situation by acceptable democratic means	52.2	53.5	30.0	25.2
Do not endorse the outlawing of Rakah	84.2	81.4	24.3	20.0
Hardline orientation				
Would prefer the Jewish-Zionist character of the state to democracy if they conflict	16.4	42.3	76.2	79.0
Advocate a strong-arm policy toward the Arabs in Israel	18.0	8.2	67.7	83.8
Feel that it is impossible to trust most Arabs in Israel	19.9	33.3	94.1	92.6
Consider Arabs in Israel as a certain or substantial danger to national security	50.4	68.4	79.6	50.2
Consider the closing of the socioeconomic gap between Arabs and Jews as neither an urgent nor important state goal	7.1	22.4	76.7	85.7
Advocate the outlawing of Rakah	15.8	18.6	75.8	80.0
Exclusionist orientation				
Advocate the idea that Israel should seek and use any opportunity to encourage Arabs to leave the state	6.9	28.4	53.6	100.0
Are totally unwilling to have an Arab as one's superior in a job	12.1	14.5	49.4	100.0
Feel that the state does too much for the Arabs in Israel	3.1	7.9	28.2	100.0

These marked differences extend virtually to all questions of coexistence (Table 19.3). To cite just a few examples, 33% of the conciliationists, 46% of the pragmatists, 67% of the hardliners, and 83% of the exclusionists hold that neighborhoods should be separate for Arabs and Jews; 20%, 42%, 73%, and 86%, respectively, are unwilling to have Arab friends; 7%, 27%, 52%, and 76%, respectively, reject the Arab minority's right to live in Israel with full civil rights; and 0%, 4%, 16%, and 33%, respectively, maintain that the most appropriate solution to the Arab minority problem is to force them out of Israel.

Table 19.3 Jewish Orientation Types by Selected Attitudes

	Concilia-tionists	Pragma-tists	Hard-liners	Exclu-sionists
Total	7.6	33.5	36.2	22.7
Hold that Jews should not adopt Arab values and habits in addition to their own	21.1	35.1	55.9	72.9
Disapprove of the view that Arab culture is an important part of Israel's national culture	33.4	56.6	70.9	81.4
Disapprove of the Arab minority's right to live in Israel with full civil rights	7.3	27.1	52.0	75.9
Maintain that Israel should strengthen its Jewish-Zionist character despite having an Arab minority	40.0	67.5	82.5	90.3
Believe that Arabs cannot be equal citizens in Israel as a Jewish-Zionist state and cannot identify themselves with the state	43.6	33.3	51.2	67.6
Favor Jewish settlement of Judea and Samaria	11.9	32.4	52.7	78.3
Hold that neighborhoods should be separate for Arabs and Jews	32.6	45.8	66.9	83.0
Oppose the establishment of an Arab university	36.8	49.7	67.5	69.5
Oppose the possibility that Arabs organize independently, like Orthodox Jews, in order to advance their vital interests	23.9	37.0	61.6	77.8
Oppose state recognition of an Arab public body as the representative of Israeli Arabs	32.6	32.7	54.0	73.4
Hold that the most appropriate solution to the problem of the Arabs in Israel is				
To live as an equal people in Israel as a non-Jewish state	11.1	2.5	3.6	0.3
To live as a national minority with equal rights	79.6	54.0	23.5	8.2
To live in Israel only if resigned to their minority status in a state designed for Jews	9.4	39.1	56.7	58.1
To force them out of Israel	0.0	4.4	16.2	33.4
Oppose the extension to Arab localities of the same special assistance given to Jewish development towns	8.6	32.7	55.3	83.2
Favor an increase of surveillance over most Arabs in Israel	16.6	36.6	83.6	95.6
Oppose the Arab use of licensed demonstrations	14.6	18.1	42.7	70.9
Oppose the Arab use of general strikes	67.9	65.9	81.2	87.4
View most Arabs in Israel as primitive	24.0	19.3	44.8	62.5
Unwilling to have Arab friends	19.8	41.6	72.6	86.0

These divergent views enrich our understanding of the political outlooks of the four types and allow sketching the following portraits of the orientation of each group toward the Arab minority.

Conciliationists

Although constituting less than one tenth of the Jewish public and being able to count on the support of only the small, Zionist leftist political parties, the conciliationists draw on the high democratic and moral principles to which the Jewish state is formally committed. They are true believers in Arab-Jewish coexistence and in the satisfactory absorption, without assimilation, of Arabs into Israeli life if Jews would undertake the necessary "conciliation." They believe that the state should treat Arabs as a national minority having equal status, but without the state's compromising its Jewish-Zionist mission. They firmly acknowledge the Arab minority's right to live in Israel with full civil rights, and most are confident that Arabs can actually be equal citizens in Israel as a Jewish-Zionist state and can identify themselves with it. In their opinion, equal treatment of Arabs, which is expected in a political democracy, should take precedence over Israel's Jewish-Zionist character if the two collide.

Conciliationist Jews believe in greater equality between Arabs and Jews in all areas. Hence they call on Israel to adopt as an important, urgent state goal the closure of the Arab-Jewish socioeconomic disparity. They endorse a variety of steps to equalize opportunities, including the extension of special assistance to Arab localities and schools, hiring of Arab university graduates by the civil service and the Jewish economy, and enactment of a special anti-discrimination law.

These most liberal Jews are staunch supporters of cultural and social integration without amalgamation between the two national groups. They wish to see Arab culture cherished as an integral part of Israel's national culture and expect fellow Jews to adopt Arab values in addition to their own. Their views stem from a broader perspective that extols a certain degree of biculturalism as a vehicle for fostering coexistence. Accordingly, the mixing of some neighborhoods and schools and the complete integration of political parties are advocated in order to promote interethnic contact.

The conciliationists' liberalism is best reflected in their sensitivity to Arab civil rights. Although they would rather have Arabs integrated into the Jewish majority, they defend Israeli Arabs' right to control Arab education and religious institutions as well as to establish independent Arab organizations, such as a university, a trade union, and a press. Since Arabs are to be accepted as a national minority with equal rights, a national Arab leadership that truly represents their interests should be recognized by the state. Nevertheless, conciliationists do not favor the use by Arabs of extra-parliamentary means of struggle (like general strikes) because such tactics may alienate the Jewish public.

Of all Jews, the conciliationists are the most tolerant. They not only trust Arabs but also do not doubt the Arabs' ability to reach Jewish levels of development, and they are also willing to have Arab friends and even Arab bosses.

In the eyes of conciliationists, Arabs are basically trustworthy, loyal citizens, requiring neither increased surveillance nor strong-arm countermeasures to contain them. Although conciliationists disagree with Israeli Arabs on how to resolve the Palestinian question, they respect dissident opinions and dismiss such dissent as grounds for suspecting the Israeli Arabs' allegiance to the state.

Pragmatists

The one third of Jews who are classified as pragmatists are persons who generally concur with the status quo that the Labor Party fashioned during its 1948-77 rule and who sympathize with the strategy of Labor-oriented Jewish Arabists, as articulated by Shmuel Toledano, who served as the Prime Minister's Advisor on Arab Affairs from 1965 to 1976. According to this strategy, as long as the Israeli-Arab dispute lasts, there is no solution to the problem of Israeli Arabs; yet, it is feasible to keep them as acquiescent, law-abiding citizens. To that end, Israeli Arabs should be placed under economic and political controls; on the other hand, they should be granted civil rights, opportunities, and a stake in the existing system. Israel must strike a "moderate" course, assuring Arabs some benefits and partial integration and applying manipulation rather than confrontation.

The pragmatists share in common many of the conciliationists' liberal views. Both accept the Arab minority's right to live in Israel with full civil rights; both believe that Arabs can be equal citizens and can identify with the Jewish state; and both agree that Arabs should be trusted and integrated into Israeli society. The size, however, of the pragmatists' majority that takes these and many other liberal stands is smaller than that of the conciliationists.

The two types differ markedly on the wider question of how to strike a balance between Zionism and democracy. Whereas conciliationists are consistent in favoring democracy and extending equality to Israeli Arabs without renouncing Zionism, the pragmatists are inconsistent and ambivalent on the issue. Most pragmatists wish to strengthen Israel's Jewish-Zionist character despite the presence of an Arab minority, and most reject the idea that Israel is a common homeland for Arabs and Jews. At the same time, most of them are willing to yield the Zionist mission of the state when it clashes with the democratic, egalitarian treatment of the Arabs. Although the pragmatists think that Israel does enough for Israeli Arabs and that the closing of the socioeconomic gap between Arabs and Jews need not be an urgent state goal, they are nonetheless ready to offer the Arabs special help in order to raise their standards. At the same time, pragmatists will not give up the principle that Jews are entitled to preferential treatment in the Jewish state.

Hardliners

The hardliners bank on the ideology of the Likud camp, as articulated by spokesmen like cabinet minister Ariel Sharon. They tolerate Arabs, but only to the extent that the latter are resigned to life in a state geared to serve Jews, Judaism, and Zionism. Arabs who accommodate themselves should be rewarded with civil rights and opportunities, whereas others should be put in check and possibly made to suffer deprivation. Since Arab subversion is a real danger, the hardliners feel that Israel must defend itself by applying extensive and expanding controls as needed.

Hardliners are totally committed to Israel as a Jewish-Zionist state and to its strengthening as such. They are undecided on the question whether Israeli Arabs can be equal citizens and can identify themselves with Israel as a Jewish-Zionist state, because some Arabs are perceived as being capable of accommodating themselves and, hence, as deserving equal rights while others are not. At any rate, the hardliners' devotion to Israel's Jewish-Zionist mission is so firm that it justifies the suspension of democratic rights for, and the equal treatment of, Arabs whenever necessary.

The overwhelming majority of hardliners feel that most Arabs in Israel cannot be trusted. Hence they approve various measures to restrict Arab political behavior. Arabs should not, for example, be allowed control of their separate institutions such as schools, and they should not be permitted to form such independent nationalist frameworks, as an Arab university. Additional restrictions on Arab natural increase, land holdings, expressions of identification with the PLO, street demonstrations, and so forth are also endorsed. At the same time, any steps to promote equality between Arabs and Jews are opposed. All these views are in line with the general position that in a Jewish state, Jews are entitled to a superior status.

Hardliners do not believe in the cultural and social integration of Arabs and Jews. They reject the notion that Arab culture should be regarded as part of the national culture, and a majority of the hardliners object to fostering biculturalism among Jews. The status quo of institutional separation is accepted, with the understandable exception that, in order not to enable Arabs to muster power, political parties should not be separate.

Exclusionists

The one fifth or more of Jews who are labeled exclusionists are in many ways "super hardliners" who feel that the cost of control over Israeli Arabs will be prohibitively high for the Jews. Hence, the only solution is to exclude Arabs from the state. Although only Kach, the Rabbi Kahane-led political movement, explicitly articulates this ideology, it is in fact shared by wider Jewish circles.[3] For this reason, the exclusionists in the sample are more numerous and more moderate than the extreme, quasi-fascist Jew that Kahane wants to fashion in Israel.

The exclusionists believe in Jewish supremacy in Israel, although some of them reason that part of the Israeli Arab community can reconcile itself to a subordinate status and may stay in the country. The majority of exclusionists, however, think that most Arabs cannot be expected to accept Jewish superiority, particularly as long as the Arab world sees the Jewish state as an alien body in the region. In consequence, it is argued, most Israeli Arabs are and will remain rejectionist and subversive. Therefore, Israel should dispense with them, the sooner the better.

The exclusionists take consistently uncompromising stands toward Israeli Arabs. In their view, Israeli Arabs are not entitled to live in Israel with full rights, they cannot be equal and cannot identify with the state, and they should not receive equal treatment in a state that was created for and tailored to serve only Jews. Biculturalism is rejected because it might undermine the national Jewish culture, and social integration is even more opposed for fear of assimilation. Arabs are perceived as untrustworthy, and a policy of increasing surveillance over them and all kinds of restrictions is called for.

Differences in Behaviors

Since Arab-Jewish contacts are not common, it is difficult to distinguish among the four orientation types in their respective behaviors vis-à-vis Arabs. Two indicators are available, however, and both show differences in behavior among the various Jewish types.

---

[3]After the banning of Kach from participation in the 1988 national elections, the idea of transfer of the Arab population is championed in the Knesset by the new Moledet ("Homeland") Party and partially by the Tehiya and Zomet parties (these ultranationalist parties hold together seven seats). However, none of them advocate the transfer of Israeli Arabs. Yet all of them make implicit threats of disenfranchisement if Arabs continue not to fulfill a duty of military or civil service.

First, Jewish types differ in friendship with Arabs. While 77.5% of all the Jews in the study do not have Arab friends, this overall proportion breaks down as follows: 60% among the conciliationists, 71% among the pragmatists, 81% among the hardliners, and 85% among the exclusionists (Table 19.4). These figures reveal, nevertheless, that even liberal Jews lack meaningful contact with Arabs, and that much of their tolerance is an abstract openness rather than a concrete experience.

Table 19.4 Jewish Orientation Types by Selected Behaviors

	Concilia-tionists	Pragma-tists	Hard-liners	Exclu-sionists
Do not have Arab friends	59.7	70.9	81.2	85.3
Voting in the 1977 national elections				
Shelli, Independent Liberals, Citizens Rights Movement, Democratic Movement for Change	40.3	24.7	10.2	1.9
Labor	41.6	29.3	28.5	21.9
Likud (including Shlomzion)	16.9	39.5	46.9	57.4
Religious parties	1.3	6.4	14.3	18.8

More crucial is the divergence in voting behavior. Of the conciliationists, 42% voted for Labor in the 1977 Knesset elections and 40% for Shelli, Citizens Rights Movement, Independent Liberals, and Democratic Movement for Change; of the pragmatists, 39.5% voted Likud, 29% Labor, and 25% the small leftist parties; of the hardliners, 47% voted Likud and 28.5% Labor; and of the exclusionists, 57% voted Likud, 22% Labor, and 19% for the religious parties (Table 19.4). The real differences between the types are much greater than those reflected in these figures because of the bifurcation of Israeli politics. For instance, 82% of the conciliationists in 1977 cast their vote for the Labor camp as against 76% of the exclusionists who voted for the Likud camp.

Determinants

These behaviors with regard to friendship with Arabs and voting patterns, which both influence and are influenced by orientation types, are included in the following three sets of factors that predispose or reinforce liberal or illiberal orientations among Israeli Jews:

1. *Susceptibility.* Education, religious observance, and ethnic origin are the most commonly mentioned determinants of behavior toward the Arabs. That formal education increases the dominant majority's tolerance toward minorities is a recurrent finding in many attitudinal surveys (e.g., Ehrlich, 1973). Religious observance, in contrast, tends to be associated with intolerance of non-coreligionists. This is particularly true in Israel, where Orthodoxy, the least tolerant of the various branches of Judaism,

reigns and joins with a strong nationalism. With regard to the ethnic division within the dominant group, it is often the disadvantaged segment that is the less tolerant. In Israel, it is generally assumed that Oriental Jews take more anti-Arab positions than Ashkenazim for one or a combination of the following factors: memories of suffering at the hands of Arabs in the Diaspora, lower education, direct competition with Israeli Arabs for the same jobs and resources, and a way of disowning Arab cultural traits in order to be accepted by Ashkenazim.

2. *Contact.* It is a common theme that under certain conditions, contact with minority members dispels stereotypes, facilitates understanding, and fosters tolerance among members of the dominant group. Although these conditions do not prevail in Israel, it is possible that contact that extends to visiting may result in a more liberal orientation toward the Arab minority.

3. *Political subculture.* Political subcultures differ in degree of tolerance toward minorities. Israeli political subcultures are largely forged by political parties or blocs, with Shelli, the Citizens Rights Movement, Mapam, Democratic Movement for Change, and Independent Liberals propagating a conciliationist orientation toward the Arab minority; Labor a pragmatist orientation; Likud, Tehiya, and the religious parties a hardline orientation; and Kach preaching an exclusionist orientation. It is thus suggested that voting for a party does shape one's orientation toward Israeli Arabs.

When the five variables in these three sets of predisposing factors are regressed on orientation types, all are found to be statistically significant and together to account for 24% of the variance on the typology (R=0.49) (Table 19.5). The variables are ranked in the following order of predictive power:

1.   Education (explains 11% of the total variance)
2.   Religious observance (explains an additional 9%)
3.   Voting (another 3%)
4.   Being on visiting terms with Arabs (additional 0.5%)
5.   Ethnic origin (additional 0.5%)

If voting is excluded, on the grounds that the types are constructed to approximate political orientations, a change in the order of the predictive power of the four other factors is evident. The two best predictors are education and religious observance, jointly explaining 18.5% of the total variance on orientation. On the other hand, ethnicity trails at the end, lacking a direct impact, but it does influence orientation indirectly through education, religious observance, and voting. In fact, voting, education, ethnicity, and religious observance are intercorrelated and indicative of a political subculture.

Table 19.5 Regression Analysis of Predictors of Jewish Orientation Types

	N	r	R	Beta
All five predictors, including voting				
Education	1,069	−0.34	0.34	−0.12407*
Religious observance	1,081	−0.33	0.43	−0.18462*
Voting in the 1977 Knesset elections (Labor camp/Likud camp)	1,069	−0.31	0.46	0.27961*
Visiting terms with Arabs	1,064	−0.18	0.48	0.18680*
Ethnic origin (Orientals/Ashkenazim)	978	−0.28	0.49	−0.19902*
The three best predictors, excluding voting				
Education	1,069	−0.34	0.34	−0.15562*
Religious observance	1,081	−0.33	0.43	−0.26201*
Visiting terms with Arabs	1,064	−0.18	0.45	−0.17369*

*Statistically significant at 0.000 level.

These factors also combine to make certain social background variables into good indicators of orientation toward Israeli Arabs.[4] The

Table 19.6 Jewish Orientation Types by Selected Background Factors

	Total	Concilia-tionists	Pragma-tists	Hard-liners	Exclu-sionists
Total	100.0	7.6	33.5	36.2	22.7
Education					
0-8	100.0	3.6	22.9	37.0	36.5
9-12	100.0	6.7	32.2	41.2	19.9
13+	100.0	15.0	49.3	26.2	9.4
Religious observance					
Religious	100.0	3.1	15.3	40.8	40.4
Traditional	100.0	2.6	31.5	43.6	22.2
Secular	100.0	14.8	43.3	26.8	15.0
Ethnic origin					
Oriental	100.0	3.7	24.3	39.1	32.9
Ashkenazic	100.0	11.0	40.2	35.6	13.2
Father's country of birth					
Yemen	100.0	2.6	14.5	37.7	45.2
Morocco	100.0	2.4	25.0	42.3	30.3
Algeria, Tunisia, Libya	100.0	1.5	18.7	46.3	33.6
Syria, Lebanon, Egypt	100.0	9.0	42.1	24.9	24.0
Iraq	100.0	1.2	27.1	45.7	26.0
Turkey, Greece, Bulgaria	100.0	6.8	25.9	40.7	26.6
Rumania	100.0	7.3	32.3	43.1	17.3
Soviet Union	100.0	10.9	44.3	26.4	18.4
Poland	100.0	10.9	44.3	35.0	9.9
Germany	100.0	15.4	40.4	34.1	10.1

[4]Types are not distinguished by age (r=0.06) and gender (r=0.06), however.

conciliationist type tends to be found disproportionately among the university educated, the secular, and Ashkenazim, especially German Jews (Table 19.6). Pragmatists are more likely to be drawn from the better educated and less religious than the average and from among Ashkenazim. Hardliners are inclined to originate from the undereducated, the religious, and Orientals. The exclusionists are overrepresented among the religious and Orientals, particularly Yemenite Jews.

20

Implications of the Typologies

Several implications may be deduced from the analysis of the two typologies. First, factionalism within each of the communities is shown to be as genuine and appreciable as the split between them. The internal divisions are strikingly similar in the number and relative size of the four types (Table 18.1 and Table 19.1). On each side, there are two large middle types and two small extreme ones. With the exception of the rejectionists, Arabs share in common the acceptance of Israel, insistence on equality, and a two-state solution to the Israeli-Palestinian dispute. They disagree, however, on the extent of their rejection of Israel's Jewish-Zionist character and on the means of struggle. With the notable exception of the exclusionists (whose proportion among Jews is 3.5 times higher than the proportion of rejectionists among Arabs), the Jews are willing to have an Arab minority in their midst, but they are internally divided on their demands of the Arabs and on the amount of equality they are prepared to extend to them.

Second, significant asymmetry between the two typologies is noticeable. All the Jewish types have parallels in ideological and political movements or parties. This is also true of the Jewish exclusionists, who draw on the support of Kahane's movement as well as on sections of the Tehiya, Likud, and religious parties. On the other hand, the Arab rejectionists are prevented by the authorities from forming a statewide organization that acts ideologically and politically. No less important is the Arab reservationists' lack of an ideological and political base. The establishment of such a base, probably through the founding of a predominantly Arab political party that is eligible for inclusion in a coalition government, would strongly activate Arab factionalism, boost Arab negotiating power, and transform Arab-Jewish relations.[1]

And third, genuine internal factionalism in the two communities started to soften Arab-Jewish polarity. Both factionalisms have begun to exercise a positive impact on Arab-Jewish coexistence. They have a certain destereotyping effect. The Arabs are increasingly conscious of the fact that the Jews are neither uniform in views nor united in actions against them; the same holds for the Jews, too. The growing mutual awareness of the other's internal diversity and discord enables increasing numbers of Arabs and Jews to seek understanding, cooperation, and alliance from segments congenial to them in the other side.

These general implications of the typologies will be further elaborated below.

Destereotyping

Since both sides hold negative stereotypes of each other, a certain degree of mutual destereotyping may be a major function of the typologies. The Jewish public tends to perceive Israeli Arabs as being disloyal (because of their massive support for the PLO), and as potentially subversive. Arabs appear as falling wholly into the rejectionist type. Even the better informed Jewish Arabists are trapped in their own stereotyping, dichotomizing Israeli Arabs into "positive" and "negative." In the eyes of these Jewish experts, "positive" Arabs approximate the accommodationist type, whereas most Arabs constitute an undifferentiated negative mass.

The fourfold Arab typology can assist in blunting Jewish stereotyping by demonstrating that only a minority of less than one tenth are rejectionist whose dissident views are not shared by the overwhelming majority of Arabs.

The Arab typology may not only correct Jewish misconceptions but also reinforce the more realistic images Arabs have of themselves. In daily life, Arabs apply their own typifications of fellow Arabs. The accommodationists are labeled "regime supporters" (Rajel Al-Hokuma," "Sultawi") or "moderates" ("Motadel"). The oppositionists are known as "Front supporters" ("Jabhawi"), viz., backers of the Rakah-led Democratic Front for Peace and Equality. The rejectionists are often referred to as "nationalists" ("Kawmiyyi"). Because the typology is readily recognizable by Arabs and corresponds to a certain degree with their one experiential typology, it is more acceptable to them and, as a result, is more likely to refine and publicize their own folk typifications. It may thus contribute to

[1]As mentioned earlier, Darawshe's new, Democratic Arab Party which won a seat in the 1988 Knesset elections, is likly to fill this void and lead the reservationists.

the institutionalization of Arab orientation types, i.e., turning them into publicly known social statuses.

The Jewish typology may perform a similar destereotyping task for Arabs. Although Arabs, like minority members in general, make finer distinctions than Jews do, they also stereotype the Jews as hostile, racist, exploitive, and domineering. In Israeli Arab eyes, the Jews are hardliners or worse. The perception of the Israeli Jew as intransigent is as widespread among Israeli Arab leaders as among the rank and file.

The fact, however, that two fifths of the Jews are classified as more liberal pragmatist and conciliationist types should provide a corrective to the Arab inordinate portrayals of Jews. There is certainly a great deal of intolerance among Jews, but less than the excesses attributed to them by Arabs.

Even though these typologies themselves may in time engender their own stereotypes, the benefit of their present introduction outweighs their potential harm.

Dichotomization

The temptation to break down the four types into two is strong, indeed. Although it would achieve a gain in simplicity and clarity, dichotomization lends itself to conflicting political and scholarly uses or misuses because there are obviously several ways to dichotomize. In fact, the rationales for dichotomization are themselves revealing.

The most obvious dichotomy of Arab orientation types is between accommodationists and others. It corresponds with the standard labeling of Israeli Arabs by officials as "positive" and "negative" and with the Jewish public's image of the overwhelming majority of Arabs as anti-Israel. But its logic goes beyond sheer stereotyping and clear Jewish self-interest. Since the Jewish-Zionist character is Israel's *raison d'être*, to oppose it is to reject Israel. Hence, the reservationist and oppositionist types who accept Israel as a state but not as a Jewish-Zionist state are as non-accommodating as the rejectionist type. The real distinction is between the accommodationists (one tenth) who reconcile themselves to Arab minority status in a Jewish-Zionist state and the non-accommodationists (nine tenths) who do not. The Rakah stance, which best represents the oppositionist position, is branded dissident by the Jewish public and authorities for being unequivocally anti-Zionist.

Dichotomization of Arabs can also run the other way – rejectionists as against the rest. Paradoxically both Rakah leaders and their Arab nationalist opponents would favor such twofold division. The accommodationists, reservationists, and oppositionists share in common the acceptance of Israel as a political entity and the pursuit of a solution to their problem within it. Both are, therefore, basically conciliatory and

adjustable. The objection to Zionism of the reservationists and oppositionists and for that matter of Rakah, is amenable to revision.

The real distinction is, therefore, between the rejectionists (under one
tenth) and non-rejectionists (over nine tenths). To put it differently, the
cutting line is between "resistance" (the rejectionists) on the one hand,
and "loyal opposition" (the reservationists and oppositionists) and
"resignation" (the accommodationists) on the other. This is why activists
in the Sons of the Village Movement and the National Progressive
Movement who pride themselves on being the true dissidents, accuse the
Rakah-affiliated Arab leaders of being "reactionary," who retort by
chiding them as "adventurists" (a common term in Communist polemics).
The Rakah-affiliated Arab leaders would find this dichotomy self-serving
because it divorces them from the rejectionist Arab leaders, presents the
majority of Israeli Arabs as loyal and moderate, and enhances their claim
of being the representative ideological and political leadership of the
Arab minority.

A third possible dichotomy is to classify Arabs into "accommodating"
and "militant." The former include the accommodationists and
reservationists (three fifths) and the latter comprise the oppositionists
and rejectionists (two fifths). This regrouping of types is
methodologically defensible on the grounds that the four distinct types
are signposts on an accommodation-militancy continuum. Hence, it
makes sense to divide close to the middle.

By the same token, several dichotomies of Jewish orientation types
can be enumerated. First, there is the division between conciliationists
and others. Conciliationists (one tenth of the Jewish population) are
Zionist critics of the status quo of control over Arabs. They believe that
Arabs deserve, and can obtain, equal treatment in Israel as a Jewish-
Zionist state. They also feel that the state should shift from a policy of
domination to one of compromise and partnership, so that Arabs can be
integrated fully into the Israeli mainstream. The overwhelming majority
of Jews (over nine tenths of the public), on the other hand, support in
principle the present situation because they see no alternative to the
regulation of Arab behavior so long as the Arabs remain potential fifth
columnists and reject Zionism.

The questioning of Israel's ability to control the Arab minority in the
long run underlies a second Jewish dichotomy. The exclusionists (over
one fifth) are convinced that the Arabs are structurally unadjustable (i.e.,
unable to fit in a Jewish-Zionist Israel) and that they constitute an
impending time bomb. Hence, the only solution is to get rid of them
through voluntary or forced emigration. The non-exclusionist Jews (four
fifths) do not share these gloomy assessments. They feel that Israeli Arabs
can effectively be kept in check, and, therefore, the state should not

embark on an extreme course that would run counter to its democratic ethos and international credentials.

From another perspective, it can be argued that the distinction which really matters in contemporary Israel is between non-Zionist and Zionist Jews. In terms of the typology, this is the division between the egalitarianists, who virtually do not exist in Israel today (except among the extreme left), and the Jewish public as a whole. The egalitarianists reason that as long as Israel remains Jewish-Zionist, there will be no remedy to its Arab problem. Peaceful accommodation can be obtained only through the formation of a true binational, or secular-democratic, non-ethnic state. Since Israeli Jews reject this solution, they are bound to subjugate, manipulate, or exclude the Arab minority. Consequently, the internal differentiation of Jews into four types, as seen from this viewpoint, is a futile exercise, a hair-splitting of committed Zionists, all of whom willy-nilly treat Arabs unequally.

A fourth and last dichotomy is a common-sense division down the middle between conciliationists and pragmatists (two fifths), on the one hand, and hardliners and exclusionists (three fifths), on the other. This is a realistic division between liberals and illiberals in relation to Israeli Arabs. The liberals recognize the Arabs' right to live in Israel with equal status, favor fewer restrictions over Arabs, would make increasing concessions to secure their cooperation, prefer economic and other manipulations to outright political suppression, and, as a whole, they are relatively receptive to Arabs. In contrast, the illiberals insist on exclusive Jewish right to the land, endorse numerous restrictions and escalating surveillance over the Arabs, are willing to pay the cost of confrontation with them, and are not generally responsive to Arab needs and sensitivities.

Each of the above dichotomies of Arab and Jewish types has its own logic and can serve a special purpose. This, in a way, is a utility measure of the full-fledged typologies, which aim at providing a useful device to a variety of scientific and non-scientific potential users.

Policy

The typologies may serve as tools for formulating or evaluating public policy in Arab-Jewish relations. As indicated above, the study shows that Arab orientation types are shaped by factors which are subject to public policy. The importance of interventionist policies in the Arab sector is evident in the effects of the status assigned to particular communities by the authorities, the level of local services, visiting contacts with Jews, and the extent of loss suffered through land expropriation. The implication for policy toward the Arabs should be rather obvious. To illustrate, since Israeli Arabs who have suffered land expropriation are more likely to be militant, it is possible that a large-scale change of land policy can have a great impact on Arab orientations. That is, a policy reversal from expropriation to the granting of land to meet the growing need in the Arab population for housing, public facilities, industry, agriculture, and new towns or villages may redistribute Arab orientation to become more moderate.

Similarly, the internal Jewish factionalism, as evidenced by the typology, has two implications for policies aiming to improve Arab-Jewish relations. The first implication involves the fact that Jewish types mainly correspond to the orientations of political parties and to background factors that are strongly associated with voting (education and religious observance). This suggests that attitudinal change among Jews is more likely to be effected through alteration of the positions of the political parties on the Israeli Arab question than through programs that attempt to persuade individuals. For instance, a softening of the Likud's style and strong-arm policy toward Israeli Arabs would have a much greater moderating impact on the Jewish population than would a series of contrived encounters between Arab and Jewish high-school students.

The other implication of the growing, internal Jewish factionalism is the need for a new Arab strategy. The nearly even split between Jewish liberals and illiberals on the Arab minority question makes Israeli Arabs an increasingly valuable ally for Jewish liberals. To seize this opportunity, Israeli Arabs need an independent, predominantly Arab, political party that is acceptable to pragmatist and conciliationist Jews and to coalition governments. As polarization among Jews soars, these liberal Jews will increasingly be more willing to cooperate with Arabs and even let them enter the national power structure.

Arab and Jewish factionalisms also provide a criterion for better assessing the effectiveness of policies or actions adopted by both communities. The division of Arabs into types that differ not only in orientation but also in needs necessitates differential policies by Jews. Accommodationist and reservationist Arabs appear to be undergoing leadership and ideology crises. The Zionist establishment realizes that its traditional hold over them through appointed functionaries and dignitaries is weakening. To keep their loyalty and political support, the Labor Party modernized its Arab politics in the early 1980's. It abandoned its traditional Arab lists, coopted Arabs to its top governing bodies, allowed Arab members to organize as a faction within the party, and even let them elect their representatives to the Party's slate to the Knesset. This partial reform, however, has not really met the needs of Arab moderates who seek full integration and equality as well as a significant change in the Party's policy toward the Arab population.

At the same time, the Jewish policy has been to prevent any recognition, legitimacy, and cooperation with representatives of the oppositionist and rejectionist types, i.e., Rakah and the Sons of the Village Movement. It has also been the policy not to let an independent, nationalist Arab party of any kind arise, not even a moderate party that articulates the interests of reservationists and cooperates with Jewish parties. The fear that in time such a party might become nationalist outweighs the possible gain of weakening Rakah and further dividing Israeli Arabs.

Some Jewish hardliners call for even stricter policies. To cite just one advocate, Israeli (1980), draws on the Arab typology, presented in the 1976 study (Smooha, 1984a). He argues that the dichotomy between the small minority of accommodationists and the large majority of non-accommodationists should be the basis for Jewish policies toward Israeli Arabs. In his view the accommodationists are Israeli Arab in identity and reconciled with Israel, whereas the non-accommodationists are or are becoming Palestinian and hostile to the state. Therefore, Israel has to pursue sharply different policies toward these two kinds of Arabs. The accommodationists should be fully integrated in all areas, including politics, schools, and the army, and be granted equal opportunities. In contrast, the non-accommodationists should be denied their present Israeli citizenship (including the right to vote) as well as funds to finance education and other services. Furthermore, as Israeli resident aliens they should be allowed to join the autonomy in the West Bank and Gaza Strip if it were established.

These Jewish implemented and suggested policies ignore the substantial change in the Arab position since the mid 1970's. The Arabs have been availing themselves of Israeli democracy, waging a successful struggle for equal rights and opportunities, and defying the various controls and restrictions imposed on them. This is why Jewish efforts to coopt Arab leaders will fail. Also, it is no longer feasible to block the emergence of a predominantly Arab party that is either integrationist-coalitionable or non-rejectionist-nationalist. Any Jewish attempt to disenfranchise or limit the rights of any segment of the Arab population will be futile as well.

Arabs have to respond to Jewish policies and decide on their line of action. The possibility of forming a new, independent, Arab political party that can seek legitimacy and inclusion in coalition governments has been discussed by some Arab leaders in the 1980's. Since 1977, Rakah has also attempted to break its isolation, to gain approval, and to broaden its political base by creating alliances with Jewish groups. But since only non-Zionist splinter Jewish factions agreed to join the Front (DFPE) it formed, the strategy has so far failed. On the other hand, the rejectionists do not usually desire alliances with Jews, except cooperation on an ad hoc basis with marginal, anti-Zionist, Jewish groups (e.g., Israeli Socialist Organization).

The continuing debate between spokesmen of the rejectionist and oppositionist types on the proper Israeli Arab response is evident in the exchange between Nakhleh (1980) and Tuma (1981). Nakhleh maintains that the strategy of the Arab minority to penetrate Israeli life, to extract concessions from Jews, and to strive for rights within the established frameworks has proved ineffective. Instead, they have to switch from this Jewish "occupiers' paradigm" to a new strategy of "creating a liberation-prone mentality" that indicates "rejection of a dominant structure that acts daily to undermine our national existence." Nakhleh calls for withdrawal from parliamentary politics because "our Knesset status has forced us to start on the road of irreversible compromises which may have a negative strategic impact on our liberation struggle." He further proposes controlling Arab "local councils, consolidating regional organizations, strengthening and enlarging the networks of existing associations, and creating and sustaining a meaningful and politically oriented coalition with progressive Jewish groups which are anti-Zionists." He rejects alliances with the Zionists because they "are not willing to make the quantum leap into anti-Zionism."

In a rejoinder, the late Tuma, at the time a leading ideologist of Rakah, dismisses Nakhleh's rejectionist strategy and states the oppositionist position. The basis for the settlement of the Israeli-Arab conflict is a mutual recognition of the Israeli Jews' and Palestinians' right to self-determination and hence a two-state solution. "In the light of this," Tuma maintains, "the Arab national minority has an important role to play. They play this role with the clear assumption that they are citizens of Israel on the one hand and are not eligible for the right of self-determination on the other." Israeli Arabs have to enter alliances with any Jewish group that accepts this principle or sympathizes with the Arab struggle for equality. "In conclusion, what the Arab masses in Israel need is not a new programme of action but a development of their own programme – this means to consolidate their unity within their local democratic institutions and within the all-embracing Democratic Front for Peace and Equality." Arabs should, therefore, redouble their efforts to make the existing strategy more effective and shy away from unrealistic rejectionist ventures.

These policy statements by Israeli, Nakhleh, and Tuma allude to a far-reaching implication of the Arab and Jewish typologies for the possibility of mutual accommodation. They make clear that the fourfold typologies are relevant for differentiation and internal struggles within each community with regard to how to respond to the other side. Hence, within the Zionist establishment, pragmatists and hardliners fight for shaping public policy toward the Arabs, while criticisms are leveled against them by the conciliationists and exclusionists. In the Arab population, Rakah is fighting against both the accommodationists and rejectionists for determining the Arab position vis-à-vis the Jewish majority.

Conflict-Resolution

The analysis of internal factionalism is a vital corrective to studies of deeply divided societies which tend to stress polarization between the constituent segments and to deemphasize internal divisions. Factionalization may coexist with polarization and in time it might even undermine it. It is paradoxical that the deeper the divisions within groups, the lesser is the conflict between them (Seliktar, 1984a). This generalization should counterbalance the common belief that internal unity is necessary and desirable for intergroup accommodation. While a certain degree of unity within the subordinate group is required for waging a successful struggle and a certain degree of unity within the dominant group is needed to pursue a policy of accommodation and compromise, it is also true that peaceful conflict resolution in ethnically split societies can draw on the "overlap" of sections from the dominant and subordinate groups.

The critical question is whether Arab and Jewish factionalisms are sufficiently large and significant to create concurring sections and cross-ethnic alliances. It is doubtful if they made any difference for Arab-Jewish coexistence up to the late 1970's. Up to that time what really counted in the intergroup context was the extreme dichotomy through which each side saw the other. From the viewpoint of most Jews, Arabs were split into accommodationists and non-accommodationists, so that the difference between the reservationists, oppositionists, and rejectionists was inconsequential because all these Arabs reject Israel as a Jewish-Zionist state and decline to reconcile themselves to the state on the terms set for them by the Jews. Even though most Arab rank and file made finer distinctions among Jews, Arab leaders not affiliated with the Zionist establishment tended to think in binary terms, particularly Rakah Arab leaders who divided Jews into conciliationists and non-conciliationists, and rejectionist Arab leaders who distinguished between egalitarianists (anti-Zionists) and non-egalitarianists (Zionists).

These political choices were made in terms of perceived resemblance of opinions, potentiality for compromise, and power alignment. In consequence, each side considered only a small minority of the other group (one tenth of the Arabs, under one tenth of the Jews) as serious candidates for negotiation and cooperation. Hence, as far as the Jews were concerned, the large majority of Arabs who were classified as reservationists and oppositionists were still too far out to qualify for Jewish trust and full equality, let alone their leaders who were openly anti-Zionists. For their part, these Arab leaders saw the large segment of Jews who fit the pragmatist type as staunch backers of Jewish-Zionist supremacy and, therefore, unlikely to support Arabs in their civil and national struggle.

By the early 1980's the positive effects of internal factionalism were already evident, however. The change was prompted by the ascendancy of the Likud to power and the growing political polarization in Israeli society between the Likud and Labor camps. As a result, more Arabs and more Jews became aware of the sharpening internal fragmentation on the other side. The parity between the two political camps pushed many reservationist Arabs and pragmatist Jews – a sizable segment in each community – to discover their interdependence and common interests. This explains the large Arab turnout for the Labor Party and for the small leftist parties in the 1981 national elections.

Reservationist Arabs feel unsettled, however. They want to develop an ideological and political base of their own through which they can deal more effectively and honorably with pragmatist Jews. The consolidation of internal factionalism on both sides (i.e., the formation of a new, independent, coalitionable, political force among the Arabs and the further polarization among the Jews) will contribute to Arab-Jewish rapprochement.

Part Three

CONCLUSIONS

—

21

Trends

It is commonly believed that the 1967 Six Day War was a turning point for the worse in Arab-Jewish coexistence. During the first nineteen years of statehood, Jews became more aware and receptive toward Israeli Arabs, and policies became increasingly liberal toward them. Israeli Arabs were admitted into the Histadrut and other public institutions, the internal Arab refugees were resettled, military government in Arab areas was gradually phased out and formally ended in December 1966, confiscation of Arab lands was terminated, many Arab localities were incorporated and their services were improved, the Israeli economy opened up to absorb Arab labor, Arab educational and living standards rose dramatically, and the status of Arab women was significantly upgraded (Layish, 1975). As a result, Israeli citizenship emerged as a solid, common bond between Arabs and Jews and the two communities moved toward mutual acceptance and conciliation.

According to this widely held perspective, the 1967 war halted and even reversed the process of Arab-Jewish rapprochement. Among the Jews, the war revived and reinforced dormant, divisive forces of nationalism, religion, and ethnicity (Cohen, 1983). The neo-Revisionist ideology of Greater Israel became practicable and has been used to garner massive support which brought the Likud to power in 1977. The religious sector became more nationalistic, with messianic overtones. Shifting their backing from Labor to Likud, the new political majority of Oriental Jews, who for a variety of reasons tend to be more anti-Arab than the average, made their special contribution to the growth of intolerance toward Arabs. Jews moved to the right and became more concerned with territory, Judaism, and ethnic equality; more frustrated by the Palestinian defiance and international censure of Israeli control of the West Bank and Gaza Strip; and more fearful of the repercussions of the post-1967 Israeli Arab militancy. These changes among the Jews have weakened their sense of shared citizenship with Israeli Arabs. Jews' lingering perceptions of the Arabs as outsiders and potential subversives have also been strengthened.

In the aftermath of the 1967 war, Israeli Arabs have found themselves hard pressed to substitute their Israeli identity, loyalty, and bonds for Palestinian ones. They have resumed contacts with relatives and others in the West Bank, Gaza Strip, and Arab countries. They have been strongly lured by Palestinian nationalism and the PLO. They were no longer condemned as traitors by their people but rather honored as faithful Palestinians who take part in the national struggle (Shilo, 1982). They were also less deterred and debilitated by Israel's invincibility and strength after the 1973 war. As a result, Israeli Arabs were supposed to drift away from Israel.

Israeli Arabs were thought to be further alienated from Israel by certain potent internal forces. Their rapid natural increase instilled in them a sense of power, intensified their discontent with unmet, growing needs for family resources and social services, and heightened their feelings of deprivation relative to the rising Jewish standards. They also continued to face discriminatory policies, Jewish prejudice and intolerance, and an increasing number of right-wing, nationalist Jews with whom they disagreed sharply.

According to this common perspective, Arab radicalization and Jewish intransigence joined after 1967 to erode Arab-Jewish coexistence. Since these supposed trends concern the very core of Arab-Jewish relations, they certainly deserve the most elaborate and thorough examination. We have to settle, however, for a brief discussion here because the available evidence is still scant and scattered.

Trends among Arabs

Peres (1971) completed a pioneering survey of attitudes toward Arab-Jewish relations during 1967-68. Although his samples were not representative, it is possible to construct comparable subsamples from our 1976 and 1980 representative samples. This is accomplished by selecting from our samples only men from the eight villages and towns where interviews for the Peres survey were administered and comparing their responses to two key questions – Israel's right to exist and whether one feels more at home in Israel or in an Arab country.[1]

---

[1]One may argue that the timing of the 1967 and 1976 surveys was inappropriate because the immediate upheavals of the 1967 war and the 1976 Land Day strike negatively slanted Arab responses. These historical events, however, should be seen not as extraneous to Arab-Jewish relations but rather inherent in them.

The findings evidently do not confirm the common approach that Israeli Arabs became more rejectionist and alienated over time. Full acceptance of Israel's right of existence went up from 31% in Peres general sample to 61% in the 1976 comparison sample and to 66% in the 1980 comparison sample, whereas negation of the Jewish state dropped from 20% to 9% and to 7%, respectively (Table 21.1). Similarly, Arabs who felt more at home in Israel remained 37% during this period but those feeling more at home in an Arab country declined sharply from 48% in 1967 to 32% in 1976 and to 19% in 1980. This trend of moderation is evident among both young adults (aged 20-35) and adults (over 35 years).[2]

Table 21.1 Arabs' Views of Israel's Right to Exist and Country Where One Feels More at Home, 1967-80

	Israel's Right to Exist			Feeling More at Home		
	Accept	Have Reservations	Deny	In Israel	No Difference	In Arab Country
1967 Peres general sample[a]	31	49	20	37	15	48
1976 Smooha comparison sample	61	30	9	38	30	32
1980 Smooha comparison sample	66	27	7	37	44	19
1967 Peres young adults (20-35) sample[a]	29	44	26	35	18	47
1976 Smooha comparison sample	56	33	11	33	35	32
1980 Smooha comparison sample	54	36	10	31	50	19
1967 Peres adults (36 and over) sample[a]	54	41	5	54	18	27
1976 Smooha comparison sample	67	27	6	40	25	35
1980 Smooha comparison sample	77	20	3	48	35	17

[a] Peres, 1971, Tables 17, 18 and 22.

Our two comparable, representative surveys also show greater Arab accommodation during the 1976-80 years. When the 1980 classification of Arabs into four orientation types was applied to the 1976 sample, it was found that the rejectionists were down from 13.5% in 1976 to 6% in 1980 and oppositionists from 44% to 40%, respectively (Table 21.2).

While a change in the distribution of Arab types provides an overall summary measure of a trend in Arab attitudes, a radicalism index is a refined indicator. It is a simple, additive index composed of three items: denial of Israel's right to exist, support for unlicensed demonstrations, and endorsement of the use of violence. Radical Arabs agreeing with two or all three points dropped from 23.5% in 1976 to 10% in 1980, whereas

[2]On the other hand, a comparison of special samples of Arab high school students taken by Peres in 1967 and myself in 1976 shows radicalization. These restive teenagers, however, tend to calm down after leaving school, becoming employed, and establishing their own families.

the most moderate Arabs who disagreed with all three points rose from 47% to 63%, respectively (Table 21.3).

Table 21.2 Arab Orientation Types, 1976-80

	Arab Public	
	1976	1980
Arab orientation types		
Accommodationists	13.1	15.3
Reservationists	29.5	39.1
Oppositionists	43.9	39.9
Rejectionists	13.5	5.7
Total	100.0	100.0
Number of cases	607	1,133

Table 21.3 Arab Radicalism Index, 1976-80

	Arab Public	
	1976	1980
Radicalism Index		
0 (least radical)	47.1	62.7
1	29.5	27.8
2	19.3	7.3
3 (most radical)	4.2	2.3
Total	100.0	100.0
Number of cases	607	1,130

Table 21.4 Selected Arab Rejectionist Views, 1976-80

	Arab Public	
	1976	1980
Deny Israel's right to exist	20.5	11.0
Favor, without reservations, unlicensed demonstrations to improve Arab conditions	17.1	7.0
Favor, without reservations, use of violence to improve Arab conditions	17.9	7.5
Unwilling to have Jewish friends	42.5	30.7
Would move to a Palestinian state if it were established in the West Bank and Gaza Strip	14.4	8.3

Contrary to the radicalization perspective, the proportion of Arabs rejecting Israel or coexistence with Jews failed to increase. For instance, Arabs negating Israel's right to exist decreased from 20.5% in 1976 to 11% in 1980; Arabs unwilling to have Jewish friends dropped from 42.5% to 31%, respectively; and Arabs who would move to a Palestinian state in the West Bank and Gaza Strip – i.e., desiring to dissociate themselves completely from Israel – declined from 14% to 8%, respectively (Table 21.4).

Another sensitive indicator is national self-identity. If Arabs were truly radicalizing, they would have become more Palestinian and less Israeli in identity. This is not the case, however. When asked to choose the term which best described their identity, 57.5% in 1976 and 54.5% in 1980 selected terms with a Palestinian component but during the same period the Israeli component in Arab identity rose from 67% to 74% (Table 21.5). An integrated, Israeli Palestinian identity is gaining ground at the expense of a rejectionist, non-Israeli Palestinian identity.

Table 21.5 Arab National Self-Identity, 1976-80

	Arab Public	
	1976	1980
Define onself in one of the following terms		
Non-Palestinian Israeli (Israeli, Israeli Arab, Arab)	42.5	45.4
Israeli Palestinian (Israeli Palestinian, Palestinian in Israel)	24.6	28.8
Non-Israeli Palestinian (Palestinian Arab, Palestinian	32.9	25.7

The increase in moderation from 1976 to 1980 was probably shaped by the waning effect of the 1976 Land Day strike, fear of the Likud government, and most important – the positive impact of the peace treaty with Egypt which legitimized Israel's right to exist and accommodation with it in the eyes of Israeli Arabs.

Proponents of the Arab radicalization perspective, like Rekhess (1976, 1977), cite supporting evidence relating to changes in three spheres of Arab behavior: voting, leadership, and protest. The Arab vote for the anti-Zionist Communist Party rose considerably from 23% in 1965, to 29.5% in 1969, to 37% in 1973, and to 51% in 1977. This dramatic shift is interpreted as an increase in the no-confidence vote in the Zionist establishment and as a growth of alienation from the state (Landau, 1981, 1984). One must doubt this explanation because by voting non-Zionist, Israeli Arabs concur with the Communist Party on the following crucial points: acceptance of Israel's right to exist, support for a peaceful, democratic struggle for equal rights and opportunities, affirmation of one's Israeli Palestinian identity, and endorsement of a two-state solution to the Palestinian question. In the absence of a better alternative, Israeli Arabs back the Communist Party which is a non-nationalist, Arab-Jewish party that well represents them on all these major views. By doing so, they express a desire to achieve equality and peace as well as to register protest against unfair state policies and practices without repudiating Israel.

After 1967, a substantial shift in Arab leadership took place. The Communist Party emerged as the most central political force among Israeli Arabs, equipping them with a network of front organizations, experienced and militant leaders, and a clear ideology for struggle. The pro-establishment Arab notables and functionaries lost much of their standing and influence, to the extent that all the traditional Arab election lists, affiliated to the Labor Party, failed for the first time in the 1981 elections to win any seat in the Knesset (Al-Haj and Yaniv, 1983). At the other extreme, a rejectionist, nationalist movement (the Sons of the Village Movement) emerged in the early 1970's but was confined to the university campuses and to a number of Arab villages. This transformation is misconceived as a shift from accommodation to radicalism. The new Arab guard, however, does not negate Israel and the Arabs' minority position in it. With the exception of activists in the Sons of the Village Movement, the new leaders accept Israel as a state, reject the status quo of control, inequality, and deprivation, and wage a democratic struggle to effect change.

Similarly, protest intensified enormously. Because of strict restrictions on Arabs, Jews were dominant in protest on behalf of Arabs before 1967. Thereafter, protest was Arabized and spread to many areas of life, presenting demands for civil equality and, occasionally also claims for national rights. It took more diverse forms as well, including mass actions. In 1976, Arabs launched the first general strike, protesting forthcoming land confiscations and clashing with the police and army, leaving six Arabs dead and some wounded. Since 1967, Arab mass rallies and demonstrations have become common. As a result of the initial encounters with the Palestinians in the occupied territories during 1967-70, 400 Israeli Arabs were convicted of terrorism, but involvement of the Arab minority in hostile activities has become rare thereafter. This escalation in Arab protest should not be interpreted as a move toward extremism and rejectionism, however. After 1967, Israel proper has been democratized, allowing many deprived groups to protest. In reaction, Israeli Arabs have seized the opportunity to wage intensive protest while remaining a law-abiding, loyal minority.

Taken together, these developments indicate the transformation of Israeli Arabs from a passive, controlled population before 1967 to an active, independent, national minority thereafter. They have availed themselves of democracy to fight for equality and peace, without dissociating themselves from Israel and the Jewish majority. This change does not substantiate the radicalization perspective, but is in line with the politicization perspective, emphasizing the Arabs' growing Israelization, factionalization, and militancy. Rather than drifting toward rejectionism and extremism, they are more insistent on attaining equality and integration in Israeli society.

Trends among Jews

It is true that after 1967 the proportion and political clout of right-wing, nationalist, religious, and Oriental Jews have risen appreciably. This rise, however, may reinforce anti-Arab predispositions, but it does not necessarily constitute evidence of increasing Jewish rejection of the Arab minority. The limited direct data available on trends in the Jewish orientation toward Israeli Arabs are inconclusive, or rather fail to confirm the growing Jewish intransigence perspective.

Representative public opinion surveys, conducted since 1967 by the Israel Institute for Applied Social Research, found mixed trends among Jews. On the one hand, Jews tend to see Israeli Arabs as radicalizing. They are well aware of the continued Arab struggle for equality, the Palestinization of Arab identity, and the Arab support for the PLO and for an independent Palestinian state in the West Bank and Gaza Strip. In Jewish eyes, these views are subversive. To illustrate, a consistent majority of 85% said that most Israeli Arabs identify themselves as Palestinians, most believed that Palestinian identity is spreading among Israeli Arabs, and 68% (in a survey taken in February 1983) were of the opinion that "an Israeli Arab who defines himself as a Palestinian is disloyal to the state" (Peled and Bar-Gal, 1983:14). For the 1967-82 period, there was an increase in the percentage of Jews who believed that Israeli Arabs' loyalty to the state was diminishing: 17% to 33% in surveys conducted between the 1967 and 1973 wars, 13% to 54% in surveys taken between the 1973 war and Sadat's visit in November 1977, 36% to 70% in surveys carried out between Sadat's visit in November 1977 to October 1980, and 39% to 53% in surveys taken during Israel's war in Lebanon (July and November 1982) (ibid.:13).

On the other hand, the same surveys found liberalization of Jewish attitudes toward Israeli Arabs. A large increase in tolerance occurred between the 1967-73 inter-war period and the period from Sadat's visit in November 1977 to October 1980. It is evident in the following figures (they represent a range of percentages obtained in different surveys within each period): Jews believing that Arabs are not inferior to Jews rose from 40-42% in 1967-73 to 51-56% in 1977-80, Jews preferring Israeli Arabs to those of the territories rose from 21-42% to 57-68%, Jews supporting the introduction of Arabic in obligatory school curriculum rose from 46-56% to 65-67%, Jews who are ready to become friendly with an Arab rose from 26-32% to 59-64%, Jews willing to live in same neighborhood with Arab families rose from 19-21% to 35-41%, Jews who visited an Arab home rose from 42-45% to 54-56% , and Jews who had Arabs visiting their homes rose from 26-27% to 37-44% (ibid.:22). This increased Jewish openness coincided with the rise in the proportion of Jews who considered the loyalty of Israeli Arabs to be declining.

Greater openness among Jews is also evidenced in selected questions from our 1976 and 1980 surveys. Although the two samples differ in size and design, they are roughly representative and comparable.[3] To cite just two findings, the proportion of Jews believing that Arabs can be equal citizens in Israel as a Jewish-Zionist state and can identify themselves with it rose from 30% in 1976 to 48% in 1980 (Table 21.6). More important, the proportion of Jews willing to have an Arab superior in a job increased from 24% in 1976 to 30% in 1980.

Table 21.6 Selected Jewish Views, 1976-80

	Jewish Public	
	1976	1980
Believe that Arabs can be equal citizens in Israel as a Jewish-Zionist state and can identify themselves with it	29.8	48.4
Endorse the establishment of an Arab university	20.0	22.1
Favor the use of general strikes by Arabs	6.2	5.9
Willing to have an Arab friend	24.5	38.6
Willing to have an Arab superior in a job	23.9	30.0
Agree that Arab youth do not have reasonable chances to fulfill their occupational aspirations in Israel	23.1	26.6

More generally, the Jews are increasingly forced to think and behave in ways inclusive of Israeli Arabs. The boundaries of the Israeli identity and collectivity have become easier to penetrate and cross by Arabs. Fewer Israeli institutions can claim Jewish exclusivity after 1967 than before. The growing Israelization of the Arabs not only facilitates communication and understanding between Jews and Arabs but also urges the Jews to discover and appreciate the Arabs' Israeliness.

The gradual loss of Jewish exclusivity continues. Since the mid-1970's all the Jewish nonreligious parties have had constitutions that allow Arabs to be full members. The Histadrut launched a program to integrate Israeli Arabs in all spheres, appointed Arabs in its key institutions, and decided to disband its separate Arab department completely. Subtitles are routinely added to certain Arabic or Hebrew television programs to facilitate viewing by both publics.

Not less significant are some unprecedented, symbolic gestures that demonstrate the Jews' willingness to recognize Arabs' Israeliness and to compromise Jewish exclusivity. They include, for instance, speeches in Arabic to Israeli Arabs by President Navon, his frequent visits to Arab

---

[3]The 1976 Jewish survey was based on 148 interviews conducted in Ramat Gan and Migdal Haemeq. The sample is, however, quite representative of the Jewish population in terms of age, education, and ethnic origin.

localities, and his recurrent declaration that Arabs and Jews are destined to live together in Israel.

Since the Land Day strike in 1976, the authorities have handled the question of land expropriations with much more care and consideration compared with the stiff, unilateral, mass confiscations of the pre-1967 period. In 1976 the intention was to take over only negligible Arab land holdings in the Galilee. The evacuation of some Bedouin of the Negev from areas earmarked for military airfields in 1979 was accompanied by negotiations with them.

Virulent anti-Arab statements and actions are no longer treated with self-restraint or indifference, but are actively opposed by the Jewish public or authorities. To illustrate, the declaration by General Ben-Gal, Chief of the Northern Command, that the Arabs of the Galilee are a cancer in the Israeli body (*Al-Hamishmar*, August 10, 1979) stirred a public storm. In reaction, he was ordered by the Defense Minister to withdraw his pronouncement, which he then denied publicly.

Overall, Jews seem to have moved over the years from rejection of Israeli Arabs to ambivalence, and in some cases, even to a defensive, apologetic posture. They better understand the complex issues involved and better differentiate between "their" and other Arabs.

Trends in Arab-Jewish Relations

If the Arab radicalization and Jewish intransigence perspectives were correct, then growing estrangement, confrontation, and repression in Arab-Jewish relations should have taken place, but they have not. At the same time, certain developments transpired among both Arabs and Jews that resulted in the de-marginalization of Arabs in the Jewish state, which is a positive step toward the normalization of their status.

The status of Israeli Arabs changed markedly since the early years of the state. In the 1950's they were a segment forcibly separated from the vanquished Palestinian people; a mass of villagers, virtually without formal education, intelligentsia, and leadership; a population placed under military government; a group struggling for economic and national survival; and a new minority that had to cope with the psychology of a disadvantaged, suspected minority. By the 1980's, this peripheral Arab situation had been dramatically transformed. Today Israeli Arabs have a middle class, a network of organizations and institutions, and a strong leadership. They constitute a militant minority that avails itself of the democratic procedures to fight for equality. They have also developed ramified ties with the Palestinians beyond the Green Line while recognizing that their fate and future are linked to Israel.

Jewish orientation toward the Arab minority also underwent appreciable transformation. In the 1950's the Jews viewed Arabs as acting like a fifth column, despised them as primitive fallahins, hardly had any contact with them, and charged the authorities with the task of containing them. Today Jews hold a more differentiated and ambivalent view. They are aware of the Israeli Arabs' growing strength and militancy and their greater affinity to the Jews in loyalty, biculturalism, and destiny, compared to the Palestinians in the West Bank and Gaza Strip. Jews also take notice of the presence and participation of Arabs in many Israeli institutions, their permanent residence in Israel, and the necessity to accommodate them satisfactorily.

These shifts in Arab and Jewish positions have brought into the open previously latent tensions and conflicts between the two sides. The Arabs have begun to press such issues as land expropriations and the equitable dispensation of development funds, which they were not able to raise in the past, or which the authorities were too effective in suppressing. More generally, the Arabs have pushed for considerably greater change than the Jews are prepared to accept, or even consider.

The continuing international conflict between Israel and the Arab world as well as the Palestinian resistance in the occupied territories cast into bold relief the fundamental issues in Arab-Jewish relations in Israel. Beyond the undisputed fact of civic equality, the basic disagreement hinges on the status of the Arabs as a minority. In fact, most Arabs reconcile themselves to the existence of the State of Israel and realize that they are destined to remain a permanent minority in the Jewish state. This is precisely the reason why they are more vehement in opposing differential treatment and the restrictions of control. They wish to be treated like Israeli Jews and to be fully admitted into Israeli society. They also demand state recognition of their elected leaders, full control of their own institutions, and Jewish acceptance of their Palestinian identity and ties. These claims are presented along with a firm call to Israel to end its occupation of the territories and to acknowledge the Palestinians' right to self-determination.

Such views signify the politicization, not the radicalization, of Israeli Arabs. Rather than rejecting Israel, they challenge the intolerable status quo and demand to negotiate new terms of coexistence. From a Jewish perspective, however, this new militancy constitutes radicalization on the part of the Arabs. The Jews fear that fulfilling the Arab demands would necessitate the transformation of Israel into a binational state and that belligerent Palestinian nationalism would place its survival in jeopardy. Jews do not appreciate the growing acceptance of Israel as a state by Israeli Arabs and expect them to accept it as a Jewish-Zionist state as well.

For their part, Israeli Arabs do not appreciate the Jews' problems in accommodating them: Jews' discontent with the steady decline in Jewish exclusivity, the deep Jewish rejection of binationalism, the importance of the Holocaust in shaping the Jewish psyche, the sheer fear aroused by the Palestinians, and the backlash produced by indiscriminate Arab terrorism. Although this set of beliefs, actions, and developments among the Jews militates, in the main, against amicable Arab-Jewish relations, it does not amount to outright rejection of the Arabs. For Jews, their own resistance to further, more radical change is not the result of an intransigence grounded in self-serving, continued domination and exclusion. Rather, it stems from the basic insecurity of being a minority in the region both historically and currently, and from apprehensions over losing control and undermining the Jewish state.

The more headway Israeli Arabs make in their fight for equal rights and opportunity, the more intense will be their disagreements with Jews on the central issues of coexistence. Only then will Arabs and Jews face the most difficult aspect of the problem: how far can Arabs identify with the Jewish state?

22

Conclusion

If the Palestinian Arabs on the West Bank and Gaza Strip are treated as part of the external conflict, then the deepest division in Israel today is the split between Israel's Arab minority (650,000, 15% of the total population in 1987) and the Jewish majority. These Israeli Arab citizens are a nondominant, nonassimilating, working-class minority. They are also considered by the Jews as a dissident and enemy-affiliated minority which rejects Israel's national consensus on Zionism and potentially threatens its national security.

Arab attitudes and behavior are conceived of in terms of "a radicalization perspective," alienated and increasingly drifting away from Israel. This approach is dominant in the social sciences and among the general public, Israeli authorities, and Jewish and Arab nationalists. As such it enjoys the status of a paradigm, taken for granted even by theoretical and ideological protagonists.

Modernization, internal colonialism, and control theories concur about Arab radicalism and radicalization, which feed on the following sources: the Israeli-Arab conflict which makes Arabs prone to rejectionist, Palestinian nationalism; mounting Arab modernization which increases deprivation as family and community needs grow faster than resources; entrenched Zionism which does not enable Arabs to identify with the state; large-scale discriminatory policies against the Arabs; and excessive intolerance and rejection of Arabs by Jews.

The Arab radicalization perspective is complemented by the common "Jewish intransigence perspective." According to the latter approach, Jews are becoming increasingly alienated from Israeli Arabs in reaction to growing Arab alienation. The contributory factors to the Jewish resistance to change are the continued Arab challenge of Jewish vested interests and dominance; the steady growth of Jewish hawkishness since the 1967 war; the rise to power of the Likud and of

Oriental Jews, who share hostility against the Arabs; and the creeping annexation of the territories, which has blurred – in the Jewish mind – the distinction between Arabs on either side of the Green Line.

Together, these two perspectives portray a gloomy picture of Arab-Jewish relations. The two sides are seen as increasingly estranged and heading toward confrontation. It is assumed that Palestinization and Israelization are two poles on the same continuum, so that an increase in one is inevitably a decrease in the other. In this view, Israeli Arabs have become, since 1967, increasingly Palestinian in their national identity, have expanded their ties with fellow Palestinians, and have intensified their support for the PLO. In consequence, their Israeli identity and loyalty have simultaneously weakened. The de-Israelization of the Arabs and their growing unrest have further alienated the Jews who are generally becoming more and more threatened, nationalistic, and uncompromising.

Despite their plausibility and popularity, I find both perspectives inadequate, and I therefore suggest alternative approaches. The central theme of the alternative "Arab politicization perspective" is that the Arabs are destined to live as a permanent, Palestinian, national minority in the Jewish state and to assert themselves as a distinct, separate segment of the Palestinian people. Israelization and Palestinization are independent processes and one does not necessarily increase at the expense of the other. However, their simultaneous growth as components of Arab life poses problems for Arab-Jewish coexistence because of the current belligerency between Israel and the Palestinians and the existing Jewish-Zionist character of the state. Hence, settlement of the dispute and reshaping of Zionism would reduce or even eliminate the contradictions and tensions.

The thrust of the Arab politicization approach is that the Arabs are becoming more and more impatient with inequalities and restrictions and are engaged in a struggle to negotiate better terms of coexistence with Jews. That Arabs have sought the course of fighting from within for more equality and integration rather than choosing the route of rejectionism and antagonism is the outcome of several conditions and developments. Looming largest among them are the extension of Israeli citizenship to Arabs in 1948 and the lifting of the military administration over them in 1966. Both have cleared the way for a democratic, non-violent Arab struggle beginning in the early 1970's. The peace treaty between Israel and Egypt and the ongoing shift of the Palestinians away from rejectionism and armed resistance have also pushed Israeli Arabs into accommodation. Most important, they are increasingly aware of their higher stakes in the Israeli system and of ultimate Jewish control, despite the erosion of control as a daily routine. This awareness has forced Israeli Arabs to reconcile themselves to minority status for lack of a better alternative.

A supplementary "Jewish accessibilty perspective" suggests that Jews are reluctantly opening up to the integration of Israeli Arabs in their midst rather than turning against them. Israeli institutions are losing their Jewish exclusivity as a result of the increasing presence of Arabs. Jews are similarly more aware of Arab deprivations and grievances, and the authorities are also more responsive to Arab demands. This transformation, however, is taking place along with mounting political polarization among the Jews. Polarization in turn is dividing the Jewish public and political parties on the Arab minority question.

The Arab politicization and Jewish accessibility perspectives emphasize that the establishment of Israel in 1948 as a liberal, rather than Herrenvolk, democracy has largely determined the course of Arab-Jewish relations. The inclusion of Arabs as part of Israeli democracy has encouraged them to accommodate themselves to the state and equipped them with the peaceful means of struggle. It has also forced Jews to react to Arab grievances with concessions rather than repression. Despite the weaknesses of Israeli democracy (lack of a constitution, the existence of the 1945 Emergency Regulations, and high political intolerance), it has, since the mid 1970's, functioned well in managing the conflicts between the Arab minority and Jewish majority.

No single study could confirm or refute either perspective on Arab-Jewish relations. This study adopts the Arab politicization and Jewish accessibility perspectives. It attempts to produce new data that show their superiority over the rival perspectives in accounting for patterns and developments in the views and behavior of Israeli Arabs and Jews toward each other. More specifically, it analyzes the key issues dividing Arabs and Jews, the internal divisions within each side over coexistence, and the trends in the orientation of both communities vis-à-vis each other. The investigation of these questions is expected to shed light on the tensions and conflicts emanating from the problematic status of a Palestinian national minority in a Jewish-Zionist state.

The present study is part of a broader research project. A main component of the project consists of surveys of the Arab and Jewish populations and leaderships in 1976, 1980, 1985, and 1988. In this volume, the findings of the 1980 survey are summarized. The 1980 survey draws on face-to-face interviews with samples of 1,140 Arabs and 1,267 Jews, representing the entire adult population in Israel proper. It also includes 178 interviews with Arab and Jewish public figures, 30 from each of the 6 major political streams. Some findings from the 1976 survey are also incorporated in the study.

Three sets of findings have emerged from the study. The first set is based on the scrutiny of 13 key issues of coexistence over which Arabs and Jews differ. These are the following: ethnic stratification, cultural diversity, legitimacy of coexistence, the Israeli-Arab conflict, collective identity, institutional separation, national autonomy, group goals, leadership credibility, educational goals, strategies for change, ethnocentrism, and deprivation and alienation.

The analysis of attitudes toward these issues reveals a situation of "Arab-Jewish polarity," i.e., a majority of Arabs disagree with a majority of Jews on most of the relevant questions. The Arabs are found to be a dissident minority, whose views fall outside the Jewish consensus.

To highlight some of the disputes, the Arabs reject Israel's Jewish-Zionist features, such as Israel as a national homeland for Jews only, a permanent Jewish majority, the Law of Return, preferential treatment of Jews by the state, and exlusive Jewish state symbols. The Arabs also present the controversial demand of national autonomy, entailing control of their institutions, official recognition of their representative organizations, and the founding of new national frameworks. Other bones of contention are a two-state solution to the Palestinian problem, support for the PLO, Palestinian national identity, and the use of extra-parliamentary means of struggle, all of which are advocated by the Arabs and repudiated by the Jews.

The second set of findings concerns the considerable factionalism among both Arabs and Jews. The Arabs are divided into four orientation types, each representing a distinct minority response and corresponding to a publicly recognizable ideological-political stream. These types are accommodationists (15%), reservationists (39%), oppositionists (40%), and rejectionists (6%). The accommodationists are Arabs who accept Israel as is and believe that an improvement in Arab status can best be achieved by working through the Zionist establishment. They endorse Jewish views on most questions. The reservationists are moderate and selective in their rejection of the Jewish national consensus; they hold that the most effective way to bring about change is by forming independent organizations that cooperate and negotiate with the authorities. The oppositionists approve of Israel as a state but reject it as Jewish and Zionist. They are convinced that the Arab cause will be advanced only through independent, active opposition to the establishment. They share the stands of and support the Communist-led Democratic Front for Peace and Equality. Last of all, the rejectionists neither accept Israel nor their minority status in it, and they are willing to resort to extra-legal means of struggle if necessary. They identify themselves with the rejectionist positions taken by the Sons of the Village Movement and the Progressive

National Movement within Israel and with the Rejection Front in the Arab world.

These four Arab types differ in many areas. With regard to their background, the more militant types are more likely to be dissatisfied with local services, to be Druzes and non-Bedouin Moslems, and to come from families that suffered from land confiscations.

Similarly, the Jews are divided into four types: conciliationists (8%), pragmatists (33.5%), hardliners (36%), and exclusionists (23%). The conciliationists are prepared to extend equal rights and opportunities to the Arabs even if this requires moderating some of Israel's exclusive Jewish-Zionist characteristics. They conform to the outlooks of the Citizens Rights Movement, Mapam, Shinui, and Independent Liberals. The pragmatists espouse the Labor orientation toward the Arabs: liberal controls and sympathetic consideration of Arab needs and views, without retreating from Israel's Zionist zeal. The hardliners follow the Likud's posture that a strong-arm policy will prevent Arabs from challenging the system and induce them to accommodate themselves to Israel as is. The exclusionists wish to exclude Arabs from the state altogether or to subordinate them to Jewish rule. Their views are reminiscent of Kahane's, but are actually less extreme.

Differences in attitudes and background among the four Jewish types are pronounced. The less educated and more religious are inclined to belong to the less tolerant types. Since ethnicity and voting are strongly associated with religious observance and education, all four variables are related to Jewish orientation.

The third set of findings relates to the trend in Arab and Jewish orientations. The comparison of the 1976 with the 1980 Arab survey shows de-radicalization rather than radicalization. The proportion of oppositionists was down from 44% in 1976 to 40% in 1980, and that of the rejectionists dropped from 13.5% to 6%, respectively. These summary figures represent an overall trend which is evident in a good many attitudes. To illustrate, the proportion of Arabs denying Israel's right to exist declined from 20.5% in 1976 to 11% in 1980, and that of those defining themselves in non-Israeli Palestinian terms decreased from 33% to 26%, respectively. This decline in Israeli Arab radicalism from 1976 to 1980 could have been caused by the Egypt-Israel Peace Treaty which further legitimizes Israel in the eyes of Israeli Arabs. The increased likelihood that rejectionism would be severely punished under the new Likud government might also have had an effect.

The change in the patterns of Arab leadership, protest, and voting behavior shows a trend to militancy rather than to radicalization; viz., fighting more strongly for equality and peace while remaining firmly attached to Israel. Israeli Arab leaders have become more independent, outspoken, and active in pursuing Arab interests; Arab protest has become more recurrent, massive, and inclusive of both civil and national issues; and Arab voting has shifted to some extent away from the Jewish-Zionist parties and their affiliated Arab lists. The growing Palestinization of the Arabs has not turned into increasing hostility against Israel and the Jews because of its coincidence with the Arabs' continuing Israelization.

Similarly, the fragmentary data do not necessarily substantiate the Jewish intransigence perspective. The Histadrut, political parties, and other Jewish frameworks have promoted the integration of Israeli Arabs. State policies have become less discriminatory. The overall level of Jewish hostility against the Arab minority has not intensified. Political polarization has made the supporters of the Likud and religious parties less tolerant, while it has further liberalized the backers of the Labor and Zionist leftist parties.

Several conclusions and implications may be drawn from the study. First, the findings are more in line with the Arab politicization and Jewish accessibility perspectives than with the common Arab radicalization and Jewish intransigence perspectives. Arabs and Jews are neither disagreeing nor becoming more antagonistic to each other, but more understanding and reluctantly compromising.

Second, a new Israeli Arab, whose spirit permeates all Arab orientation types, has emerged and dominates the scene in the 1980's. The new Israeli Arab was born or educated since the establishment of the state, has at least post-primary education, has command of both Arabic and Hebrew, and is versed in both Arab and Israeli culture. He is strongly committed to democracy, considering it the best defensive weapon at his disposal in the struggle for equality as an individual and as a member of a minority. His level of aspiration is high, and he compares his achievements to those of the Jews. He accepts Israel and sees his future tied to it. He feels deprived and is willing to fight hard for equality. The new Arab in Israel is sensitive, proud, and self-assertive. He regards himself as a member of the Palestinian people, a carrier of the Palestinian culture, and a proponent of the Palestinian solution to the Israeli-Arab conflict; i.e., the formation of a PLO-headed Palestinian state in the West Bank and Gaza Strip alongside Israel. This solution is designed not for himself but for his Palestinian brethren. Being at once Israeli and Palestinian, the new Arab attempts to reconcile both of these components in his attitudes and behavior.

It is this new Israeli Palestinian Arab who presents a serious challenge to the status quo and demands to negotiate new terms of coexistence. Unlike such older Arab figures as the traditionalist, the collaborator, and the rejectionist who could easily be dismissed, the new

Arab imposes himself on the Jews and raises a number of fundamental dilemmas for them with regard to Arab identity, loyalty, and equality.

Third, the Jews refuse to recognize the Israeli Arabs' Palestinian national identity which they consider as illegitimate and subversive. Yet, continued Israeli control of the Palestinians has clearly shown that the Green Line has remained as firm as ever and that Israeli Arabs have developed as a distinct segment within the Palestinian people. They are Israeli Palestinian in identity and culture, and their fate and future are tied to Israel. Their demands are part of Israel's internal problems, and are separate from the Palestinian international question in the West Bank, Gaza Strip, and the Diaspora.

Fourth, another dilemma for the Jews is whether Israeli Arabs have become sufficiently loyal to justify the complete removal of the machinery of control over them. Control has been relaxed and eroded appreciably over the years as a result of both the growing democratization of Israeli society and the ongoing Arab struggle. For the Jews in general and the authorities in particular, the dismantling of control and the treatment of Arabs as loyal is problematic. In Jewish eyes, Israeli Arabs belong to the belligerent Palestinian people and back the PLO. From time to time, Jewish suspicions are reinforced when individual Israeli Arabs are convicted for perpetrating terrorist actions against Jews.

Fifth, the dilemma of equality is even harder and more complex than that of loyalty. The Arab struggle for equality, which has already scored significant gains, is and will be encountering Jewish resistance. Although it wins the sympathy of many Jews, most feel fearful and reluctant once they grasp its wider repercussions. It is not just that Arabs do not deserve equal rights as long as they do not assume equal duties (mostly military or civil service). Extension of full civil rights and opportunities to the Arabs would also mean the elimination of preferential treatment for Jews, who feel entitled to it in a Jewish state. Furthermore, in addition to equal, individual civil rights, the Arabs demand equal, collective national rights; i.e., the right to develop and to control their own national institutions. As far as the Jews are concerned, this is a claim to some sort of national self-determination and, therefore, a radical desire to transform Israel from a Jewish-Zionist to a binational state within the Green Line.

Sixth, it is only when Arabs become a legitimate pressure group in Israeli politics that they could make a breakthrough in their fight for equality. To this effect, they can take one or more of the following steps: fulfillment of the duty of civil or military service, formation of an Arab (or predominantly Arab) political party that is eligible for membership in coalition governments (a step in this direction was made in 1988 with the formation of the Democratic Arab Party headed by Knesset Member Darawshe), and softening the rejection of Israel's Jewish-Zionist character.

Seventh, policy toward the Arab minority emerges as a very important determinant of Arab and Jewish orientation. The degree of Arab militancy is influenced by how they are treated (the status of their community, effect of land expropriations, dispensation of funds, etc.), and not related to age, education, level of urbanization, and extent of individual modernism. Similarly, Jewish suspicions and rejection of Arabs are shaped and perpetuated by the state's treatment of the Arabs as potentially disloyal and by its application of certain controls and restrictions over them. A shift to a policy of trust, openness, equality, integration, and partnership will improve considerably the attitudes of both Arabs and Jews toward each other.

Finally, the Arab struggle for equality, acceptance, and peace and, particularly, the emergence of the new Arab have put both the Arab minority and the Jewish majority in Israel into an uneasy position. Under present conditions, it is difficult for the Arabs to reconcile their Israeli attachments with their Palestinian nationalism, and for the Jews to reconcile democracy with Zionism. Thus the settlement of the Arab minority problem in the Jewish state requires rethinking: the recasting of Zionism, of Israel's Jewish-Zionist character, of Israeli democracy, and of the Palestinian question.

Part Four

APPENDIXES

A

Methodology of Arab Sample Interview Survey

Survey methods are extensively applied to populations in advanced industrial societies. To be effective, they require both respondents' familiarity with surveys and active cooperation. Hence many doubt whether it is feasible to study, through surveys, sensitive issues among the Arab population of Israel because of its traditionalism and distrust. This is also why the 1976 and 1980 surveys, being the first national representative surveys of the attitudes of the Arabs on Arab-Jewish relations, have enjoyed much scientific and public interest, as well as aroused many methodological questions.

It is thus useful to review the methodology used in conducting the Arab sample interview survey. Since research on Israel's Jewish population is the most appropriate criterion for evaluating surveys among the Arabs, let me briefly describe first the procedures followed in the Jewish survey.

Public opinion polling is as well established in Israel as in Western countries. The Israel Institute of Applied Social Research, a non-profit organization headed by the late Louis Gutmann, started its activities back in 1949. After the 1967 war, polling expanded ever further and became regularized. Since then four major research institutes have operated, each of which takes a monthly general population survey.

The standard survey in Israel is based on face-to-face interviews using a questionnaire composed of closed-ended questions.[1] Respondents are interviewed in their homes and are assured privacy and confidentiality. A questionnaire is designed to take about half an hour to

---

[1]Telephone polling is only occasionally used in Israel because telephones are not standard in private homes.

administer. The target population includes all adult Jews (i.e., 18 years and older) living in localities within the pre-1967 borders, excluding kibbutzim.[2] An ecological sampling procedure is used. For this purpose

Table A1 Localities Surveyed in the 1980 Jewish Sample and Their Statistical Profiles

Locality	District	Population Size	Type	Opportunity Structure	Aggregate SES	% Oriental	1980 Sample
1. Tel-Aviv-Yafo	5	1	1	3	6	4	189
2. Jerusalem	1	1	1	3	5	5	86
3. Haifa	3	1	1	3	7	3	104
4. Beer Sheva	6	1	3	2	3	7	39
5. Ramat Gan	5	1	2	3	6	4	82
6. Bene Berak	5	2	2	3	5	4	38
7. Herzliya	5	2	2	3	5	5	34
8. Holon	5	1	2	3	6	5	101
9. Petah Tikva	4	1	2	3	5	5	63
10. Netanya	4	2	2	3	4	6	45
11. Rishon Letzion	4	2	2	2	5	5	53
12. Pardes Hana	3	4	4	2	4	6	32
13. Teveria (Tiberias)	2	3	2	1	2	8	28
14. Ramle	4	3	3	2	2	8	28
15. Ashdod	6	2	3	2	3	8	36
16. Yavne	4	4	5	2	1	10	23
17. Rosh Haayin	4	4	5	1	1	10	21
18. Raanana	4	3	4	3	4	6	16
19. Afula	2	4	2	1	3	7	27
20. Beit Shean	2	4	5	1	1	10	25
21. Beit Shemesh	1	4	5	1	1	9	11
22. Dimona	6	3	3	1	2	9	17
23. Mishmar Hanegev	6	7	8	3	9	2	10
24. Akko (Acre)	2	3	3	2	3	7	30
25. Kiryat Yam	3	3	2	3	5	6	31
26. Hahotrim	3	7	9	3	9	1	10
27. Gaash	4	7	9	3	8	2	10
28. Kiryat Anavim	1	7	8	3	9	1	10
29. Tzofit	4	7	6	3	9	1	11
30. Bareket	4	7	7	1	1	10	11
31. Beit Yitzhak	4	6	6	2	7	3	9
32. Ben Shemen	4	7	7	2	5	1	11
33. Brosh	6	7	7	1	1	10	10
34. Geva Karmel	3	7	7	1	3	10	11
Not known							4
Total							1,267

Key to Codes in Table:

District: 1. Jerusalem; 2. Northern; 3. Haifa; 4. Central; 5. Tel-Aviv; 6. Southern.

Population size: 1. 100,000 and over; 2. 50,000-99,999; 3. 20,000-49,999; 4. 10,000-19,999; 5. 5,000-9,999; 6. 1,000-4,999; 7. 999 or fewer.

Type: 1. Three largest cities; 2. municipality settled by Jews before 1948; 3. municipality settled by Jews since 1948; 4. urban settlement settled by Jews before 1948; 5. urban settlement settled by Jews since 1948; 6. Moshav established before 1948; 7. Moshav established since 1948; 8. Kibbutz established before 1948; 9. Kibbutz established since 1948.

Opportunity structure 1. Below average; 2. average; 3. above average.

Aggregate socioeconomic status (based on residents' socioeconomic measures): 1. Lowest, 5. average, 9. highest.

% Orientals (% Jews of Asian-African origin): 1. 0-9; 2. 10-19; 3. 20-29; 4. 30-39; 5. 40-49; 6. 50-59; 7. 60-69; 8. 70-79; 9. 80-89; 10. 90-100.

[2]Kibbutzim, constituting 4% of the adult population, are usually excluded because there is need to obtain permission to interview there.

the country is divided into strata according to two criteria: region and type of locality. The proportion of each stratum in the sample is determined by its weight among the voters in the entire population. The sample is taken in the following manner: localities are sampled in each stratum, polling tracts are chosen in each sampled locality, and streets are selected in each chosen polling tract. In each of the selected streets, apartments are sampled according to the systematic sampling method, and within each apartment and by the same method respondents are chosen. In this way 1,200 interviews are conducted within a week. As a safeguard against falsifications, the work of each interviewer is verified in every survey. A sampling error of 3% is standard for samples of this size.

The July 1980 survey of the Jewish population for the present study was contracted to an independent research institute which meticulously implemented the above standard procedures. Our interviews ran longer than usual, with 6.5% lasting more than one hour. Our sample was also larger (N=1,267 persons) and covered kibbutzim as well. Table A1 above lists the 34 localities in which fieldwork took place, each locality's demographic characteristics, and the number of interviews completed in each.

Bearing in mind these procedures for the Jewish survey, let us review and evaluate the procedures used in the Arab survey.

Procedures

Measuring Instrument

A questionnaire, consisting of 170 closed-ended questions, was the research instrument for the 1980 Arab survey. Most of the questions were attitudinal, covering various issues in Arab-Jewish relations, and the remainder (40 items) provided background information.

The Arabic questionnaire for Arabs was similar to the Hebrew questionnaire for Jews. Most of the questions were identical, but some were either deleted or modified to fit the situation of each group. Both questionnaires were pretested on small samples prior to the fieldwork, and vague or undifferentiating items were reworded or discarded.

Population and Sampling

For the purpose of this research, the Arab population was limited to those 18 years or over within Israel's pre-1967 borders.[3] It included the

[3]The Arab sample also included 45 youths (aged 16-17) in 1980 and 66 in 1976. For the sake of comparability with Arab surveys conducted after 1980 and with Jewish surveys that cover adults only, all persons under 18 were excluded from the statistics in this study.

Druzes but excluded non-Arab minorities (e.g., Circassians, Bahais), the Palestinian Arab residents of East Jerusalem, Gaza Strip, the West Bank, and the Druzes in the Golan Heights.

The sampling frame consisted of all Arab permanent localities, Bedouin encampments, and mixed Arab-Jewish towns. All these localities were stratified by region, population size, municipal status, religious composition, level of services, and percent voting for the Democratic Front for Peace and Equality (DFPE) in the 1977 national elections. Of the 115 stratified Arab permanent localities and mixed towns, 36 were selected. In addition, 2 of the 18 Northern Bedouin encampments and 4 of the 21 more populous Negev Bedouin encampments were chosen.

The complete official voter registry, which by law automatically registers all eligible voters in the country and must be published annually by the Ministry of the Interior, was used to draw a systematic random sample from each sampled locality. The number of respondents in each was proportional to its population size.

This sampling design was applied to the 1976 and 1980 Arab surveys, but the 1980 sample had another important feature. Being larger, it was possible to subdivide it into two parts (in a ratio of 60 to 40). The first part was a replication of the same 29 localities (including Bedouin encampments) and the same number of interviews in each used in the 1976 survey. The second part included two thirds of the respondents selected from 13 additional communities and one third from the 1976 localities.[4]

This special design was followed for two reasons. First, the replication of the 1976 sampling frame assures comparability, an essential criterion for a longitudinal analysis. Second, since each of the two parts of the 1980 sample is intended to represent the entire Arab population, a comparison of their findings on certain items that should remain constant furnishes a direct check of the representativeness of the 1980 sample and an indirect test of the 1976 sample as well.

Table A2 lists all the localities selected for the 1976 and 1980 Arab samples. The classification of each locality according to six sampling criteria and the number of respondents is also indicated. This table demonstrates the representiveness of both samples, as well as the comparability of the 1976 sample to the first part of the 1980 sample.

While both Arab samples applied a stratified probability sampling technique designed to yield, for the first time, a truly representative sample of Israel's Arab population for a study of Arab-Jewish relations,

---

[4]I wish to thank Henry Lever and Yochanon Peres for suggesting this design.

Table A2 Localities Surveyed in the 1976 and 1980 Arab Samples and Their Statistical Profiles[a]

	Religious Composition	Region	Municipal Status	Population Size	DFPE Vote	Level of Services	1976 Sample[b]	1980 1st Sub-Sample[b]	1980 2nd Sub-Sample[b]	1980 Sample (Total)
1. Haifa	6	1	1	1	2	3	37	41	25	66
2. Lod	1	3	1	1	2	2	27	29	–	29
3. Akko (Acre)	2	1	1	1	3	2	–	–	13	13
4. Tel-Aviv-Yafo	7	3	1	1	2	2	–	–	12	12
5. Nazareth	7	1	1	1	4	3	48	50	41	91
6. Shefaram	7	1	1	1	4	3	27	28	42	42
7. Tira	1	2	2	2	4	3	27	28	–	28
8. Baka Al-Gharbia	1	2	2	2	3	3	29	30	–	30
9. Sakhnin	2	1	2	2	4	3	28	38	27	65
10. Majd Al-Khrum	1	1	2	3	3	3	30	32	–	32
11. Daliat Al-Karmel	3	1	2	3	1	3	20	22	6	28
12. Kfar Yasif	7	1	2	3	4	3	26	29	–	29
13. Um Al-Fahem	1	2	2	1	3	3	–	–	34	34
14. Tayba	1	2	2	1	4	3	–	–	40	40
15. Yirka	3	1	2	3	2	3	–	–	14	14
16. Kfar Kana[c]	2	1	2	3	4	3	–	–	9	9
17. Maker	2	1	2	4	3	1	30	34	19	53
18. Ein Mahel	1	1	2	4	4	2	28	30	–	30
19. Jat[c]	1	2	2	4	3	3	28	29	–	29
20. Jisser Al-Zarka	1	3	2	4	1	2	25	24	–	24
21. Julis	3	1	2	4	1	2	19	21	4	25
22. Meilya	5	1	2	4	4	3	25	21	–	21
23. Pkiein	4	1	2	4	3	3	–	–	18	18
24. Fassuta	5	1	2	4	2	2	–	–	16	16
25. Faradies	1	3	2	4	2	2	–	–	27	27
26. Nahaf	1	1	2	4	3	1	–	–	26	26
27. Marja	1	2	3	5	2	1	8	8	2	10
28. Naora	1	1	3	4	1	1	18	23	–	23
29. Ibtin	1	1	3	4	2	1	16	19	6	25
30. Sajur	3	1	3	4	1	2	15	15	9	24
31. Eilut	1	1	4	4	3	1	16	14	1	15
32. Buayna	1	1	4	4	4	1	19	20	–	20
33. Akbara	1	1	4	5	1	1	7	10	–	10
34. Mouawiya	1	2	4	4	3	1	21	20	–	20
35. Bartaa	1	2	4	4	3	1	–	–	30	30
36. Busmat-Tivon	1	1	2	4	2	2	22	24	5	29
37. Hilf	1	1	4	4	1	1	13	14	1	15
38. Saayda Um Al-Ghnam	1	1	4	4	2	1	12	10	–	10
39. Huzayil	1	4	4	3	1	1	18	20	–	20
40. Aatzam	1	4	4	4	1	1	17	19	–	19
41. Abu Rabiaa	1	4	4	3	1	1	–	–	20	20
42. Atawna	1	4	4	4	2	1	–	–	19	19
Total							656	702	438	1,140

[a] Statistical profiles reflect the situation in 1980.

[b] Interviews with 18-year-olds and older only (excluding 16-17 years old – 66 in 1976 and 45 in 1980). For technical reasons there were certain minor differences in the number of interviews between the 1976 sample and the parallel 1980 first subsample.

[c] Because of an intense hamula feud during the fieldwork period, some of the interviews were conducted elsewhere.

Key to Codes in Table:

Religious composition: 1. Moslem; 2. mixed, with Moslem majority; 3. Druze; 4. mixed, with Druze majority; 5. Christian; 6. mixed, with Christian majority; 7. mixed, with no majority.

Region: 1. The Galilee; 2. Triangle; 3. Center; 4. Negev.

Municipal status: 1. Municipality; 2. local council; 3. regional council; 4. unincorporated.

Population size 1. 15,00 or over; 2. 10,000-14,999; 3. 5,000-9,999; 4. 500-4,999; 5. 499 or fewer.

DFPE vote: (% voting for the Democratic Front for Peace and Equality in 1977): 1. 0-19; 2. 20-39; 3. 40-59; 4. 60 or over.

Level of local services: 1. low; 2. medium; 3. high.

they also differed in some respects. The 1976 survey was smaller and used statistical weighting to adjust for disproportionality in representation.[5]

Sampling was also different for Arabs and Jews. Arab respondents were drawn from the electorate roster while Jewish respondents were drawn from dwelling units. Although both selection techniques are scientifically sound, the ecological one used in the Jewish sector is faster and cheaper because individuals immediately available at the time of the interviewer's first contact are interviewed without having to arrange callbacks to interview a predesignated respondent. It has, however, the possible disadvantage of letting interviewers be biased in their final selection. Lacking this drawback, the name-listing registered voter method is superior.

Fieldwork

Data were gathered through interviewing. Unlike the procedure used by the survey research firms that have a permanent, trained interviewing staff for continuing polling of the Jewish population, it was necessary each time to recruit about one hundred interviewers from among Arab university and teachers' college students, as well as school teachers. A special effort was made to locate persons from each selected community because a local interviewer usually enjoys greater cooperation. The interviewers were briefed, and their first completed interviews were checked. Gender matching of interviewers and interviewees was made but it proved to be of little consequence for most Arabs (except Druzes and some Bedouin).

The dropout rate resulting from difficult-to-locate respondents, changes of address, sojourning at other residences, misspelled names, sicknesses, and refusals was 27% in 1976 and 26% in 1980. Substitutes were used from a preselected random name roll in order to complete the quota of interviews in each sampled locality.

Interviewing procedures for Arabs were the same as those for the Jews. Each question and its possible answers were first read. The respondent was then asked to select the most appropriate answer. The presentation of all questionnaire items followed a uniform order. In cases of doubt, questions and potential answers were repeated and occasionally rephrased in order to clarify them. Interviewers were instructed not to cite any specific examples in these clarifications. They were also told to avoid conversing or exchanging views with respondents during the interview. These rules standardized the

[5]Only 24% of the interviews in the 1976 survey were with women, but their proportion was doubled through weighting of the final findings.

interviews by reducing interviewers' biases. They also saved time because 79.5% of the interviews took up to one and a half hours each.

Respondents were assured full confidentiality. Their names and addresses were not recorded on the completed questionnaires. In 53% of the cases, interviewers and interviewees were acquaintances, and the rest were not known to each other.

A total of 1,140 interviews with Arabs (conducted by Arab interviewers in Arabic) and 1,267 interviews with Jews (administered by Jewish interviewers in Hebrew) were completed during the last week of June and the first two weeks of July 1980. In the earlier surveys, 656 Arabs in a representative sample and 148 Jews in a small sample were interviewed in the summer of 1976.

Evaluation

Representativeness
Do the Arab and Jewish samples truly represent the respective Arab and Jewish populations? Given the same instrument, would other samples yield essentially similar results? The answer is probably yes. The samples are fair and unbiased. The stratified sampling technique used in the Arab samples insures representativeness according to region, population size, municipal status, religious composition, level of local services, and DFPE vote. Similarly, the Jewish sample is designed to represent a cross section of communities according to region and type of locality.

It is possible to estimate the sampling error due to random fluctuations. For a confidence level of 95%, a sample of 1,140 respondents provides for a sampling error ranging from 1.3% (for attributes distributed in a ratio of 5:95) to 2.9% (for a ratio of 50:50).[6] Sampling errors for subpopulations with 500 or more respondents do not exceed 4.5%. Hence, distributions of any entire sample and large sections thereof are reliable estimates of the characteristics of the population. But the estimates for small subpopulations (e.g., Druzes, persons with higher education) are not reliable enough and should be treated with caution. However, the differences between subpopulations are by and large reliable.

Representativeness of the Arab sample is confirmed by a comparison between the sample statistics with known population parameters. For instance, the sample distributions of age and education closely

[6]Samples of 1,200 persons have a sampling error of 3% for any population over 500,000. This is why such sample size is used for polling the Israeli Arab minority, Jewish majority, or the larger by far U.S. population.

correspond to those published by the Central Bureau of Statistics for the general Arab population. To be sure, there are always minor deviations which seldom exceed 5%. To illustrate, persons with post-secondary education are somewhat overrepresented, while persons 65 years old and over are slightly underrepresented.

The application of these direct checks shows that the Jewish sample is less representative than the Arab sample. To reduce the biases in the Jewish sample, it is stratified into 27 categories of age (18-34, 35-54, 55+) education (0-8, 9-12, 13+), and ethnic origin (father born in Israel, Asia-Africa, Europe-America), and the correct weights of each category, obtained from official annual labor force surveys conducted in 1980, are applied to them. The weighting also indirectly decreases other biases which are associated with these three socio-demographic features.[7]

Despite the weighting used in the Jewish survey, certain nondominant categories of Jews remain underrepresented. Looming largest among them are newcomers and those with a poor knowledge of Hebrew. Only 5% of the Jewish respondents report Hebrew illiteracy as compared to an estimated population rate of around 15%. Only 11% of the Jews in the study report voting for the religious parties in the 1977 national elections as compared to the actual results of 16%. Also underrepresented are residents in the country's Southern district (13% of the population but only 8% of the sample). These deviations would probably introduce a minor liberal bias in the attitudes of the Jewish sample toward Arabs.

A systematic comparison of the two parts of the 1980 Arab sample on many attributes and opinions shows no significant differences and hence confirms beyond any doubt the representativeness of the sample as a whole. As indicated above, the 1980 Arab sample is composed of two independent subsamples of 702 and 438 persons each, with two thirds of the second subsample coming from entirely different communities. These subsamples produce similar findings; for instance, 62% of the Arabs in the first subsample and 65% in the second subsample are literate in Hebrew, and 59% of each subsample accept Israel's right to exist.

The interchangeability of the two subsamples not only verifies the proper representativeness of the 1980 sample but also has two additional implications. First, it implies that the 1976 sample, which is comparable to the first 1980 subsample, is representative. Second, the comparability

---

[7]This weighting was also applied to Van Leer survey of the Jewish population (some of its findings are incorporated in this study). This is why statistics which we weighted from the Van Leer survey slightly differ from the unweighted statistics reported in the published report of that survey (Zemah, 1980).

between the two 1980 subsamples and the 1976 sample allows for straightforward comparisons in order to establish longitudinal trends.

Reliability

Would answers be similar if the same respondents were reinterviewed a short time later, interviewed by somebody else, or asked questions and offered answers worded or ordered differently? It is immaterial whether an individual respondent would answer exactly the same with lapse of time, change of interviewer, or shift of phrasing or order. The response distribution of the sample is what matters, and it is much less likely to fluctuate randomly than individual answers.

Although these objections to the reliability of survey data apply in general, they could be particularly levelled against the Arab data. Two specific points stand out. One is the low educational standard of the Arab population: 20% have no schooling at all and 48% have primary education only. Furthermore, the lack of "Western sophistication" could cause serious comprehension difficulties resulting in distorted information. The other doubt stems from the Arabs' public image as "fickle-minded," incapable of giving stable answers.

The available tests refute these potential objections and show Arab responses to be as reliable as Jewish ones.

1. *Estimated comprehension.* The interviewers rate the degree of comprehension shown by Arab respondents to be, overall, satisfactory: 84% have full or reasonable understanding, 15% lack certain understanding, and only 1% lack any understanding. The ratings of the Jewish respondents are similar: 79%, 16%, and 5%, respectively.

2. *Consistency in response.* A thorough examination reveals that Arab responses are highly consistent between items and problem areas. A direct test is provided by a repetition of one question in the 1980 questionnaire. At the beginning of the interview respondents were asked if neighborhoods should be separate for Arabs and Jews; past the middle of the interview they were asked if neighborhoods should be integrated for Arabs and Jews. The survey shows that 42% of the Arabs in the first question and 37% in the second question favor separation, 18% and 26% have reservations, and 40% and 37% oppose it. This strong consistency, despite a different wording of the question and despite the wide exposure to many issues in Arab-Jewish relations placed between the two questions, is not lower than the internal response consistency shown by the Jews: 60% and 59% endorse separate neighborhoods, 17% and 26% have reservations, and 23% and 15% object to them.

In fact, consistency is sufficiently large to classify 89% of the Arabs, like 85% of the Jews, into discernible pre-defined, politically prevalent, complex orientation types. The coherent, internal structure of the data demonstrates that Arab responses as a whole are informed and dependable rather than misunderstood and erratic.

3. *Stability over time.* A repeated measurement of the same unalterable characteristic can test the stability of responses. Unvariable information on sensitive factual matters is likely to be reliable. To illustrate, in 1980 65.5% of the land-owning Arab respondents and in 1976 65% report that they were affected over the years by land expropriations. Similarly, 21% and 23.5%, respectively, report they were of refugee origin (i.e., their families became "internal refugees" as a result of the 1948 war).

By the same token, logically stable attitudes are in fact stable. While we do not have two consecutive Arab samples within the same year, it is possible to compare Jewish responses to some questions in the July 1980 sample with those of the Van Leer survey taken six months earlier. It was found that 41% of the Jews in July and 34% in January unreservedly approve of the expropriation of Israeli Arab lands for Jewish development. Likewise, 36% and 43%, respectively, feel that Israel does more than it should for its Arab population. This stability suggests that opinions regarding Arab-Jewish issues are firm and predictable rather than capricious.

Validity

Are respondents telling the "truth"? This is the most crucial yet most difficult question to tackle. In addition to the ordinary impediments in eliciting "real" opinions in public surveys, two special obstacles stand out in the case of the Arab minority. One is excessive "social desirability" (Sohlberg, 1976). Potential bias is presumably caused by the strong predisposition of Arabs to answer according to what is expected or socially acceptable regardless of their own beliefs. Second, there may be a rather serious problem of trust. As many as 66% of the Arabs in the 1980 sample agree that it is impossible to trust most Jews. Since most Arabs mistrust Jews, many could misrepresent their responses because they fear that the information might be used against them personally or against the Arab minority collectively.

If social desirability is supposed to pressure Arabs to answer with an eye to the norm-setting Jewish views or to respond with less hostility, these two built-in biases could slant Arab data toward greater accommodation. Actually, in reaction to the survey findings, one political commentator has protested that only if Arabs were to be individually placed in "safe" rooms where they could express themselves freely, the sample answers would be uniformly anti-Israel.

But is this really the case? Instead of guessing how Arabs would have responded under imaginary circumstances of absolute impunity, it would be more beneficial to record the steps taken to explore validity checks in the study. The following are worth noting:

1. *Timing.* The general atmosphere in 1976 was, no doubt, more congenial for surveying Arabs than it was four years later. The fieldwork for the first survey was carried out in the summer, i.e., five to eight months after the Land Day strike of March 30, 1976. The strike encouraged an ongoing process of Arabs becoming more openly critical and less fearful of Jews. In fact, many Arabs were enthusiastic about participating in the survey in order to ventilate their opinions. Indeed, 79% of the Arabs and 84% of the Jews in the 1976 survey agree fully or partially with the observation that since the 1973 war Arabs have overcome their apprehension of Israeli authorities. This openness helped secure Arab cooperation and hence obtain more accurate information.

While their willingness to speak up increased, Arabs had shifted from an offensive to defensive posture in reaction to restrictive measures taken by the government in 1980. The Likud government, which came to power after the completion of the 1976 survey, was indifferent to Arabs but in 1979-80 it became increasingly impatient with growing Arab criticism of Israel, mounting identification with the Palestinians in the occupied territories and the PLO, and recurrent clashes with Jewish university students. The government first made warnings and threats. It then issued confinement injunctions to about one dozen Arab leaders and students and also passed an amendment in the Knesset to the "Terror Act 1948" so that persons who expressed public sympathy with the PLO could be persecuted.

As a result of the rising personal costs of Arabs' militancy and their resulting guarded stance, our interviewers were received with less enthusiasm and more anxiety in 1980. It is difficult to estimate how much additional self-restraint Arab respondents exercised and which subgroups were more apprehensive. However, fear did not suppress other Arab statements that would be considered extremist by Jews. To illustrate, the fact that 60% of the Arabs polled in 1980 and 58% in 1976 report participation in the 1976 Land Day strike shows that in the 1980 survey Israeli Arabs did not try to hide their militancy. Furthermore, 48.5% of the Arabs in 1980 maintain that the PLO truly represents Israeli Arabs and 61% even say that they would rejoice at or justify Fedayeen actions in which Israeli Jews were killed.

2. *Estimated trust.* The survey was designed to win the respondents' trust. The assurance of anonymity, the use of Arab fieldwork coordinators, and the use of Arab interviewers (who in half of the cases knew the respondents personally) were only some of the measures adopted. According to the interviewers' assessments, during 37% of the interviews the atmosphere was characterized by full trust, 53% by

reasonable trust, 9% by some mistrust, and only in 1% by total mistrust. Trust was greater when the interviewer and the respondent were acquaintances and among the more educated. More important, trust was poorly correlated with radicalism in orientation. Mistrust should not have, therefore, caused an underrepresentation of radicals in the sample. It is possible that some portion of the 26% who dropped out from the original list of respondents did so because of mistrust, but those who refused were not necessarily radicals. They probably include as many accommodating persons who also preferred not to express their reservations about the regime.

3. *Estimated validity.* Interviewers estimate the overall validity of the information provided by the respondents as satisfactory or better. In 24% of the cases information is rated as very good, 38% as good, 32% as sufficient, and only 7% as unsatisfactory. Perceived validity correlates highly with perceived trust ($r = 0.65$) and comprehension ($r = 0.68$), and to some extent with acquaintanceship ($r = 0.21$) and education ($r = 0.26$). The significant fact that validity bears virtually no relationship to radicalism ($r = 0.03$) means that accommodationist and rejectionist Arabs are judged to be equally accurate in their responses.

4. *Contrast groups.* The study differentiates well between groups that are likely to differ. Several highlights will suffice. The disagreement between Arabs and Jews on many issues is found, as expected, to be deep and pervasive. And, the views of different Arab leadership groups, which are known for their ideological divergence, differ considerably. Druzes and Northern Bedouin are predictably less militant than Christians, Negev Bedouin, and non-Bedouin Moslems. Arabs who report they suffered from land expropriations, or took part in the 1976 Land Day strike, are also more potentially militant than the others. The systematic confirmation of these observed differences between known groups helps to validate the information supplied by the respondents.

5. *Coherence.* The consistency of stands taken on related issues, the link between attitudes and reported behavior, and the relationship between life-situations (background) and orientations demonstrate an underlying logical structure to the data that is not likely to be accidental. The answers have reasonable "construct validity," that is, they form ordered patterns and "make sense."

6. *Cross-validation.* The Arab findings are not a function of a specific survey time or sample. The consistency between two independent, representative samples taken four years apart lends credence to the results. The favorable retesting of the 1976 data in the 1980 survey constitutes major cross-validation.

To conclude, the 1976 and 1980 Arab surveys demonstrate that, contrary to scientific doubts and public misconceptions, the use of standard survey methods to study Arab opinion on controversial matters is feasible. The result is data which pass the usual checks of representativeness, reliability, and validity.

B

The Questionnaire

Following is an English translation of the questionnaire used for interviewing both Arabs and Jews. Except where indicated, the Arabic-language questionnaire was identical in content and form to the Hebrew-language version. Questions that were presented to Arabs only are marked by an asterisk, and those posed to Jews only are identified by two asterisks.

Interviewer's Introduction to Arab Respondents

The Jewish-Arab Center at the University of Haifa is conducting a survey of Arab-Jewish relations in Israel. For this purpose, 1,200 persons, representing Arabs all over the country, were chosen. You are one of those who were randomly selected for this sample. A similar sample of Jews was also selected for the study. The goal of the research is to ascertain the attitudes of Arabs and Jews toward each other.

All of the information that you provide will be used for scientific objectives only. Hence there is no need to know your name and address and they will not be recorded. Your answers will serve to understand better the situation of Arabs in Israel, and your cooperation is very important.

The questions that I will present to you do not have right or wrong answers. The purpose is to learn about your stands on a number of topics. I hope that you will take this opportunity to express your opinions freely.

I will read to you the question and the answers related to it, and you are requested to choose the answer that suits you most.

Interviewer's Introduction to Jewish Respondents

I am an interviewer from the Dahaf Research Institute, which is an independent institute for social research. We conduct public opinion polls on various subjects. You were randomly selected as one respondent. Your answers will remain anonymous and be used for scientific objectives only.

The subject matter of the survey this time is Arab-Jewish relations in Israel. The goal of the study is to ascertain the attitudes of Jews toward the Arabs of Israel: i.e., the Arabs who are Israeli citizens and live within the Green Line.

Every question has a number of answers, and you are requested to choose, only after hearing all the possible answers, the one that suits you most.

Text of the Questionnaire[1]

1   *Case number.*

5   *To what extent are you interested in problems relating to relations between Jews and Arabs in Israel?*
           1 Much   2 To an appreciable degree   3 To some degree
           4 No

6   *To what extent are you interested in politics?*
           1 Much   2 To an appreciable degree   3 To some degree
           4 No

7   *(For Arab respondents:) How often do you have contact with Jews? (For Jewish respondents: "Jews" reads "Arabs.")*
           1 Daily   2 Quite often   3 Sometimes   4 Almost Never

8   *(For Arab respondents:) Do you have Jewish friends and have you visited their homes over the past two years? (For Jewish respondents: "Jewish" reads "Arab.")*
           1 Have no Jewish/Arab friends
           2 Have Jewish/Arab friends but have not visited them
           3 Have Jewish/Arab friends and have visited their homes over the past two years

9   *(For Arab respondents:) Are you willing to have Jewish friends? (For Jewish respondents: "Jewish" reads "Arab.")*
           1 Definitely willing   2 Willing
           3 Willing, but prefer Arab/Jewish friends
           4 Wants to have Arab/Jewish friends only

[1]The item numbers here are the variable numbers used in the codebook of the computerized records rather than the original numbers in the questionnaire. For this reason there are gaps in the numbers (e.g., 1, 5, 6...128, 205, etc.) although all items are reproduced as they appear in the original questionnaire.

10   *Are you willing to live in a mixed neighborhood?*
      1 Definitely willing   2 Willing
      3 Willing, but prefer Arabs/Jews   4 Want Arabs/Jews only

11   *Do you think that schools should be separate for Arabs and Jews?*
      1 Yes   2 Uncertain   3 No

12   *Do you think that residential quarters should be separate for Arabs and Jews?*
      1 Yes   2 Uncertain   3 No

13   *Do you think that political parties should be separate for Arabs and Jews?*
      1 Yes   2 Uncertain   3 No

14   *Do you know how to read and write in any language (i.e., can you write a simple letter)?*
      1 Yes   2 No

15   *Do you know how to read and write in Arabic (i.e., can you write a simple letter in Arabic)?*
      1 Yes   2 No

16*   *Which Arabic newspaper have you read recently?*
      1 Did not read any newspaper, but can read Arabic
      2 Al-Anba
      3 Al-Ittihad
      4 An East Jerusalem newspaper
      5 Al-Anba and Al-Ittihad
      6 Al-Anba and an East Jerusalem newspaper
      7 Al-Ittihad and an East Jerusalem newspaper
      8 Al-Anba, Al-Ittihad and an East Jerusalem newspaper
      9 Cannot read Arabic

18*   *Which newspaper and broadcasts do you trust most?*
      1 Official, non-partisan Israeli newspapers and broadcasts
      2 Israeli newspapers of the Jewish left like "Haolam Haze" and "Al-Hamishmar"
      3 Rakah newspapers
      4 Non-Israeli newspapers and broadcasts from the occupied territories, Arab states, or Europe

19   *(For Arab respondents:) Do you know enough Hebrew to conduct a conversation with an Israeli Jew? (For Jewish respondents: "Hebrew" reads "Arabic," "Jew" reads "Arab.")*
      1 Yes   2 No

20   *Do you read and write Hebrew (i.e., can you write a simple letter in Hebrew)?*
      1 Yes   2 No

21   *Have you read a Hebrew newspaper recently?*
      1 Yes   2 No   3 Cannot read Hebrew

22   *What is your opinion of the possibility that modern values and practices will prevail in Israel?*
1 In favor   2 Have reservations   3 Against

23   *Should Arabs in Israel learn modern values and practices from Jews?*
1 Yes   2 Uncertain   3 No

24   *Should Arabs in Israel adopt Jewish values and practices in addition to their own?*
1 In favor   2 Uncertain   3 Against

25   *Should Jews in Israel adopt Arab values and practices in addition to their own?*
1 In favor   2 Uncertain   3 Against

26   *Which of the following goals is most desirable for Arab education in Israel today?*
1 To live as a loyal minority member in a Jewish state
2 To love Israel as the common homeland of its two peoples, Arab and Jewish
3 To be a member of the Palestinian people

27   *Which o f the following goals is most desirable for Jewish education in Israel today?*
1 To live as a loyal citizen
2 To love Israel as the common homeland of its two peoples, Arab and Jewish
3 To be a member of the Jewish people

28   *Which language should be the dominant language of the public and state institutions in Israel?*
1 Hebrew   2 Hebrew and Arabic equally   3 Arabic

29   *Should Arab culture be treated as an important part of Israel's national culture?*
1 In favor   2 Have reservations   3 Against

30   *The State of Israel is:*
1 Homeland of Jews only
2 Common homeland of Jews and Arabs
3 Homeland of Arabs only

31   *Should the State of Israel within the Green Line retain a Jewish majority?*
1 Yes   2 No

32   *Should the State of Israel prefer Jews or Arabs?*
1 Prefer Jews to Arabs considerably
2 Prefer Jews to Arabs to some extent
3 Treat both equally
4 Prefer Arabs to Jews to some extent
5 Prefer Arabs to Jews considerably

33   *(For Arab respondents:) Do you accept Israel's right to exist? (For Jewish respondents:) Do you accept the Arabs' right to live in Israel as a minority with full civil rights?*
       1 Yes   2 Have reservations   3 No

34   *(For Arab respondents:) Do you accept Israel's right to exist within the Green Line as a Jewish-Zionist state?*
       1 Yes   2 Have reservations   3 No

       (For Jewish respondents:) How important is it for you that Israel will remain a Jewish-Zionist state?
       1 Very important   2 Important
       3 Not too important   4 Not important

35   *(For Arab respondents:) It is said that it is all right to use any means necessary to abolish Israel's Jewish-Zionist character. What is your opinion? (For Jewish respondents: "to abolish" reads "to retain.")*
       1 Yes   2 Have reservations   3 Against

       Indicate if you are in favor, have reservations, or are against the use of each of the following means against groups that oppose the Jewish-Zionist character of the state.

36**   *Denial of a license to publish a newspaper.*
       1 In favor   2 Have reservations   3 Against

37**   *Denial of registration to incorporate as a voluntary association.*
       1 In favor   2 Have reservations   3 Against

38**   *Use of administrative detention without a trial of the group members.*
       1 In favor   2 Have reservations   3 Against

39**   *Outlawing.*
       1 In favor   2 Have reservations   3 Against

40**   *Deportation from the country of the group members.*
       1 In favor   2 Have reservations   3 Against

41*   *The United Nations General Assembly adopted a resolution that Zionism is a racist movement. Do you agree with this resolution?*
       1 Agree   2 Have reservations   3 Disagree

42   *What is your opinion of the Law of Return, i.e., the law that accords only to the Jews the right of citizenship upon arrival in Israel?*
       1 Retain as is   2 Retain under certain circumstances   3 Repeal

43   *Do you think that Israel should devote all its attention to its Jewish and Arab residents and stop its efforts for Jewish immigration and for Jews in the Diaspora?*
       1 Definitely yes   2 Yes   3 No   4 Definitely no

44   *Do you think that Arabs can be equal citizens in Israel as a Jewish-Zionist state and can identify themselves with the state?*
       1 Yes   2 Possibly   3 Doubtful   4 No

45 *Should the special departments for Arab affairs such as the Office of the Prime Minister's Adviser on Arab Affairs and the Arab Department in the Histadrut be abolished?*
1 In favor of abolishment   2 Have reservations
3 Against abolishment

46 *Should a compulsory civil service be imposed on Arabs in Israel as long as they are exempted from a compulsory military service?*
1 Yes   2 Only under certain circumstances   3 No

47 *Should Arabs control and manage their own system of education?*
1 In favor   2 Have reservations   3 Against

48 *Should Arabs control and manage the various Arab departments?*
1 In favor   2 Have reservations   3 Against
4 In favor of abolishing the Arab departments

49 *What is your opinion of establishing an independent Arab university?*
1 In favor   2 Have reservations   Against

50 *What is your opinion of establishing an independent , new Arab press, radio or television station?*
1 In favor   2 Have reservations   3 Against

51 *What is your opinion of establishing an independent Arab trade union?*
1 In favor   2 Have reservations   3 Against

52 *What is your opinion of establishing an independent, new, nationalist Arab political party?*
1 In favor   2 Have reservations   3 Against

53 *Which political organization is most desirable for Arabs in Israel under the present circumstances?*
1 To join existing Jewish parties as individuals with equal status
2 To form Arab parties that can reach agreement or cooperate with the existing Jewish parties
3 To belong to non-Zionist parties composed of Arabs and Jews
4 To establish independent nationalist Arab parties
5 No political party organization at all

54* *Suppose that in the next elections to the Knesset, an independent nationalist political party that aimed to promote the interests of the Arabs in Israel were established by the Arab intelligentsia. Would you be willing to vote for it?*
1 Yes   2 Under certain circumstances   3 No

55 *Do you consider Rakah (Israeli Communist Party) to be truly representative of the interests of Arabs in Israel?*
1 Definitely yes   2 Yes   3 No   4 Definitely No

56 *Do you consider the Committee for Defence of Arab Lands to be truly representative of the interests of Arabs in Israel?*
1 Definitely yes   2 Yes   3 No   4 Definitely no
5 Have not heard of the Committee

57* *In assessing your socioeconomic achievements today, with whom do you compare yourself most?*
1 Arabs in Arab countries
2 Arabs in the West Bank and Gaza Strip
3 Inhabitants of the Western World
4 Jews in Israel
5 Palestinian Arabs during Mandatory Palestine

58 *How do you regard the present socioeconomic gap between Jews and Arabs in Israel?*
1 Large 2 Medium 3 Small

59 *How do existing government policies affect the present socioeconomic gap between Jews and Arabs in Israel?*
1 Reduce it 2 Neither reduce nor widen it 3 Widen it

60 *Some say that Arabs in Israel enjoy equal job opportunities, except in jobs related to national security. What is your opinion?*
1 Agree 2 Have reservations 3 Disagree

61 *Do you think that Arab youth have reasonable chances of fulfilling their occupational aspirations in Israel today?*
1 Yes 2 Possible 3 Doubtful 4 No

62 *To what extent are you satisfied with being an Israeli citizen?*
1 Definitely satisfied 2 Satisfied 3 Not too satisfied
4 Not satisfied 5 Not satisfied at all

63 *Are you satisfied with the cultural and educational services in your place of residence?*
1 Definitely satisfied 2 Satisfied 3 Not too satisfied
4 Not satisfied 5 Not satisfied at all

64* *Where would you feel more at home, in Israel or in an Arab country?*
1 More in Israel 2 More in an Arab Country 3 No difference

65 *Do you feel alien in Israel in your style of life, practices, and values?*
1 To a great degree 2 To a considerable degree
3 To some degree 4 Do not feel alien

66 *Do you feel that your relations with Jews are on an equal footing? (For Jewish respondents: "Jews" reads "Arabs.")*
1 Always 2 In most cases 3 Often
4 Almost never 5 Have no contact with Jews/Arabs

67* *When you learn about a Fedayeen action in which Jewish citizens were killed, how do you feel?*
1 Rejoice and justify action 2 Rejoice but do not justify action
3 Sadden but justify action 4 Sadden and do not justify action

Indicate the degree to which you are satisfied with each of the following.

68*   *The President of the State.*
        1 Very satisfied   2 Satisfied   3 Indifferent
        4 Dissatisfied   5 Very dissatisfied

69*   *The Prime Minister.*
        1 Very satisfied   2 Satisfied   3 Indifferent
        4 Dissatisfied   5 Very dissatisfied

70*   *The Knesset.*
        1 Very satisfied   2 Satisfied   3 Indifferent
        4 Dissatisfied   5 Very dissatisfied

71*   *Democracy in Israel.*
        1 Very satisfied   2 Satisfied   3 Indifferent
        4 Dissatisfied   5 Very dissatisfied

72*   *Freedom of expression in Israel.*
        1 Very satisfied   2 Satisfied   3 Indifferent
        4 Dissatisfied   5 Very dissatisfied

73*   *Israel Defence Forces.*
        1 Very satisfied   2 Satisfied   3 Indifferent
        4 Dissatisfied   5 Very dissatisfied

74*   *The courts.*
        1 Very satisfied   2 Satisfied   3 Indifferent
        4 Dissatisfied   5 Very dissatisfied

75*   *The police.*
        1 Very satisfied   2 Satisfied   3 Indifferent
        4 Dissatisfied   5 Very dissatisfied

76*   *Medicine.*
        1 Very satisfied   2 Satisfied   3 Indifferent
        4 Dissatisfied   5 Very dissatisfied

77*   *Education and culture.*
        1 Very satisfied   2 Satisfied   3 Indifferent
        4 Dissatisfied   5 Very dissatisfied

Let us proceed to questions regarding the Israeli-Arab conflict.

78   *What is your stand on settlements in Judea and Samaria?*
        1 In favor   2 Have reservations   3 Against

79   *What is your stand on the peace treaty between Israel and Egypt?*
        1 In favor   2 Have reservations   3 Against

80   *What is you stand on the autonomy plan as a basis for settling the Palestinian problem?*
        1 In favor   2 Have reservations   3 Against

81   *Do you think that Israel should recognize the Palestinians as a nation?*
      1 Yes   2 Only under certain circumstances   3 No

82   *Which borders of the State of Israel are you prepared to compromise on in order to reach a peace settlement?*
      1 All of Mandatory Palestine where a new state will be established instead of Israel
      2 1947 UN partition borders
      3 Pre-1967 borders, including retreat from East Jerusalem
      4 Pre-1967 borders with certain modifications
      5 Present borders with willingness to compromise also in Judea and Samaria
      6 Present borders with certain modifications

83   *Do you think that Israel should recognize the PLO as the authoritative representative of the Palestinian people?*
      1 Yes   2 Only under certain circumstances   3 No

84*   *Do you think that the PLO should recognize the State of Israel?*
      1 Yes   2 Only under certain circumstances   3 No

85   *Are you in favor of establishing a Palestinian state in the West Bank and Gaza Strip alongside Israel?*
      1 Yes   2 Only under certain circumstances   3 No

86   *Should Israel recognize the Palestine refugees' right of repatriation to Israel within the Green Line?*
      1 Yes   2 Only under certain circumstances   3 No

87   *(For Arab respondents:) Should the Palestinians give up the demand for the right of repatriation if this is necessary to reach a peace settlement? (For Jewish respondents:) Should the Jews give up East Jerusalem if this is necessary to reach a peace settlement?*
      1 In favor   2 Have reservations   3 Against

88*   *Do you think that the Arabs in Israel should fashion a special compromise position of their own on the Israeli-Arab conflict or be an integral part of the struggle of the Palestinian people?*
      1 Fashion a special compromise position of their own
      2 Be an integral part of the struggle of the Palestinian people

89   *Which one of the following political bodies offers the best solution to the Israeli-Arab conflict?*
      1 Gush Emunim, or Tehiya   2 Likud   3 Labor
      4 Shelli   5 Rakah   6 PLO

90*   *Do Jews outside Israel today constitute a people or a religious community only?*
      1 People   2 Religious community only

91*   *Do Jews in Israel today constitute a people or a religious community only?*
      1 People   2 Religious community only

92   *Is the term "Israeli" appropriate in describing your identity?*
     1 Very appropriate   2 Appropriate
     3 Not too appropriate   4 Not appropriate at all

93   *Is the term "Palestinian" appropriate in describing your identity? (For Jewish respondents: "Palestinian" reads "Jew.")*
     1 Very appropriate   2 Appropriate
     3 Not too appropriate   4 Not appropriate at all

94* *How would you define yourself if you had to choose one of the following alternatives?*
     1 Arab   2 Palestinian Arab   3 Israeli Arab
     4 Israeli   5 Israeli Palestinian
     6 Palestinian in Israel or Palestinian Arabs in Israel
     7 Palestinian

95   *How would you define Arabs in Israel if you had to choose one of the following alternatives?*
     1 Arabs   2 Israeli Arabs
     3 Israelis   4 Palestinian Arabs   5 Israeli Palestinians
     6 Palestinians in Israel or Palestinian Arabs in Israel
     7 Palestinians

96   *To what extent is there a relationship between the problem of Arabs in Israel and the Palestinian problem?*
     1 This is one common problem
     2 This is primarily one problem with slightly different expressions
     3 These are two problems that are somewhat interrelated
     4 These are two separate problems

97* *To whom do you feel closer, to Arabs in the West Bank and Gaza Strip, or to Jews in Israel?*
     1 Arabs in the West Bank and Gaza Strip
     2 Jews in Israel
     3 No difference

98   *To whom are Arabs in Israel more similar in style of life and daily behavior?*
     1 More similar to Arabs in the West Bank and Gaza Strip
     2 More similar to Jews in Israel
     3 Similar to both
     4 Different from both

99* *What was your stand on the Education Day strike that was held recently (on May 27, 1980)?*
     1 Was in favor   2 Had reservations
     3 Was against   4 Have not heard of this strike

100* *How many times during the past year did you pay social or business visits to the West Bank and Gaza Strip?*
     1 Never   2 Several times a year   3 Once a month
     4 Several times a month   5 Several times a week

101*   *Do you maintain ties with relatives living across the Green Line or in Arab*
         countries?
         1 Yes   2 No, but have relatives there
         3 Do not have relatives there

102   *Should the Israeli government recognize a certain Arab public body as the*
         authoritative representative of the Arabs in Israel?
         1 Definitely yes   2 Yes   3 No   4 Definitely no

103   *What is your view of Arab self-rule in the Galilee and Triangle?*
         1 In favor   2 Have reservations   3 Against

104*   *If a Palestinian state were to be established in the West Bank and Gaza Strip,*
         are you willing to let the Galilee and Triangle remain integral parts of Israel?
         1 Definitely willing   2 Willing
         3 Not willing   4 Definitely not willing

105*   *If a Palestinian state were to be established in the West Bank and Gaza Strip,*
         would you feel better as an Arab citizen in Israel?
         1 Yes   2 Possible   3 Doubtful   4 No

106*   *If a Palestinian state were to be established in the West Bank and Gaza Strip,*
         would you like to move there?
         1 Yes   2 Perhaps   3 No

107   *Which of the following settlements of the problem of Arabs in Israel are you*
         willing to compromise with?

         (For Arab respondents:)
         1 The Arabs will live in Israel as a people with full rights
         2 The Arabs will move to a Palestinian state to be established in the West
           Bank and Gaza Strip
         3 The Arabs will live in a Palestinian state to be established in the West
           Bank, Gaza Strip, Galilee, and Triangle
         4 The Arabs will live in a secular-democratic state to be established in all
           of Palestine in place of Israel

         (For Jewish respondents:)
         1 Willing only to let Arabs live outside Israel
         2 Willing to let Arabs live in Israel, only if they are resigned to their
           minority status in a state designed for Jews
         3 Willing to let Arabs live in Israel as a national minority with full rights
         4 Willing also to let Arabs live as an equal people in Israel as a non-
           Jewish state

108**   *Should Arabs in Israel be allowed to organize independently, like Orthodox*
         Jews, in order to advance their vital interests?
         1 In favor   2 Have reservations   3 Against

109   *Should the closing of the socioeconomic gap between Arabs and Jews be an important and urgent state goal?*
1 Yes, an important and urgent state goal
2 Yes, an important but not urgent state goal
3 Not so important and not so urgent
4 Not important and not urgent

110   *Do you consider the Committee of Heads of Arab Local Councils to be truly representative of the interests of Arabs in Israel?*
1 Definitely yes   2 Yes   3 No
4 Definitely no   5 Have not heard of the Committee

111*   *Do you consider the Sons of the Village Movement or the Progressive National Movement to be truly representative of the interests of Arabs in Israel?*
1 Definitely yes   2 Yes   3 No
4 Definitely no   5 Have not heard of these movements

112   *Do you consider the PLO to be truly representative of the interests of Arabs in Israel?*
1 Definitely yes   2 Yes   3 No   4 Definitely no

113   *To what extent is it possible to improve the Arab situation by acceptable democratic means, such as persuasion and political pressure?*
1 To a great extent   2 To a substantial extent
3 To a certain extent   4 To almost no extent

Are you in favor, have reservations, or are against the use of each of the following means to improve the situation of Arabs in Israel?

114   *Protest actions abroad.*
1 In favor   2 Have reservations   3 Against

115   *General strikes.*
1 In favor   2 Have reservations   3 Against

116   *Boycotts of institutions or plants.*
1 In favor   2 Have reservations   3 Against

117   *Licensed demonstrations.*
1 In favor   2 Have reservations   3 Against

118   *Unlicensed demonstrations.*
1 In favor   2 Have reservations   3 Against

119   *Resistance with force.*
1 In favor   2 Have reservations   3 Against

120   *Do you think that residential quarters should be mixed for Arabs and Jews?*
1 Yes   2 Uncertain   3 No

121*   *What did you do during the Land Day strike (on March 30, 1976)?*
       1 Willingly went to work (or to study) as usual
       2 Unwillingly went to work (or to study)
       3 Unwillingly did not go to work (or to study)
       4 Willingly did not go to work (or to study)
       5 Unemployed, retired, housewife, neither working nor studying, sick,
          etc.

122*   *Did you participate during the past two years in a demonstration protesting the treatment of Arabs in Israel?*
       1 Never   2 Once or twice   3 Three or more times

123   *How will you react if the government will deny groups which criticize the regime the right to hold demonstrations?*
       1 Will agree   2 Will have reservations   3 Will oppose

124   *How will you react if the government will deny Arabs in Israel the right to hold demonstrations?*
       1 Will agree   2 Will have reservations   3 Will oppose

125   *Are security restrictions on Arabs in Israel justified as long as the Israeli-Arab conflict persists?*
       1 Yes   2 To some extent   3 No

126** *What is your opinion of imposing restrictions on Arabs in Israel to prevent them from becoming a majority in the country?*
       1 Agree   2 Have reservations   3 Disagree

127** *Should Israel seek and use any opportunity to encourage Israeli Arabs to leave the state?*
       1 Agree   2 Have reservations   3 Disagree

128** *Should the Knesset enact a law providing for the dismissal of a civil servant or a university student who publicly declares support for the PLO?*
       1 Agree   2 Have reservations   3 Disagree

205** *What is your opinion on outlawing Rakah?*
       1 Agree   2 Have reservations   3 Disagree

206*   *Have you endured harassment by the authorities or economic suffering as a result of expressing opinions or taking actions to effect the present conditions of Arabs in Israel?*
       1 Not at all
       2 Endured political harassment, but not economic suffering
       3 Endured economic suffering, but not political harassment
       4 Endured political harassment and economic suffering

207*   *Do you fear harassment by the authorities or economic suffering if you act strongly to change the situation of Arabs in Israel?*
1 Not at all
2 Fear political harassment, but not economic suffering
3 Fear economic suffering, but not political harassment
4 Fear political harassment and economic suffering

208** *Are you willing to have an Arab as your own personal doctor?*
1 Definitely willing   2 Willing
3 Willing, but prefer a Jew   4 Want a Jew only

209** *Are you willing to have an Arab as your superior in a job?*
1 Definitely willing   2 Willing
3 Willing, but prefer a Jew   4 Want a Jew only

(For Arab respondents:) Indicate with which of the following statements on Jews in Israel do you agree or disagree. (For Jewish respondents: "Jews" reads "Arabs.")

210   *(For Arab respondents:) Most Jews in Israel do not care about self-respect and family honor.*

(For Jewish respondents:) Most Arabs in Israel will never reach the level of development Jews have reached.
1 Agree   2 Disagree

211   *(For Arab respondents:) Most Jews in Israel are exploitive.*

(For Jewish respondents:) Surveillance over most Arabs in Israel should be increased.
1 Agree   2 Disagree

212   *It is impossible to trust most Jews in Israel. (For Jewish respondents: "Jews" reads "Arabs.")*
1 Agree   2 Disagree

213   *(For Arab respondents:) Most Jews in Israel are racist.*

(For Jewish respondents:) Most Arabs in Israel are primitive.
1 Agree   2 Disagree

214   *(For Arab respondents:) Do you accept the right to exist of Israel within the Green Line?*
1 Yes   2 Have reservations   3 No

(For Jewish respondents:) Today Israel within the Green line is a Jewish-Zionist state in which an Arab minority lives. What is your opinion of the Jewish-Zionist character of the state?
1 It should be strengthened   2 It should remain the same
3 It should be mitigated

215**   *What would you prefer if the egalitarian-democratic character of the state
         stands in contradiction to its Jewish-Zionist character and you must choose
         between them?*
         1 Would prefer the egalitarian-democratic character
         2 Would prefer the Jewish-Zionist character

216**   *What is your opinion of expropriation of Arab lands within the Green Line for
         Jewish development?*
         1 Agree   2 Have reservations   3 Disagree

217**   *Does the State of Israel do enough for Arabs in Israel?*
         1 Yes, it does too much   2 It does enough
         3 No, it does too little

218   *What should be the policy of the state toward Arabs in Israel?*
         1 Continuation of the present policy
         2 Increase in surveillance over Arabs
         3 Achievement of equality and integration with Jews
         4 Allowing Arabs to organize independently and become partners in
           state institutions
         5 Granting Arabs a separate legal status like the autonomy offered to
           Arabs in the West Bank and Gaza Strip

219   *Should Israel do its utmost to have most Jews and most Arabs in Israel
         command the two languages, Hebrew and Arabic?*
         1 Definitely yes   2 Yes   3 No   4 Definitely no

         *Indicate the extent to which each of the following statements regarding Arabs in
         Israel is true or not.*

220*   *Arabs in Israel hate Jews.*
         1 True for almost all of them
         2 True for a large proportion of them
         3 True for a certain proportion of them
         4 True for a small proportion of them
         5 True for only individual instances or not true at all

221*   *Arabs in Israel are loyal to the State of Israel.*
         1 True for almost all of them
         2 True for a large proportion of them
         3 True for a certain proportion of them
         4 True for a small proportion of them
         5 True for only individual instances or not true at all

222*   *Arabs in Israel have reconciled themselves to Israel's existence.*
         1 True for almost all of them
         2 True for a large proportion of them
         3 True for a certain proportion of them
         4 True for a small proportion of them
         5 True for only individual instances or not true at all

223* *Arabs in Israel rejoice at Israel's suffering.*
1 True for almost all of them
2 True for a large proportion of them
3 True for a certain proportion of them
4 True for a small proportion of them
5 True for only individual instances or not true at all

224* *Arabs in Israel are torn between their loyalty to the state and loyalty to their people.*
1 True for almost all of them
2 True for a large proportion of them
3 True for a certain proportion of them
4 True for a small proportion of them
5 True for only individual instances or not true at all

225* *Do you sense any difference between Likud and Labor attitude toward Arabs in Israel?*
1 Labor attitude is better
2 Likud attitude is better
3 No difference

Indicate whether you are in favor, have reservations, or are against each of the following measures to improve Arab conditions in Israel.

226** *The extension to Arab localities of the same special assistance given to Jewish development towns.*
1 In favor   2 Have reservations   3 Against

227** *The extension to Arab schools of the same special assistance given to disadvantaged Jewish schools.*
1 In favor   2 Have reservations   3 Against

228** *Opening up employment in the state, public, and private sectors for Arab university graduates.*
1 In favor   2 Have reservations   3 Against

229** *Repeal of the practice to extend benefits to army veterans or to their relatives.*
1 In favor   2 Have reservations   3 Against

230** *Allocation of lands and funds to establish new Arab towns.*
1 In favor   2 Have reservations   3 Against

231** *Enactment of a special punitive law against discrimination in employment, housing, etc., on religious or national grounds.*
1 In favor   2 Have reservations   3 Against

232** *Alteration of state symbols such as the flag and anthem, so that Arabs also can identify themselves with them.*
1 In favor   2 Have reservations   3 Against

233**   *Do you consider Arabs in Israel to be a danger to national security?*
            1 To a great degree   2 To a considerable degree
            3 To a certain degree   4 No

234   *(For Arab respondents:) If you have to assign yourself to one of the following groups with regard to the attitude of Arabs in Israel toward the state, which one would you choose?*

            1 Arabs who believe in coexistence with Jews and in acting only through state institutions to improve the Arabs' situation in the country

            2 Arabs who believe in coexistence with Jews and in acting through both state institutions and independently

            3 Arabs who believe that different terms of coexistence with Jews have to be worked out and this should be done through independent struggle

            4 Arabs who believe that coexistence with Jews in a Jewish-Zionist state is impossible and a struggle should be waged to establish another state in place of Israel

       (For Jewish respondents:) What is your opinion of a strong-arm policy toward Arabs in Israel?
            1 In favor   2 Have reservations   3 Against

       Let us proceed now to general topics.

235   *With regard to the observance of religious tradition, what do you consider yourself?*
            1 Very religious   2 Religious
            3 Religious to some extent (for Jewish respondents: traditional)
            4 Not religious (for Jewish respondents: secular)

236*   *What is your opinion of the traditional practice of loyalty to one's hamula against other hamulas?*
            1 Retain as is   2 Modify   3 Abolish

237   *(For Arab respondents:) What should be the average number of children per Arab family in Israel today? (For Jewish respondents: "Arab family" reads "family.")*
            1 One or two children   2 Three   3 Four
            4 Five   5 Six or more

238*   *Do you allow a young single Arab girl to have a boyfriend?*
            1 Yes, allow   2 Allow to some extent   3 No

239   *Since 1948, has there been any expropriation of lands owned by you, your brothers, sisters, parents, or children?*
            1 Yes, much   2 Yes, some   3 No, but own land   4 Own no land

240*   *Did your family or the family of your father become a refugee family as a result of the 1948 war?*
            1 No   2 Yes

241   *Are you a member of any party? Which one?*
        1 Not a member   2 Labor   3 Mapam
        4 Herut   5 Liberals   6 Democratic Movement for Change
        7 Citizens Rights Movement, Independent Liberals
        8 National Religious Party   9 Agudat Israel, Poale Agudat Israel
        10 Shelli   11 Rakah   12 Rafi   13 Tehiya   14 Other

243   *For what list did you vote in the last elections to the Knesset (in May 1977)? (Jewish respondents' answers are recorded in Question 251.)*
        1 Likud, Shlomzion   2 Labor
        3 Democratic Movement for Change   4 National Religious Party
        5 Agudat Israel, Poale Agudat Israel
        6 Citizens Rights Movement, Independent Liberals   7 Shelli
        8 Women's Party, Plato-Sharon, Social Renewal Movement (Ben-Porat), Beit-Israel (Yamini)
        9 Democratic Front for Peace and Equality (Rakah)
        10 United Arab List, Reform Arab List, Coexistence and Justice List
        11 Other   12 Did not vote

245   *For which list would you vote if elections to the Knesset were held today? (Jewish respondents' answers are recorded in Question 243.)*
        1 Likud   2 Labor   3 National Religious Party
        4 Agudat Israel, Poale Agudat Israel
        5 Democratic Movement, Change
        6 Citizens Rights Movement, Independent Liberals   7 Shelli
        8 Tehiya   9 DFPE (Rakah)   10 Arab lists
        11 Sephardic or Oriental lists   12 Other lists
        13 Undecided   14 Would not vote

247*   *For which one of the following lists would you vote in the next elections to the Knesset?*
        1 An independent, nationalist Arab party, if it were established
        2 An independent Arab list that can negotiate or cooperate with Jewish parties, if it were established
        3 An Arab list affiliated to a Jewish party
        4 A Jewish party (Labor, Likud, National Religious Party, etc.)
        5 DFPE or Rakah   6 None of the above
        7 Undecided, or would not vote

248*   *For which list did you vote in the last elections to the local councils (in November 1978)?*
        1 A Jewish list   2 A list affiliated to a Jewish party
        3 DFPE or Rakah
        4 A list of the Sons of the Village Movement or an affiliated list
        5 Other local lists   6 Did not vote
        7 Elections were not held in my locality

249*   *Did your hamula support the list that you voted for?*
        1 Yes   2 No   3 Do not know
        4 Have no hamula   5 Did not vote
        6 Elections were not held in my locality

250*   *For which list would you vote if elections to local councils were held today?*
        1 A Jewish list   2 A list affiliated to a Jewish party
        3 DFPE or Rakah
        4 A list of the Sons of the Village Movement or an affiliated list
        5 Other local list   6 Undecided   7 Would not vote
        8 My locality lacks municipal status

251*   *(Jewish respondents' answers to Question 243.)*

        Now let me get some information about you.

260   *Do you or your family have a car?*
        1 No   2 Yes

261   *Gender.*
        1 Male   2 Female

262   *Age (recorded in two digits).*

264   *Personal status.*
        1 Single   2 Married   3 Widowed   4 Divorced

265   *Number of unmarried children.*
        1 None   2 One or two   3 Three or four
        4 Five or six   5 Seven or more children

266*   *Is your spouse (in the last marriage) your cousin (i.e., a daughter of your
        father's brother)?*
        1 Yes   2 No

267*   *Your spouse (in the last marriage) is from:*
        1 Same hamula and same locality
        2 Same hamula but different locality
        3 Same locality but different hamula
        4 Different hamula and different locality

268   *Are you, or any of your brothers, sisters, or parents, married today to a Jew?
        (For Jewish respondents: "a Jew" reads "a member of the other ethnic group,
        i.e., Ashkenazi if you are non-Ashkenazi, or non-Ashkenazi if you are
        Ashkenazi.")*
        1 No   2 Yes, myself   3 Yes, my brother, sister or parent

269*   *How many of your hamula members live in your locality?*
        1 Fewer than 100 person   2 100-500
        3 501-1,000   4 More than 1,000

270   *Education (last class in school completed).*
      1 No schooling   2 Incomplete primary   3 Complete primary
      4 Incomplete secondary   5 Complete secondary
      6 Post-secondary, incomplete higher   7 Complete higher

271   *Religion.*
      1 Druze   2 Moslem   3 Greek-Catholic
      4 Greek-Orthodox   5 Other Christian   6 Jew

272   *What do you do in the main?*
      1 Employed (including soldier in professional army)
      2 Unemployed (seeking work)
      3 Retired   4 Housewife   5 Student
      6 Soldier in compulsory service

273   *Are you the head of a family (a husband, a father; a single living separately; or a divorced, or a widowed woman living separately)?*
      1 Yes   2 No

274   *Work status of head of family.*
      1 Employee   2 Employer   3 Self-employed
      4 Member of cooperative or Moshav
      5 Kibbutz member   6 Unpaid family member
      7 Head of family is unemployed, retired, housewife, student, or soldier
        in compulsory service

275   *Is the head of family a tenured employee?*
      1 Yes   2 No   3 Head of family is not an employee

276   *Who is the employer of the head of family?*
      1 Jewish   2 Arab
      3 Public institution (State, Histadrut, Local Government, Jewish Agency,
        University, etc.)
      4 Other   5 Head of family is not an employee

277   *Job classification of head of family.*
      1 Scientific and academic worker
      2 Other professional, technical, and related worker
      3 Top administrator and manager
      4 Other administrator and manager
      5 Top clerical and related worker
      6 Other clerical and related worker
      7 Big merchant
      8 Other sales worker

9 Service worker

10 Farm owner or manager

11 Skilled agricultural worker

12 Unskilled agricultural worker

13 Skilled worker in industry, mining, building, transport, and other skilled worker

14 Other worker in industry, mining, building, transport, and other unskilled worker

15 Head of family is unemployed, soldier in compulsory service, student, retired, divorced or widowed housewife living separately

279**   *Were you born in the country or abroad?*
1 In the country   2 Abroad

280**   *Father's country of birth.*
1 Born in Israel   2 Morocco, Tangier   3 Algeria, Tunisia, Libya
4 Iraq   5 Yemen and Southern Yemen   6 Syria, Lebanon, Egypt
7 Turkey, Bulgaria, Greece   8 Other countries in Asia and Africa
9 U.S.S.R.   10 Poland   11 Rumania   12 Germany
13 Anglo-Saxon countries   14 Other countries in Europe and America

282**   *Year of immigration.*
1 Immigrated before 1948   2 1948-51   3 1952-56
4 1957-60   5 1961-65   6 1966 or later   7 Born in Israel

283**   *If you have to define yourself in terms of ethnic origin, which one of the following would you choose?*
1 Oriental   2 Sephardic   3 Ashkenazic   4 Mixed

We are through. Thanks for your cooperation.

Following is the interviewer's report, to be completed at the end of the interview.

284*   *Respondent's subsample.*
1 Main (same localities as in the 1976 survey)
2 Additional (localities not included in the 1976 survey)

285*   *Respondent's sampling listing.*
1 Included in original list   2 Included in replacement list

286   *Duration of interview.*
1 Up to one hour   2 One hour to less than one and one half hours
3 One and one half hours or more

287*   *Do you personally know the respondent?*
1 Yes   2 No

288   *What was the degree of understanding shown by the respondent?*
1 Lack of understanding   2 Certain lack of understanding
3 Reasonable understanding   4 Full understanding

289   *Was there an atmosphere of trust during the interview?*
       1 Lack of trust   2 Certain lack of trust
       3 Reasonable trust   4 Full trust

290   *What was the overall reliability of the information given by the respondent?*
       1 Not reliable   2 Sufficient   3 Good   4 Very good

291   *(For Arab interviewers:) If you have to assign yourself to one of the following groups with regard to the attitude of Arabs in Israel toward the state, which one would you choose?*
       1 Arabs who belive in coexistence with Jews and in acting only through state institutions to improve the Arabs' situation in the country
       2 Arabs who belive in coexistence with Jews and in acting through both state institutions and independently
       3 Arabs who believe that different terms of coexistence with Jews have to be worked out and this should be done through independent struggle
       4 Arabs who believe that coexistence with Jews in a Jewish-Zionist state is impossible and a struggle should be waged to establish another state in place of Israel

       (For Jewish interviewers:) What was the overall attitude of the respondent toward Arabs in Israel?
       1 Very sympathetic   2 Sympathetic   3 Neutral, mixed
       4 Hostile   5 Very hostile

292   *Respondent's locality.*

294   *Research group.*
       1 Arab public
       2 Arab leaders affiliated to the Zionist establishment
       3 Arab leaders affiliated to DFPE (Rakah) or independent Arab leaders
       4 Arab leaders active in the Sons of the Village Movement or in the Progressive National Movement
       5 Jewish public
       6 Dovish Jewish leaders
       7 Jewish Arabists (Jewish functionaries in separate Arab departments)
       8 Hawkish Jewish leaders

295   *Interviewer's code.*

299   *Respondent's nationality.*
       1 Arab   2 Jew

References

Abraham, Sameer Y. 1983. "The Development and Transformation of the Palestine National Movement." Pp. 391-425 in *Occupation: Israel over Palestine*, edited by Naseer Aruri. Belmont, MA: AAUG Press.

Al-Haj, Majid. 1986. "Adjustment Patterns of the Arab Internal Refugees in Israel." *International Migration* 24, 3: 651-74.

_____. 1988a. "The Sociopolitical Structure of Arabs in Israel: External vs. Internal Orientation." Pp. 92-122 in *Arab-Jewish Relations in Israel: A Quest in Human Understanding*. Bristol, IN: Wyndham Hall Press.

_____. 1988b. "Social and Political Aspects of the Contact between Palestinians on Each Side of the Green Line." Pp. 41-56 in *Twenty Years since the Six-Day War*, edited by Arnon Soffer. Haifa: The Jewish-Arab Center, University of Haifa. (Hebrew).

Al-Haj, Majid and Avner Yaniv. 1983. "Uniformity or Diversity: A Reappraisal of the Voting Behavior of the Arab Minority in Israel." Pp. 139-64 in *The Elections in Israel 1981*, edited by Asher Arian. Tel Aviv: Ramot Publishing, Tel Aviv University.

Amir, Yehuda. 1976. "The Role of Intergroup Contact in Change of Prejudice and Ethnic Relations." Pp. 245-305 in *Toward the Elimination of Racism*, edited by P.A. Katz. New York: Pergamon Press.

_____. 1979. "Interpersonal Contact between Arabs and Israelis." *The Jerusalem Quarterly* 13 (Fall): 3-17.

Arian, Asher. 1985. *Politics in Israel: The Second Generation*. Chatham, NJ: Chatham House.

Avineri, Sholomo. 1986. "Ideology and Israel's Foreign Policy." *The Jerusalem Quarterly* 37 (Fall): 3-13.

Bachrach, Peter and Morton Baratz. 1962. "Two Faces of Power." *American Political Science Review* 56: 947-52.

Benjamin, Avraham and Rachel Peleg. 1977. *Higher Education and Arabs in Israel*. Tel Aviv: Am Oved. (Hebrew).

Benvenisti, Meron. 1987. *The West Bank Data Base Project 1987 Report: Demographic, Economic, Legal, Social and Political Developments in the West Bank*. Jerusalem and New York: The Jerusalem Post.

Caspi, Dan and Mitchell A. Seligson. 1983. "Toward an Empirical Theory of Tolerance: Radical Groups in Israel and Costa Rica." *Comparitive Political Studies* 15, 4: 385-404.

Claude, Inis. 1955. *National Minorities*. Cambridge: Harvard University Press.

Cohen, Erik. 1983. "Ethnicity and Legitimation in Contemporary Israel." *The Jerusalem Quarterly* 28 (Summer): 111-24.

Cohen, Raanan. 1985. *Processes of Political Organization and Voting Patterns of Arabs in Israel (In Four Election Campaigns to the Knesset, 1973-1984)*. Two Parts. M.A. Thesis. Tel Aviv: Department of the Middle East, Tel Aviv University. (Hebrew).

Ehrlich, Howard J. 1973. *The Social Psychology of Prejudice*. New York: Wiley-Interscience.

Eisenstadt, S.N. 1985. *The Transformation of Israeli Society*. London: Weidenfeld and Nicolson.

Elazar, Daniel J. 1986. *Israel: Building a New Society*. Bloomington, IN: Indiana University Press.

Esman, Milton. 1973. "The Management of Communal Conflict." Public Policy 21, 1 (Winter): 49-78.

Flapan, Simha. 1979. *Zionism and the Palestinians*. London: Croom Helm.

Galnoor, Itzhak. 1982. *Steering the Polity: Communication and Politics in Israel*. Beverly Hills, CA: Sage.

Geffner, Ellen. 1974. "An Israeli Arab View of Israel." *Jewish Social Studies* 36: 134-41.

Gorny, Yosef. 1987. *Zionism and the Arabs, 1882-1948: A Study of Ideology*. Oxford: Oxford University Press.

Hall, Raymond (ed.). 1979. *Ethnic Autonomy: Comparative Dynamics*. New York: Pergamon Press.

Hanson, Jim. 1979. "On How to Live with Survey Research." *Contemporary Sociology* 8, 5 (September): 677-87.

Hareven, Alouph (ed.). 1983. *Every Sixth Israeli: Relations between the Jewish Majority and the Arab Minority in Israel*. Jerusalem: The Van Leer Jerusalem Foundation.

Harkabi, Yehoshafat. 1970. *Arab Attitudes to Israel*. Jerusalem: Israel Universities Press.

_____. 1988. *Israel's Fateful Hour*. New York: Harper and Row.

Harris, W.W. 1980. *Taking Root: Israeli Settlement in the West Bank, the Golan Heights and Gaza Strip, 1967-1980.* New York: Wiley.

Heller, Mark. 1983. *A Palestine State: Implications for Israel.* Cambridge, MA: Harvard University Press.

Hilf, Rudolf. 1979. "The Other Dimension of Peace." *New Outlook* 22, 4 (May-June): 44-50.

Hofman, John E. 1977. "Identity and Intergroup Perception in Israel." *International Journal of Inter-Cultural Relations* 1, 3: 79-102.

_____ .1982. "Social Identity and the Readiness for Social Relations between Jews and Arabs in Israel." *Human Relations* 35, 9: 727-41.

Horowitz, Dan. 1987. "Israel and Occupation." *The Jerusalem Quarterly* 43 (Summer): 21-36.

Horowitz, Donald C. 1985. *Ethnic Groups in Conflict.* Berkeley and Los Angeles: University of California Press.

Israeli Communist Party. 1985. *Report of the 20th Congress.* Haifa: Israeli Communist Party. (Hebrew).

Israeli, Raphael. 1980. "Arabs in Israel: The Surge of a New Identity." *Plural Societies* 11, 4 (Winter): 21-29.

Jiryis, Sabri. 1976. *The Arabs in Israel.* New York: Monthly Review Press.

_____ . 1979. "The Arabs in Israel, 1973-1979." *Journal of Palestine Studies* 8, 4 (Summer): 31-56.

Kahane, Meir. 1981. *They Must Go.* New York: Grosset and Dunlap.

_____ . 1987. *Uncomfortable Questions for Comfortable Jews.* Secaucus, NJ: L. Stuart.

Katzenell, Jack. 1987. "Minorities in the IDF." *IDF Journal* 4, 3 (Fall): 40-45.

Kelman, Herbert C. 1988. "The Palestinianization of the Arab-Israeli Conflict." *The Jerusalem Quarterly* 46 (Spring): 3-15.

Kimmerling, Baruch. 1985. "Between the Primordial and the Civil Definitions of the Collective Identity: Eretz Israel or the State of Israel?" Pp. 262-83 in *Comparative Social Dynamics,* edited by Erik Cohen, Moshe Lissak, and Uri Almagor. Boulder and London: Westview Press.

Klein, Claude. 1987. *Israel as a Nation State and the Problem of the Arab Minority: In Search of a Status.* (Mimeographed). Tel Aviv: International Center for Peace in the Middle East.

Kopilevitch, Emanuel. 1973. "Education in the Arab Sector: Facts and Problems." Pp. 323-34 in *Education in Israel,* edited by Haim Ormian. Jerusalem: Ministry of Education and Culture. (Hebrew).

Lam, Zvi. 1983. "The Status of a Minority is Determined by the Political Culture of the Society." *Akhvah* 1 (Spring): 9-12. (Hebrew).

Landau, Jacob M. 1969. *The Arabs in Israel: A Political Study.* Oxford: Oxford University Press.

_____. 1981. "Alienation and Strains in Political Behavior." Pp. 197-212 in *The Arabs in Israel,* edited by Aharon Layish. Jerusalem: Magnes Press. (Hebrew).

_____. 1984. "The Arab Vote." Pp. 169-89 in *The Roots of Begin's Success,* edited by Dan Caspi, Abraham Diskin and Emanuel Gutmann. London: Croom Helm.

Lanternari, Vittorio. 1980. "Ethnocentrism and Ideology." *Ethnic and Racial Studies* 3, 1 (January): 52-66.

Layish, Aharon. 1975. "Social and Political Change in Arab Society in Israel." Pp. 81-87 in *The Palestinians,* edited by Michael Curtis, Joseph Neyer, Chaim Waxman, and Allen Pollach. New Brunswick, NJ: Transaction.

LeVine, Robert A. and Donald T. Campbell. 1972. *Ethnocentrism: Theories of Conflict, Ethnic Attitudes and Group Behavior.* New York: Wiley.

Lewin-Epstein, Noah and Moshe Semyonov. 1986. "Ethnic Group Mobility in the Israeli Labor Market." *American Sociological Review* 51, 3 (June): 342-51.

Lewy, Arieh, Chanan Rapaport and Mordechai Rimor. 1978. *Educational Achievements in the Israeli School System: A Cross National Comparative Study.* Tel Aviv: Ramot Educational Systems. (Hebrew).

Lieblich, Amia. 1983. "Level of Intelligence and Its Structure in Various Groups and Minorities in Israel." Pp. 335-57 in *Between Education and Psychology,* edited by Mordechai Nissan and Uriel Last. Jerusalem: Magnes Press. (Hebrew).

Liebman, Charles. 1988. "Conceptions of 'State of Israel' in Israeli Society." *The Jerusalem Quarterly* 47 (Summer):96-107.

Liebman, Charles and Eliezer Don-Yehiya. 1984. *Religion and Politics in Israel.* Bloomington, IN: Indiana University Press.

Lustick, Ian. 1980. *Arabs in the Jewish State: Israel's Control of a National Minority.* Austin, TX: University of Texas Press.

_____. 1988a. "A Political Role for Israeli Arabs." *Davar.* March 16. (Hebrew).

_____. 1988b. "Creeping Binationalism within the Green Line." *New Outlook* 31, 7 (July): 14-19.

_____. 1988c. "The Voice of a Sociologist: The Task of a Historian; The limits of a Paradigm." Pp. 9-16 in *Books on Israel,* edited by Ian Lustick. Albany, NY: SUNY Press.

Mar'i, Sami K. 1978. *Arab Education in Israel.* Syracuse, NY: Syracuse University Press.

McCord, Arline and William McCord. 1979. "Ethnic Autonomy: A Socio-Historic Synthesis." Pp. 426-36 in *Ethnic Autonomy: Comparative Dynamics*, edited by Richard Hall. New York: Pergamon Press.

Merton, Robert K. 1957. *Social Theory and Social Structure*. Rev. Ed. Glencoe, IL: Free Press.

Mi'ari, Mahmoud. 1975. *A comparative Survey of the Curricula of the Schools in the Arab Sector.* (Mimeographed). Jerusalem: Educational Programs Project. (Hebrew).

_____. 1987. "Traditionalism and Political Identity of Arabs in Israel." *Journal of Asian and African Studies* 22, 1-2: 33-44.

Ministry of Education and Culture (Yadlin Committee). 1972. *Basic Goals of Arab Education.* (Mimeograped). Jerusalem: Ministry of Education and Culture. (Hebrew).

Ministry of Education and Culture. 1976. *The Education in Israel in the Eighties.* (Mimeographed). Jerusalem: Planning Project of Education for the Eighties. (Hebrew).

Nakhleh, Emile A. 1977. *The Arabs in Israel and their Role in a Future Arab Israeli Conflict. A Perception Study.* (Mimeographed). Alexandria, VA: Abott Associates.

Nakhleh, Khalil. 1975. "Cultural Determinants of Palestinian Collective Identity: The Case of the Arabs in Israel." *New Outlook* 18, 7 (October-November): 31-40.

_____. 1977a. "The Goals of Education for Arabs in Israel." *New Outlook* 20, 3 (April-May): 29-35.

_____. 1977b. "Anthropological and Sociological Studies of the Arabs in Israel: A Critique." *Journal of Palestine Studies* 6, 4 (Summer): 41-70.

_____. 1979. *Palestinian Dilemma: Nationalist Consciousness and University Education in Israel.* Shrewsbury, MA: Association of Arab American University Graduates.

_____. 1980. "Palestinian Struggle Under Occupation." *Arab World Issues. Occasional Papers No. 6*: 1-16. Belmont, MA: Association of Arab-American University Graduates.

_____. 1982. "The Two Galilees." *Arab World Issues.* Occasional Papers No. 7: 1-27. Belmont, MA: Association of Arab-American University Graduates.

Nakhleh, Khalil and Elia Zureik (eds.). 1980. *The Sociology of the Palestinians.* New York: St. Martin's Press.

Peled, Tsiyona. 1979. "On the Social Distance between Arabs and Jews in Israel." *The Israel Institute of Applied Social Research Bulletin* 50: 8-10. (Hebrew).

Peled, Tsiyona and David Bar-Gal. 1983. *Intervention Activities in Arab-Jewish Relations: Conceptualization, Classification and Evaluation.* Research Report Submitted to the Ford Foundation through Israel Foundations Trustees. (Mimeographed). Jerusalem: The Israel Institute of Applied Social Research.

Peleg, Ilan. 1987. *Begin's Foreign Policy, 1977-1983: Israel's Move to the Right.* New York: Greenwood Press.

Peres, Yochanan. 1970. "Modernization and Nationalism in the Identity of the Israeli Arab." *The Middle East Journal* 24, 4 (Autumn): 479-92.

_____. 1971. "Ethnic Relations in Israel." American Journal of Sociology 76, 6 (May): 1021-47.

Peres, Yochanan, Avishai Ehrlich and Nira Yuval-Davis. 1970. "National Education for Arab Youth in Israel: A Comparative Analysis of Curricula." *Jewish Journal of Sociology* 12, 2 (December): 147-64.

Peres, Yochanan and Zippora Levy. 1969. "Jews and Arabs: Ethnic Group Stereotypes in Israel." *Race* 10, 4 (April): 479-92.

Peres, Yochanan and Nira Yuval-Davis. "Arab Students' Attitudes toward Jews as Individuals and toward the State of Israel." *Megamot* 17, 3: 254-61. (Hebrew).

Peri, Yoram and Johnnie Goldberg. 1985. *Are the Orientals More Hawkish?* Discussion Paper No. 7. (Mimeographed). Tel Aviv: International Center for Peace in the Middle East. (Hebrew).

Plascov, Avi. 1981. *A Palestinian State? Examininig the Alternatives.* Adelphai Papers No. 163. London: The International Institute for Strategic Studies.

Rapaport, Chanan, Matatyahu Peled, Mordechai Rimor and Chaim Mano. 1978. *Arab Youth in Israel: Knowledge, Values and Behavior in the Social and Political Spheres.* Research Report No. 211. Publication No. 594. (Mimeographed). Jerusalem: Szold Institute.

Rekhess, Elie. 1976. *The Arabs in Israel After 1967: The Exaserbation of the Orientation Problem.* (Mimeographed). Tel Aviv: Shiloah Center, Tel Aviv University. (Hebrew).

_____. 1977. *Arabs in Israel and the Land Expropriations in the Galilee: Background, Events and Implications, 1975-1977.* Sekirot No. 53. (Mimeographed). Tel Aviv: Shiloah Center, Tel Aviv University. (Hebrew).

_____. 1979. "Israeli Arab Intelligentsia." *The Jerusalem Quarterly* 11 (Spring): 51-69.

_____. 1986a. "The Arab Village in Israel: A Renewed National Political Center." Ofakim Bageographia 17-18: 145-60. (Hebrew).

_____. 1986b. *Between Communism and Arab Nationalism: Rakah and the Arab Minority in Israel (1965-1973)*. Doctoral Dissertation. Tel Aviv: Tel Aviv University. (Hebrew).

Robins, Edward A. 1972. "Attitudes, Stereotypes and Prejudice among Arabs and Jews in Israel." *New Outlook* 15, 9 (November-December): 36-48.

Schermerhorn, R.A. 1970. *Comparative Ethnic Relations*. New York: Random House.

Scholch, Alexander (ed). 1983. *Palestinians Over the Green Line*. London: Ithaca Press.

Schnall, David J. 1979. *Radical Dissent in Contemporary Israeli Politics*. New York: Praeger Press.

See, Katherine O'Sullivan and William J. Wilson. 1988. "Race and Ethnicity." Pp. 223-42 in *Handbook of Sociology*, edited by Neil J. Smelser. Beverly Hills, CA: Sage.

Seligson, Mitchell A. and Dan Caspi. 1983. "Arabs in Israel: Political Tolerance and Ethnic Conflict." *Journal of Applied Behavioral Science* 19, 1: 55-66.

Seliktar, Ofira 1984a. "The Arabs in Israel: Some Observations on the Psychology of the System of Controls." *Journal of Conflict Resolution* 28, 2 (June): 247-69.

_____. 1984b. "Ethnic Stratification and Foreign Policy in Israel: The Attitudes of Oriental Jews towards the Arabs and the Arab-Israeli Conflict." *The Middle East Journal* 38, 1 (Winter): 34-50.

Shafir, Gershon. 1984. "Changing Nationalism and Israel's 'Open Frontier' on the West Bank." *Theory and Society* 13: 803-27.

Shamir, Michal. 1986. "Realignment in the Israeli Party System." Pp. 267-96 in *The Elections in Israel 1984*, edited by Asher Arian and Michal Shamir. New Brunswick, NJ: Transaction.

Shamir, Michal and John L. Sullivan. 1983. "The Political Context of Tolerance: The United States and Israel." *The American Political Science Review* 77, 6 (December): 911-28.

Shapira, Yonathan. 1977. *Democracy in Israel*. Ramat Gan: Massada. (Hebrew).

Shilo, Gideon. 1982. Israeli Arabs in the Eyes of the Arab States and the PLO. Jerusalem: Magnes Press. (Hebrew).

Shimshoni, Daniel. 1982. *Israeli Democracy*. New York: Free Press.

Shipler, David. 1987. *Arab and Jew: Wounded Spirits in the Promised Land*. New York: Penguin.

Simpson, George and Milton Yinger. 1972. *Racial and Cultural Minorities*. 4th Ed. New York: Harper and Row.

Smith, Anthony D. 1979. "Towards a Theory of Ethnic Separatism." *Ethnic and Racial Studies* 2, 1 (January): 22-37.

Smooha, Sammy. 1976. "Ethnic Stratification and Allegiance in Israel: Where do Oriental Jews Belong?" *Il Politico* 41, 4: 635-51.

_____. 1978. *Israel: Pluralism and Conflict.* Berkeley and Los Angeles: University of California Press.

_____. 1980. "Control of Minorities in Israel and Northern Ireland." *Comparative Studies in Society and History* 22, 2 (April): 256-80.

_____. 1982. "Existing and Alternative Policy towards Arabs in Israel." *Ethnic and Racial Studies* 5, 1 (January): 71-98.

_____. 1983. "Minority Responses in Plural Societies: A Typology of the Arabs in Israel." *Sociology and Social Research* 67, 4 (July): 436-56.

_____. 1984a. *The Orientation and Politicization of the Arab Minority in Israel.* Haifa: The Jewish-Arab Center, University of Haifa.

_____(ed.). 1984b. *Social Research on Arabs in Israel, 1977-1982: A Bibliography.* Vol. 2. Haifa: The Jewish-Arab Center, University of Haifa.

_____. 1987a. "Jewish and Arab Ethnocentrism in Israel." *Ethnic and Racial Studies* 10, 1 (January): 1-26.

_____. 1987b. *Social Research on Jewish Ethnicity in Israel, 1948-1986: A Review and Selected Bibliography with Abstracts.* Haifa: Haifa University Press.

Smooha, Sammy and Ora Cibulski. 1987. *Social Research on Arabs in Israel, 1948-1976: An Annotated Bibliography.* Vol. 1. Haifa: The Jewish-Arab Center, University of Haifa.

Soffer, Arnon. 1986. "The Territorial Struggle between Jews and Arabs in Eretz Israel." *Ofakim Bageographia* 17-18: 7-23. (Hebrew).

_____. 1987. "Geography and Demography in Eretz Israel in the Year 2000." (Mimeographed). Haifa: Geography Department, University of Haifa. (Hebrew).

_____. 1988. *The Demographic and Geographic Situation in Eretz Israel: Is It the End of the Zionist Vision?* Haifa: Author's Printing. (Hebrew).

Sohlberg, Shaul. 1976. "Social Desirability Responses in Jewish and Arab Children in Israel." *Journal of Cross-Cultural Psychology* 7, 3 (September): 301-14.

Sprinzak, Ehud. 1986. "Kach and Kahane: The Emergence of Jewish Quasi-Fascism." Pp. 169-87 in *The Elections in Israel 1984*, edited by Asher Arian and Michal Shamir. New Brunswick, NJ: Transaction.

Sullivan, John L., Michal Shamir, Nigel Roberts and Patrick Walsh. 1984. "Political Intolerance and the Structure of Mass Attitudes: A

Study of the United States, Israel and New Zealand." *Comparative Political studies* 17, 3 (October): 319-44.

Sumner, W.G. 1906. *Folkways*. New York: Ginn.

Tehon, Ori. 1979. "The Radicalization of the Arabs in Israel." *Migvan* 37 (June): 28-29. (Hebrew).

Tessler, Mark A. 1977. "Israel's Arabs and the Palestinian Problem." *The Middle East Journal* 31, 3 (Summer): 313-29.

_____. 1980. "Arabs in Israel." *American Universities Field Staff Reports* 1, Asia: 1-25.

Tiryakian, Edward A. 1968. "Typologies." *International Encyclopedia of Social Sciences* 16: 177-86.

Toledano, Shmuel. 1974. Interview. *Maariv*. November 22. (Hebrew).

Tuma, Emil. 1981. "Reply to Nakhleh's 'Liberation Mentality'." *New Outlook* (June): 30-33.

Vander Zanden, James. 1972. *American Minority Relations*. 3rd Ed. New York: Ronald Press.

Wirth, Louis. 1945. "The Problem of Minority Groups." Pp. 347-72 in *The Science of Man in the World Crisis*, edited by Ralph Linton. New York: Columbia University Press.

Zemah, Mina. 1980. *The Attitudes of the Jewish Majority towards the Arab Minority in Israel*. Interim Report. (Mimeographed). Jerusalem: The Van Leer Jerusalem Foundation. (Hebrew).

Zureik, Elia T. 1979. *The Palestinians in Israel: A Study in Internal Colonialism*. London: Routledge and Kegan Paul.

Index